THERE IS NO SUCH THING AS A SOCIAL SCIENCE

Directions in Ethnomethodology and Conversation Analysis

Series Editors:
Stephen Hester, University of Wales, UK
David Francis, Manchester Metropolitan University, UK

Ethnomethodology and Conversation Analysis are cognate approaches to the study of social action that together comprise a major perspective within the contemporary human sciences. This perspective focuses upon naturally occurring talk and interaction and analyses the methods by which social activities are ordered and accomplished. From its origins within sociology, EM/CA has ramified across a wide range of human science disciplines, including anthropology, social psychology, linguistics, communication studies and social studies of technology. Its influence is international, with large and active research communities in many countries, including Japan, Australia, Canada, France, The Netherlands, Denmark and Sweden as well as the UK and USA.

The International Institute of Ethnomethodology and Conversation Analysis is the major association of EM/CA researchers worldwide. It was set up in 1978 by Prof. George Psathas to provide a forum for international collaboration between scholars working in the field of studies of social action and to support their work through conferences and publications. It published several books in EM/CA in association with University Press of America. Now reconstituted under the direction of Francis and Hester, supported by an international steering committee, the IIEMCA holds regular conferences and symposia in various countries.

This major new book series will present current work in EM/CA, including research monographs, edited collections and theoretical studies. It will be essential reading for specialists in the field as well as those who wish to know more about this major approach to human action.

Other titles in this series

Orders of Ordinary Action: Respecifying Sociological Knowledge
Stephen Hester and David Francis
ISBN 978-0-7546-3311-2

The Academic Presentation: Situated Talk in Action
Johanna Rendle-Short
ISBN 978-0-7546-4597-9

Institutional Interaction: Studies of Talk at Work
Ilkka Arminen
ISBN 978-0-7546-4285-5

There is No Such Thing as a Social Science
In Defence of Peter Winch

PHIL HUTCHINSON
Manchester Metropolitan University, UK

RUPERT READ
University of East Anglia, UK

WES SHARROCK
University of Manchester, UK

ASHGATE

Published by
Ashgate Publishing Limited
Gower House
Croft Road
Aldershot
Hampshire GU11 3HR
England

Ashgate Publishing Company
Suite 420
101 Cherry Street
Burlington, VT 05401-4405
USA

www.ashgate.com

British Library Cataloguing in Publication Data
Hutchinson, Phil
    There is no such thing as a social science : in defence of
    Peter Winch. - (Directions in ethnomethodology and
    conversation analysis)
    1. Winch, Peter 2. Social sciences - Philosophy
    I. Title II. Read, Rupert J., 1966- III. Sharrock, W. W.
    (Wes W.)
    300.1

Library of Congress Cataloging in Publication Data
Hutchinson, Phil.
    There is no such thing as a social science : in defence of Peter Winch / by Phil Hutchinson, Rupert Read, and Wes Sharrock.
        p. cm. -- (Directions in ethnomethodology and conversation analysis)
    Introduction: The legendary PC -- Beyond pluralism, monism, relativism, realism, etc. : reassessing Peter Winch -- Winch and linguistic idealism -- Seeing things for themselves : Winch, ethnography, ethnomethodology, and social studies -- Winch and conservatism : the question of philosophical quietism.
    Includes index.
    ISBN 978-0-7546-4776-8
    1. Philosophy and social sciences. 2. Winch, Peter. I. Read, Rupert J.,
1966- II. Sharrock, W. W. (Wes W.) III. Title.

    B63.H88 2008
    300.92--dc22

2008009813

ISBN 978-0-7546-4776-8

Mixed Sources
Product group from well-managed forests and other controlled sources
www.fsc.org Cert no. SA-COC-1565
© 1996 Forest Stewardship Council
FSC

Printed and bound in Great Britain by
MPG Books Ltd, Bodmin, Cornwall.

Contents

Preface

It is now 50 years since the publication of Peter Winch's *The Idea of a Social Science and its Relation to Philosophy* (*ISS*). Fifty years on, Winch's book is no less controversial, no less relevant and no less read. Students in philosophy, anthropology, economics, politics, psychology and sociology, have and will continue to find Winch's arguments of central relevance to their own concerns.

The landscape of the social studies can appear to have changed somewhat over the past 50 years. Where Positivism was once dominant, students are now confronted with what can appear like a marketplace of methodologies and theories. In many ways, and contrary to the orthodox understanding of Winch, this makes *ISS* even more relevant now than when it appeared in 1958. For this marketplace of methodologies and theories can obscure from view the common assumptions underpinning all of those approaches, assumptions that Winch's writings expose as seriously flawed.

Winch's arguments have been widely misunderstood. In this book we seek to offer both a corrective to some of the most widespread and pervasive of those misunderstandings and issue a call to genuine dialogue to those who still find themselves in disagreement with Winch's central concerns, as expressed in *ISS* (and a number of subsequent articles).

This book has been co-authored by the three of us. The three of us have been discussing Winch (and Wittgenstein) in various fora for much of our academic lives (for one of us that covers much of the 50 years since the publication of *ISS*). We co-organise (along with Dave Francis, Philippe Rouchy and Christian Greiffenhagen) the annual *Mind and Society* seminar series, hosted over the past 15 years in Manchester and Cambridge. We have met, along with graduate students and colleagues, on regular occasions over the years in the Senior Common Room at Manchester University and in the Grafton Arms, Manchester to discuss issues explored in the following pages.

Our chief debt of thanks, therefore, goes to all those who have attended *Mind and Society* over the years and those who have attended Wes Sharrock's Wednesday afternoon discussion group in the SCR (a venue which increasingly seems to be seen by the university as a corporate hospitality suite and banquet hall rather than a senior common room). These discussions are often the highlight of the week for those involved, a time when we can discuss and argue about those things that interest us most. We should also like to thank Jean Sanders for compiling the index.

Phil would like to thank madeleine kennedy-macfoy. Rupert would like to thank Juliette Harkin, Theodore Schatzki and the students who have attended his philosophy of social science class at UEA over the years. Wes would like to thank 'agreeable colleagues'. Any mistakes are ours, of course.

Introduction

The Legendary Peter Winch and the Myth of 'Social Science'

Rejecting the Very Idea of a Social Science

J.L. Austin (1962, p. 2), once remarked that in philosophy one often observes that there is the bit where it's said and the bit where it's taken back. Well, we have titled this book, somewhat boldly, some might say brashly, but certainly intentionally provocatively, *There is No Such thing as Social Science.* That is where we say it. Will we now begin taking it back? Well, of course the answer to that question will depend on the use to which we are putting the word 'science' in our title, in claiming there is no such thing as a social science. Is the use to which we put that term consonant with ordinary English usage or are we, in some sense, leaving ourselves open to a charge of gerrymandering by employing a marginal, specialised or contentious use of 'science' so that we might more easily say that there is no such thing as a social science?

To come at this from another vantage point, let us state what we are not against and what we are not saying there is no possibility of. We are not against analytical rigour; such rigour is, of course, crucial to most serious modes of inquiry. Nor are we against a programme of social inquiry which accords a deal of importance to the revision of its claims in light of further (relevant) observations of various kinds; it is, of course, inquiry and not the production and defence of doctrine that practitioners in the social studies are undertaking.

Indeed, we would be willing to go further. We will even allow that the practice of social inquiry can (and does) on occasion learn from the practices undertaken in other modes of inquiry and on occasion these might be those modes of inquiry known as the natural sciences.

One might be inclined to retort that in this case, given what we have just said, we must concede that there *is* such a thing as a social science; that we have just furnished our readers with 'the bit where we take it back'. Well, our reasons for resisting such a concession are as follows. Rigour, openness to having one's claims revised in light of further study and openness to learning[1] from other modes of inquiry are not

---

1 Of course, there are diverse ways in which such learning can take place. One can for instance learn from the (natural) sciences in social inquiry by loose analogy, without in the slightest being committed to regarding one's own inquiry as itself scientific. An intriguing example of roughly this, on our reading, is Thomas Kuhn's borrowings from Darwin and other natural scientists, in the substance of his own philosophising. See Sharrock and Read (2002).

enough for those who claim to be defenders of the idea of a social science against those whom they take to be their opponents. Analytic rigour is a *pre-eminent* mark of English-speaking philosophy; but, on Wittgensteinian grounds we would wish to contest strenuously any claim that such philosophy is itself scientific. 'Openness to having one's claims revised in light of further study' is a pre-requisite for being an historian—hardly thereby making history a science. 'Openness to learning from other modes of inquiry' is essential for polymaths and spiritual seekers and … Enough said.[2] No; there is always a further claim, of one kind or another, made in order to justify labelling one's inquiries 'scientific'. It is this further claim in all its variants to which we object. This further claim might be methodological:

- There is an identifiable scientific method and this ought to be employed if one intends to make a claim to do something scientific.

Or it might be substantive (or, sometimes, more specifically 'ontological'):

- Social scientific findings are reducible to the findings of the natural sciences.

Put another way one might say the following. The term 'science' and 'scientific' can be employed in one way to do no more than to denote a certain spirit of inquiry. Alternatively those terms might be employed in such a way as to invoke a specific method (or class of methods) of inquiry. And, sometimes the term is employed or invoked such that it denotes a set of specific substantive claims made by practitioners in certain domains of scientific enquiry (e.g. physics, biology, neuroscience and so on), to which the claims of one's own inquiry (anthropology, sociology, psychology, etc.), are reducible.[3] The latter of this trio and the second of the two varieties of reductionism is often referred to as ontological reductionism. We here call it substantive reductionism; we prefer the term 'substantive reductionism' to 'ontological reductionism' in the present context so as to allow for a broader casting of our net, as it were. There are some reductionists who, while being reductionists in the substantive sense would not obviously be ontological reductionists. Those who seek to reduce sociological claims to evolutionary psychological claims, for example, are not merely methodological reductionists, simply arguing for what they take to be legitimate scientific methods (as does, for example, McIntyre 1996 and 2006), but are substantive reductionists, in that they reduce the sociological to the

---

2   Though far more, in fact, could be said here. For instance: the huge irony of the programmatic, science-aping nature of 'social science' is that in this regard it manifestly fails to successfully ape (natural) science—for (real) sciences developed not through aping other sciences, but through actual empirical etc. study that eventually issued, through anomaly, crisis and revolution, in paradigms that gave birth to more unified or at least novel research traditions. *In the very act* of attempting to copy (natural) science, 'social science' invalidates its own scientific pretensions—for science did not and does not proceed by such copying. (For detailed exposition of this argument, see Sharrock and Read 2002, *passim.*)

3   There are, of course, many uses of the words 'science' and 'scientific'. We make no attempt here at a taxonomy.

evolutionary psychological:[4] the claims of the former, if valid, will always be simply the claims of the latter. This said, they are not necessarily committed to ontological reductionism.

We might therefore express the above in the form of questions as to what meaning one attaches to the term 'social science',

- Is one talking of social science as scientific in terms of it being conducted in the scientific spirit: its practitioners acting in accordance with certain intellectual virtues?
- Is one talking of social science being scientific in terms of its method being one that is shared with the (or some of the) natural sciences, reducible in terms of methods employed? Or
- Is one talking of social science as scientific in terms of it being reducible to one or other of the natural sciences, reducible in terms of the substance of their claims?

While substantive reductionism is (sadly) both common and prominent in recent philosophical work on consciousness, for example (e.g. Patricia Churchland's (1989) and Paul Churchland's (1988) neuroreductionism), it is, relatively speaking, less-so in the social sciences. However, it is present, even gaining a degree of prominence. Evolutionary psychology would be one example; varieties of materialism would be others.[5] For, evolutionary psychology's misnomer not withstanding, it reduces psychological claims (and sociological ones, where it cares to) to evolutionary biology.[6] However, our targets—those we have in mind in titling our book as we do—are also the methodological reductionists.

One might then paraphrase our title to the somewhat less snappy, though less open to misunderstanding, 'There is no such thing as a social science on the model of either methodological or substantive reductionism.' Why are we so sure there is no such thing? Well this question is what we seek to answer in the chapters that follow; but, in short, there is no such thing as a social science on the model of methodological or substantive reductionism, because to be committed to methodological or substantive reductionism is to be committed to *a priorism*; it is to be committed to something—a method or the relevant explanatory factors in one's explanation of social action—prior to one's investigation. The correct method, if one wishes to speak so, is read off the

---

4   See, for example, John Alcock (2001).

5   See for instance Colin Campbell (1996); compare Sharrock's criticisms thereof, and Read's (both in Coulter and Watson (eds), 2008).

6   We are not here denying that 'evolutionary psychology' (sociobiology) has anything going for it: it is obvious and trivial that some social phenomena have roots in biological adaptation from previous epochs. What we have against sociobiology is principally its scientistic and programmatic ambition to reduce most important social phenomena to those roots—it stands in dire risk, among other things, of thereby blighting our ability to understand the phenomena in question. In short: it tends toward crudity, in its portrayal of the practices it would explain and to leave us *less* clear about many social phenomena than we were before we started. In that regard, its failing is indicative and prototypical of the diminishment of understanding that 'social science' can produce.

nature of the phenomena. To embrace a particular methodology from another domain of inquiry owing to its success in that domain is, one might say, ironically contrary to the scientific spirit: it is to fail to act in accordance with the intellectual virtues.[7]

It will be retorted that it is we who are being *a prioristic* ... How can we say ahead of time that there cannot be a science of *x*?—Well then, must we consider the possibility that there must be a science of morals? A science of abstract objects? A science of things beginning with the letter 'e'?[8]

The question is, upon whom the onus falls to show that there can be or is a science of *x* (where *x* is society). We submit that the onus is on our opponents to demonstrate an intelligible sense in which there can be a science of *x* in this case, just as in the above cases.[9] It is not us but our opponents, the 'mainstream' who have the orthodoxy of academic structures on their side (there are far more faculties of 'Social Science' than of 'Social Studies'), who are being *a prioristic* and dogmatic: whenever they insist, overtly or covertly, that there is only one legitimate method of human inquiry or knowledge-acquisition, they are ruling out the possibility that there may be several, or many. They are already convinced, before any discussion begins, that science is the alpha and omega of epistemic respectability; whereas we are open-minded. They are convinced that, to be worth anything, social study must be social science; we keep looking[10] for whatever social study actually is and can be.

Let us put our case still more plainly here, for reductionists will continue to resist and will, no doubt, accuse us of something akin to anti-reductionist 'hand-waving', 'knee-jerk' anti-reductionism, or along with such luminaries as Pinker and Dennett, simply dismiss us as yearning fantasists who either know not what we

---

7   Thus the first of our bullet-pointed questions above, we are employing to pose a serious problem for those who would, as most apologists for social science would, be inclined to answer either the second or the third (or both of those) of the bullet-pointed questions with some kind of 'Yes'.

8   For more developed argument and examples, see Read (2008).

9   The attempt to argue for the possibility of a hard science of sociology is surely inappropriate for someone who really believes that such a possibility can be realised, since the most convincing proof of their point would be the delivery of just that science. The appropriate thing to do would be to work out that science. Those who have taken the obligation to walk the walk, not just talk the programme, have failed and failed dismally to produce anything but caricatures of understanding or cumbersome machineries for saying not very much of a genuinely informative kind.

10   This expression of ours is intended to echo Sextus Empiricus's brilliant description of the alternative to positive and negative dogmatisms, in chapter 1 of book 1 of his 'Outline of Pyrrhonism' (see http://people.uvawise.edu/philosophy/phil205/Sextus.html), 'some have claimed to have discovered the truth, others have asserted that it cannot be apprehended, while others again go on inquiring'. We 'go on inquiring' after or 'keep on searching' for—keep an open mind to—methods and truths that are not scientific or not scientifically-arrived at, rather than—absurdly—denying that science has efficaciously inquired into anything or—dogmatically and scientistically—insisting that *only* science has efficaciously inquired into anything.

mean by 'reductionism' or fail to give adequate sense to the term.[11] Our case is that reductionism in terms of methodologies or substantive claims is counter to the *spirit* of scientific inquiry, and it is the *spirit* of scientific inquiry that is primary. The 'scientific spirit'—what one *wanted* out of attaching the qualities of science to one's endeavour in the first place—militates against both methodological and substantive reductionism in the social studies.

In Defence of Peter Winch?

To our subtitle; why defend Peter Winch? Is he not, as so-often presented, a minor diversion in mid-twentieth century philosophy of social science? Has intellectual culture not moved on, and overcome Winch, as philosophy in general has moved on from the diversion that was linguistic philosophy? Was Gellner not correct in dismissing Winch's work as a voguish and 'profoundly mistaken doctrine'?[12] This seems to be the dominant narrative. Similarly, we often hear the refrain that Winch was railing against positivism,[13] but none of us are positivists now. So, no need to read Winch then.

Social Studies as Philosophy

It is now exactly a half-century since Winch wrote his provocatively polemical little book, *The Idea of a Social Science*. When Winch refers to 'science' or the 'natural sciences' in *ISS* he usually explicitly refers to the '*experimental* sciences'. Some contemporary defenders of social studies as science (defenders of the idea of a social science), such as Roy Bhaskar and Lee C. McIntyre, believe this leads those who criticise them to begin with flawed premises, for their conceptions of science (they have very different conceptions) do not demand that the conducting of experiments are essential to a science. But this rejection of Winch, were it to be/when it is aimed at him, does not work. Even those natural sciences such as geology and astronomy for which large parts of their respective domains of inquiry are not amenable to subjecting to reproducible experiments are not non-experimental in any logical

---

11 Dennett remarks, "The term that is most often bandied about in these conflicts, typically as a term of abuse, is 'reductionism'. Those who yearn for skyhooks call those who eagerly settle for cranes 'reductionists', and they can often make reductionism seem philistine and heartless. But like most terms of abuse, 'reductionism' has no fixed meaning" (Dennett 1995, 80). In a similar manner Pinker writes, "Attempts to explain behavior in mechanistic terms are commonly denounced as 'reductionist' or 'determinist'. The denouncers rarely know exactly what they mean by those words, but everyone knows they refer to something bad" (Pinker 2002, 10). Dennett's drawing of an analogy between his critics and some mythical yearners for skyhooks is somewhat cheap and maybe even gratuitous. To dismiss (even by inference) those who do not share one's approach as yearning for something nonsensical like 'skyhooks' is nothing more than a cheap and empty rhetorical move, gaining him nothing. We are very far from seeking 'skyhooks'; indeed, by contrast, we remain resolutely on the ground.

12 See Gellner 'Concepts and Society', footnote 1, in Wilson, B.R. (ed.) (1970).

13 See, for example, Bhaskar (1998 [1979]), p. 2.

sense, though they are in practice (largely) non-experimental. Put another way: the unavailability of conditions under which experiments can be reproduced in some of the natural sciences is allegedly similar to a sense in which reproducible experiments are often unavailable to the social scientist. However, this practical unavailability of experimental conditions, though it is well worthy of both ethical and methodological reflection in the *social* case[14] is *not* the locus of the main issue to which Winch draws attention. Winch, as we discuss below, draws attention to the fact that questions in social studies are *logically distinct* from those in the natural sciences.

So, what were Winch's claims? Well, one of his concerns in his *the Idea of a Social Science and its Relation to Philosophy* (hereafter *ISS*) was to disabuse social studies of the obsession with methodology and refocus attention onto the genuine loci of significance in their investigations: meaningful human actions. In short, Winch sought to pull one away from an obsession (which continues unabated) with identifying a methodology so that instead one might spend one's efforts on the identification and understanding of action. Unfortunately Winch's efforts, by and large, went unrewarded. The scientistic obsession with method went deep, very deep. So deep in fact that when someone like Winch came along and tried to treat the obsession he was misunderstood as making a call for a new, distinctive method of social inquiry of his own, replacing the idea of covering laws with the Wittgensteinian notion of rule-following. This was not Winch's intention. Winch was concerned to demonstrate that the social scientist has good reason to look somewhere other than the natural sciences for guidance. In a profound but very predictable irony, Winch was read—(re-)interpreted—through the distorting lens of scientism. Scientism, so powerful a cultural urge that Winch could help relatively few others to overcome it, and so was largely read as simply offering a variant form of it.[15]

Winch's claim in fact was that the central misunderstanding current in the social studies was the desire or tendency to see them as a branch, a new or proto- branch but a branch all the same, of the sciences; when rather one should see the social studies as much more akin to a branch of philosophy. This has been and is resisted by Winch's critics, philosopher and social scientist alike. The resistance is founded in a misunderstanding of the nature of philosophy, which Winch addresses in the opening chapter of *ISS*. The inertia of those who are resistant to social studies being philosophical rather than scientific stems from their being in thrall to a latent but thought-constraining picture of philosophy as either an inferior pretender to science or as a master science: a science of the most general.

Winch writes,

> The argument runs as follows: new discoveries about real matters of fact can only be established by experimental methods; no purely *a priori* process of thinking is sufficient

---

14 What would a genuine controlled 'economic experiment' look like, for instance? Could it really happen at all, outside a thoroughly authoritarian state in which the answer to the experiment was in effect guaranteed before one started by repression of any human effort to resist that answer? (Think Friedman's Chile).

15 We shall detail in the body of this book some moments where early Winch unfortunately provided hostages to fortune in making this misreading of him too easy; these moments were very largely overcome, in later decades of Winch's life and work.

for this. But since it is science which uses experimental methods, while philosophy is purely *a priori*, it follows that the investigation of reality must be left to science. On the other hand, philosophy has traditionally claimed, at least in large part, to consist in the investigation of the nature of reality; either therefore traditional philosophy was attempting to do something which its methods of investigation could never possibly achieve, and must be abandoned; or else it was mistaken about its own nature and the purport of its investigations must be drastically reinterpreted (*ISS*, p. 8).

Winch continues to show how this argument fails. It fails because of equivocation on the word 'reality'.

The difference between the respective aims of the scientist and the philosopher might be expressed as follows. Whereas the scientist investigates the nature of particular real things and processes, the philosopher is concerned with the nature of reality as such and in general. Burnet puts the point very well ... when he points out that the sense in which the philosopher asks "what's real?" involves the problem of man's relation to reality, which takes us beyond pure science. "We have to ask whether the mind of man can have any contact with reality at all, and, if it can, what difference this will make to his life". Now to think that this question of Burnet's could be settled by experimental methods involves just as serious a mistake as to think that philosophy with its a *priori* methods of reasoning could compete with experimental science on its own ground. **For it is not an empirical question at all but a** *conceptual* **one. It has to do with the** *force of the concept* **of reality. An appeal to the results of an experiment would necessarily beg the important question, since the philosopher would be bound to ask by what token those results themselves are accepted as "reality"** (ibid., pp. 8-9, emboldened emphasis ours).

So, Winch at once defends a discrete realm of philosophical inquiry; a realm where appeal to experimental results simply begs the (philosophical) question. And he further claims that social studies either belong to this realm or are closer to it than they are to the realm of the experimental natural sciences. The point, to be clear, is that a question is a philosophical question if that which is in question involves, has intrinsic to it, a question as to the subject of the question's criteria for identity. If it does then to try to answer the question through appeal to experimental methods begs the question; to conduct an experiment one has to have already established the identity of the subject of the experiment; it is only then that we can talk meaningfully of conducting the experiment and of the experiment having established anything. Consider: the question as to whether God exists is not the same kind of question as the question as to whether unicorns exist, nor even whether an invisible man exists (as featured in H G Wells's novella). For in asking whether God exists we are asking what would count as Him, and what would count as Him existing: would we have to be able to see Him, must He be tangible, and must He be locatable? Unless the question as to whether unicorns exist is using the name in a radically different way to its usage in English then we have no problems similar to those we encounter with the God question. (Problems indexed preliminarily, indeed, by capitalisation of the 'H' in 'Him'.)

Consider another question. The question as to whether there are any dodos living on the island of Mauritius is a question for which we can easily establish criteria for answering (as we have done, and answered). We can establish criteria for what we are calling a 'dodo', what we count as its being 'on the island of Mauritius' and so on. Once we've established the criteria, producing a living dodo on the island would settle the question, just as agreeing that we have conducted an exhaustive study of Mauritius and found no evidence of living dodos will establish the contrary.[16]

In contrast, if someone, a sceptic, were to ask whether anything exists outside our thoughts, producing for them a living dodo as evidence of something that exists outside their thoughts will simply beg the question. Indeed, consider that their asking the question in the first place indicated that asking questions of an interlocutor had not satisfied them of the reality of the external world—the externality of the interlocutor. All these things, everything, is what they question the reality of, for they are questioning reality *per se*: reality as a realm constitutively independent of their own thoughts. Pointing at something, even taking the questioner by the hand and leading them to touch the thing, having it peck their fingers, leaves their question untouched if not, presumably, their fingers. For the sceptic can simply respond that the thing pointed to, just as with the person pointing, does not *really* exist, for you (who? ...) have yet to demonstrate its reality, its existence outside the mind (the only mind that really exists). The question posed was a question about the nature of reality in general. What was/is then in question is what *counts* as real. Providing the sceptic with something that one would ordinarily count as evidence of the existence of that particular thing is to offer 'something' to the sceptic as evidence, the status of which their question had already cast in doubt, not just as evidence but as *anything* outside of their own thoughts. We are not implying here that such sceptical questions are unanswerable, that one must concede the sceptic's point.[17] We are saying, with Winch who follows Wittgenstein,[18] *that the idea that one can refute such sceptical questions by recourse to experimental methods is deeply confused.*[19] The sceptic's

---

16 And pretty much the latter is what has actually happened: there *are* no dodos on Mauritius. Of course, as with those who hold out for the existence of the Loch Ness monster, there might well always be those who insist that we might still find a dodo on Mauritius, just as we might one day find Nessy in Loch Ness and little green humanoids on the planet Mars, all previous attempts to do so not withstanding. But such resistance is psychological not logical, as it were; for such resistance is based in a *desire* for the dodo to exist or for Nessy to exist, or for (human-like) life on Mars. It is not based on lack of criteria for what would count as a dodo or for what would count as Nessy and so on. (Some might object to the example of the Loch Ness monster in that it is not established what sort of creature it is we are looking for. However, we have a clear idea what it isn't: dolphin, seal, shoal of fish, beaver, submarine made to look like a large sea creature, and so on.)

17 Far from it—we would suggest indeed that they can ultimately be shown to the sceptic to be nonsensical (see for explication many of the essays in *Wittgenstein and Scepticism*, edited by Denis McManus 2004).

18 See especially Wittgenstein's *On Certainty*.

19 It is well worth comparing here, section xiv of Part II of Wittgenstein's *PI* (the very close of the book, as Anscombe and Rhees arranged it): "The confusion and barrenness of psychology is not to be explained by calling it a 'young science'; its state is not comparable with that of physics, for instance, in its beginnings ... For in psychology there are experimental methods and *conceptual confusion* ... The existence of the experimental method makes us

question is a philosophical question about the nature of reality. It is thus a question about the place the concept of reality has in the lives of those who have grasped it, those who have a life with that concept.

How does this relate to social studies? Well consider a further, third, question: are any altruistic actions undertaken on the island of Mauritius in a designated period of time? You might answer no to this question, having read a book by the populist evolutionary theorist (and former non-executive Chairman of Northern Rock bank) Matt Ridley; a book bought for you (as a 'gift') by your—as you now realise—self-serving mother. However, we suggest to you that you might want to consider the case of our friend Reuben, his dog, Spot and his Aunt, Bola (from Mauritius). Reuben's dog Spot required a rather expensive operation on one of his claws. Aunty Bola sold her house and her belongings and moved into a hostel so as to provide funds to pay for Spot's claw operation. You 'point out' that Reuben's Aunty Bola was merely acting from self-interest.[20] The reasons you might provide for such a response to us are many and easily imagined, and there is little need to rehearse them here. The point we wish to make is simply that what is in question, what is intrinsic to the question as to whether there exist altruistic actions, is the question as to what one would count as such an action. The criteria for altruistic actions, taken in abstraction from the meanings those (altruistic) actions have for those undertaking them, is up for grabs, as it were; whether an action is altruistic or not is not something that can be settled by experimental methods. It is rather a purpose-relative and occasion-sensitive matter. To abstract from the purpose of the action and its occasion is to abstract from that which conveys upon the action its identity. So, imagine the most generous act possible and then imagine a non-altruistic motive for that action. One can always be suggested, with a little thought, and rejecting the validity of such a suggestion is not achieved by simply pointing to the original action as originally imagined.

So we have our three questions,

1. Are there any dodos alive on Mauritius?
2. Does 'the world beyond my thoughts' exist?
3. Are there any 'truly altruistic' acts?

So question 1 is an empirical question; questions 2 and 3 are conceptual questions. They are in one important sense questions about the meaning of the words 'world' and 'altruism', respectively. The answer to question 1 can be settled empirically, by producing a dodo (or, equally, by thoroughly checking Mauritius for dodos and

---

think we have the means of solving the problems which trouble us; though problem and method pass one another by".

20 The explanation from self-interest that you insist upon might be grounded in some theory to which you subscribe regarding the evolved behaviour of the human species, the place of the keeping of pets in that evolution and possibly also of the evolutionary-function of the neatness of one's pet's claws: Spot having neat claws means he is likely to be a more attractive mate to other dogs in the park of a morning, which means Reuben, too, has more chance of striking up a relationship with possible mates who are also dog-owners or dog-walkers. It is in the species' interest that Aunts have nephews in relationships that are likely to bear fruit, and so on. Spot's claw has more significance put like that …

finding none, which is in effect what hunters and alien vermin did to this island and to this unfortunate species in remarkably short order, some time ago now). The answers to questions 2 and 3 cannot be so settled. We might put the difference as being one of scope. Empirical questions rest upon agreement in criteria; it is *only* because we agree that we can even talk of something being evidence without begging the question of those to whom we are providing said evidence. Conceptual questions are questions wherein and whereby such agreement cannot be assumed in abstraction from specific occasions and purposes.[21] What this means is that the craving for generality which is central to the idea of a social science is undercut by the nature of that which the social scientist seeks to explain: its occasion sensitivity and it purpose relativity.[22]

Why do we go to such lengths to make our point here? Well, as we noted above, Winch is often misunderstood. So, once again, it is not the unavailability of the conditions for reproducible experiments in the social studies which drives Winch's claims in *ISS*. It is rather the nature of questions in the social studies that, Winch claims, have more in common with philosophical questions than with scientific questions.

Resisting Winch: Reaffirming Social Science

Now, there has been considerable resistance to the implications that Winch took to follow from this (social studies as philosophy, rather than science). One prominent and trenchant recent advocate of Hempelian deductive-nomological methods in the social studies, Lee C. McIntyre, argues for what we termed above 'methodological reductionism'. While he claims to not reject what he terms 'interpretivism' (we challenge this as being an apposite term for denoting Winch's discussions, below) McIntyre argues that

> [I]n order to understand the meaning of human action, we must attempt to put it in context, and at least part of the ideal context would include an account of the causes that led up to the event itself. The ... example of interpreting the meaning of a film is instructive. Could one really be a film critic if one knew nothing about how films were made? That is, even if one were concerned with only understanding the "meaning" of the film as a "text" and

---

21 No absolute line or gulf is being suggested here between empirical and conceptual (for explication, see for instance Kuhn's work and Wittgenstein's *On Certainty*). That a complicated grey area certainly exists is irrelevant to the distinction between empirical and conceptual remaining a sound and useful one, Quinian qualms notwithstanding. (Those qualms, we submit, are no more pressing than the Sorites paradox.)

22 'Occasion-sensitivity' is Charles Travis's term (Travis 2008). We borrow it because we find it apposite to our purpose here; we use it in a way which does not necessarily draw upon Travis's arguments, though we do by-and-large agree with those arguments, and (highly) recommend them to our readers who are interested in some of the central questions in philosophy. 'Purpose-relativity' of the meaning of actions does not entail Relativism—about culture or truth, and so on—but means only to draw attention to how the identity of an action is intimately related—we might say internally related—to the purpose of the action. More on this below and in subsequent chapters.

only sought to give an interpretation of it in order to evaluate its quality, wouldn't one also have to know something about the causal genesis of film? Wouldn't one need to know about editing, producing, and sound direction? Are these really alien to the interpretation of a film's meaning? Surely we must care to know whether some of the subtleties in the final product were intentional—or whether they were artefacts of the medium itself.

Perhaps the same is true for the interpretation of human action. Even if one professes to be concerned solely with interpreting human action, there may still be a role for causal inquiry. One must know something about prior events that led up to the action as well as how the decision to act was formulated. What were the factors that influenced the thoughts the agent had? Could he or she have acted differently? To what extent was the action a function of intentions versus constraints imposed by other "human" factors? Was the actor tired, desperate or hungry—had he or she just had a fight with someone? How do people normally act under these circumstances?

Thus, one may conclude that interpretive and nomological modes of explanation need not exclude one another; although given their differing commitments to what it is most important to have explained about human behaviour, they will inevitably be at odds with one another about the proper focus of our inquiry (McIntyre 1996, pp. 129-130).

There is much here that could with reasonable charity be heard as unobjectionable. But, insofar as there is a case here for Hempel and against Winch, what does that case really amount to? The implied distinction between levels of description is misguided; as if there is an interpretive and a causal 'level', both being ways of describing 'the same thing' only from different 'perspectives'. Describing a punch in a way which does not involve the intentions of the person throwing the punch *is no longer a description of a **punch*** but a description of a type of movement. This aside, what does McIntyre provide us with by way of examples of putatively causal influences on a meaningful action? He writes: 'What were the factors that influenced the thoughts the agent had? Could he or she have acted differently? To what extent was the action a function of intentions versus constraints imposed by other "human" factors? Was the actor tired, desperate or hungry—had he or she just had a fight with someone? How do people normally act under these circumstances?' (ibid.). These are all things which can and would, where relevant, be easily included in any account of the meaning of an action and none of these examples are obviously examples of factors which must be, are best, or even fruitfully explained by subsumption under covering laws. (Though, needless to say, various 'natural laws' will be *potentially* 'relevant to'/in play in the situation under description, even if rather remotely—e.g. perhaps biological 'laws' covering the function of water in the body.)[23] Whether someone could have acted otherwise, in acting as they did, is not obviously best

---

23 One reason why it is worth pointing this triviality out is the danger—a danger that Winch sometimes lets his formulations foment—that Winch (likewise, Wittgenstein, or Kuhn) will be (mis-)interpreted as an 'Idealist' or Anti-Realist of some kind. The *whole person*, the whole 'rational animal', and not just their 'mental life', is what interests Winch/Wittgenstein; and indeed the whole person in their *worldly situation*. Not just biological but also ecological (as well as physical) 'laws' are ultimately 'in play' in the—in any—situation. But this is, as we note, trivial and obvious, not a cause either for scientistic ecstasy or schadenfreude.

captured by the deductive-nomological method, as McIntyre seeks to establish. It is best captured by knowing something about the actor as a person and their relation to the context, the social situation. Of course if the only 'alternative' to acting as they did would imply acting in violation of the laws of physics then that does not so much serve as a reason for acting as the person did, but makes manifest a constraint upon their actions. But saying this does not mean that we see such constraints as *beyond* or *outside* the meaning of the action. Such things are the *background* against which the action *has sense*. One's description of the meaning of a leap of joy has no more sense (cannot be said to have that meaning) devoid of its background context than a smile devoid of its face.

Similarly, questions as to whether a film is shot on film, or on video, or HD digital are the background against which a critic makes his appraisal and pens his judgement of the film. The critic is not oblivious to the practice, logistics and material constraints of film-making. When it is pertinent to what he wants to convey about the film he will refer to elements of the practice explicitly; when it is not judged pertinent to what he is claiming regarding the film's meaning he will leave such things in the background, as the unsaid non-manifest context, so to speak. Some critics might think that the use of extreme close-ups shot from an extreme distance through a telephoto lens (when the decision to do so is purely aesthetic), rather than, as is standard, shot close-up to the subject with a standard lens, is relevant to the point they wish to make in their appraisal and interpretation of the film. Others will think it merely an inconsequential stylistic tic of the director. Either way, such things are not thought of as any more beyond the limits of interpretation of a film than the constraints of gravity are thought beyond the limits of interpretation of a person's Earthly actions, it is merely that in both cases sometimes they are relevant to the point being made and thus should be a factor in one's description and sometimes they are not so relevant and can be left *entirely* in the background, *simply* assumed.

However, we would not want to stop here; it is instructive to really try to imagine what it would be for a film critic to be oblivious to the basic practice, logistics and material constraints of film making, or a sociologist or anthropologist to be oblivious to basic physical and biological realities. Would such a person—let's call them 'McIntyre's film critic' and 'McIntyre's interpretivist sociologist'—be recognisably a critic or a sociologist; would they even be recognisably *members* of our culture? They would rather resemble members of a (rather extreme and exotic) cargo cult. In the case of 'McIntyre's film critic' would he not be as (or, even more) likely to believe the actors on screen to be Gods called into existence by the folding down of cinema seats and the drawing back of velvet curtains? For if the film critic really knows nothing of the basic practice, logistics and material constraints of film making he knows nothing of what is and is not a film. Similarly, 'McIntyre's interpretivist sociologist' who knows simply nothing of physical and biological reality; what could he meaningfully say that we would understand? How could *he* live? We say this not in an attempt to refute anything McIntyre writes but merely to show that the dichotomy he sets up makes little sense. 'Interpretivists' (as McIntyre identifies non-Hempelians) are neither oblivious to physical reality nor do they think it always insignificant to their inquiries (though of course the degree of significance regarding a particular account of a particular action might well be what gives rise to many debates between sociologists of all kinds).

One thing that is raised by a discussion such as that initiated by what McIntyre writes (above) is how Winch is usually discussed, by would-be friend and would-be foe alike. That is, as one of the 'interpretivist' or '*Verstehen*' school in the philosophy of social science. Now, in one sense there is no problem with Winch being claimed or identified as a member of this school, if membership is open simply to those who oppose positivism and materialism in the philosophy of social sciences and favour some form of analysis which accounts for the meaning of social action. However, there are crucial differences between Winch and other prominent interpretivists, and the difference raises questions as to whether calling Winch an interpretivist is perspicuous. In short (for we discuss this in subsequent chapters) Winch follows Wittgenstein in drawing a vital distinction between interpreting a rule and grasping/ following/obeying it. What it is to understand a social action is to grasp the meaning of the action as do the participants. One does not generally go through a process of interpreting another's words as they engage in conversation—one *hears* the words. Similarly, one does not interpret the punch; one sees it (one would hope). The thought that interpreting must be taking place in both cases is born of prejudice and results in fallacy. This fallacy we might dub the fallacy of extensional primacy. This fallacy is born of the tendency to think that what is real or what has ultimate significance, what is primary, is that which is extensionally described, with all other intensional descriptions being merely ways of 'tarting-up' this perhaps more authentic but certainly more primary extensional world (The gendered descriptor here is salient: 'extensionalism', a close cousin to physicalism, is a fantasy of 'hard' science, psychologically-attractive to a gendered wish to avoid 'softness'). The fallacy has its roots in empiricism (and flowers in some forms of reductionism) and the idea that it is we, our minds, that add the meaning onto the world or the sense impressions caused by the (bare, unclothed or mechanical) world.

The German *Verstehen* can be translated as either 'understanding' or 'interpretation'. If Winch is to be seen as close to the *Verstehen* tradition, then we would favour the former translation, with the rider that when we say that what we seek is 'understanding' we are saying no more than that we seek to understand the action, in a perfectly everyday, sense. We do not seek understanding in some abstract sense, only available through application of one or another 'methodology'. One seeks understanding in that one seeks to grasp the meaning (in the same way) as ordinary members of the culture do. Expertise in social understanding is a maturational art, not a science open to expertise in any 'academic' sense of *that* word. There is and can be no *elite* of independent experts in (the genuine content of) social science. In an important sense, we are *all* practical experts—as, very roughly, we are all (all writers or readers of this book, in an important sense) experts in practical use of the English language.

Participants in a conversation do not need to constantly be interpreting each others' words. Social actors interacting within society need not constantly be interpreting the meanings of each others' actions. There is no *process* of understanding running along which enables them to see the meaning in each other's actions and words. This is where Winch differs from *Verstehen* theorists such as Collingwood and Charles

Taylor. So; one should *not* fall into the trap of seeing understanding as some sort of mysterious property, like some non-rational emotive capacity. This seems to be Manicas's concern,

> We must not think of *verstehen* as some sort of special, intuitive, sympathetic understanding, **a reliving of the experience of others.** *Verstehen* is something we do all the time. We are engaged in *verstehen* in **judging that** a person on a ladder is painting the house, in **judging that** the expression on another's face is distress produced by our careless remark, and so forth. We learned to do this, indeed, when we learned to use language. There is nothing dubious about such **judgements** since, as with **any judgement,** they **require evidence** and may, subsequently, be rejected (Manicas, P.T. 2006, 64, emboldened emphasis ours).

Now, we can very much take Manicas's point about *Verstehen* not being 'a sort of special, intuitive, sympathetic understanding, a reliving of the experience of others'. Indeed, it is rather (as ordinary understanding, rather than as extraordinary interpretation) what 'we do all the time'; there is nothing magical or queer about it. However, it is also, as we noted above, not something that draws decisively or (usually) *at all* on evidence (cf. our discussion of the three questions: of the dodo, of reality, and of altruism). Manicas is guilty of not paying close enough attention to the different uses to which we put 'to judge'/'judgement'. One's judgement as regards a *fact* or a material state of affairs is made when the resources for *knowing* and thus for stating the fact are not fully available to one. It falls to one then to judge rather than apprehend and state the fact, *x*, in the form of a true proposition: *x* is *y*; when the fact, *x*, is fully disclosed then the question of evidence becomes redundant and there is no need to talk of judging that *x* is thus and so. To invoke Austin's discussion in *Sense and Sensibilia*, we judge there to be a pig in the vicinity only when the pig is not before us: we judge a pig to be in the vicinity on the evidence provided by the trough of partially eaten turnips, the fresh trotter marks in the mud of the fenced-off area, and so on. If and when the pig emerges from the sty and stands grunting and snuffling before us this is not further evidence of a pig being in the vicinity, making our judgement stronger, but it is rather the moment at which judgement is made redundant as we have apprehended the fact: here is a pig.[24]

Judgement regarding the meaning of a social action is not of this variety of judgement. For the use of 'judgement' in the case of empirical matters, the only use Manicas sees, is, we might say, internally related to the concept of evidence. In contrast, judgements regarding the meaning of social action are not so related to the concept of evidence. For, as we explained above, the meaning of social actions

---

24 As Austin puts the scenario (in his unmistakable style): 'The situation in which I would properly be said to have *evidence* for the statement that some animal is a pig is that, for example, in which the beast itself is not actually on view, but I can see plenty of pig-like marks on the ground outside its retreat. If I find a few buckets of pig food, that's a bit more evidence, and the noises and the smell may provide better evidence still. But if the animal then emerges and stands there plainly in view, there is no longer any question of collecting evidence; its coming into view doesn't provide me with more *evidence* that it's a pig, I can now just *see* that it is, the question is settled' (Austin 1970, p. 115).

is not an empirical matter—it is a conceptual one. A judgement as to the meaning of a social action comes into play (as opposed to our merely/simply *grasping* the meaning) when the meaning is not fully to hand, when it is beyond our grasp. This might happen in situations where the context is unclear, where we are observing another culture (people with seemingly very different ways of doing things to us) and so on. There are situations where while we cannot see the pig we can judge there to be a pig (or not), just as there are situations where while we haven't grasped the meaning of an action we judge it to mean x or y or z. This similarity is what leads Manicas, and others, astray; it leads them astray for the similarity ends here. Judging there to be a pig in the vicinity, like judging there to be dodos on Mauritius, is rendered redundant by production of a pig or (hypothetically, as once upon a time one could do) of a dodo on Mauritius. Judging whether a dance is a war dance or simply an entertaining way of passing the evening, is not settled by pointing at the dance in question, no more than judging an act to be altruistic is settled by pointing at the action. The action's identity is a conceptual not an empirical matter.

Beyond Science: Winch's Continued Relevance

McIntyre and Manicas both want to defend some sort of naturalism in the philosophy of social science. McIntyre is defending Hempelian deductive-nomological methods and Manicas a version of 'realist' philosophy of social science. We would not wish to leave our readers with the impression that it is only naturalists such as McIntyre and Manicas that need take note of Winch's writings. It was in the 1940s that Robert Merton (1968 [1949]) tried to popularise the earlier pronouncement of that 'Dean of social science' W. I. Thomas that 'a science which hesitates to forget its founders' is lost, challenging sociologists and other social theorists to give up pondering over the work of their predecessors and to get on with some empirical research and theory-building that would be sufficiently focussed to support knowledge accumulation. This campaign did not succeed. Stephen Cole's (2001) edited collection *What's Wrong With Sociology?* and Lee C. McIntyre's (2006) *The Dark Ages* testify that there are not many who are willing to describe what has gone on in 'empirical social science' since Merton's day as involving anything much worth calling progress. McIntyre's book is a full-scale recognition of how little progress sociology has made in Merton's terms, for it is a reiteration of Merton's complaint that we are largely bereft of *scientific* understanding of how society works and how its problems might be solved.

Contemporary sociology in Britain and Europe, in contrast, is often *very much* a function of the way in which its history is understood, the main most recent contributions to 'Sociological Theory' proper offering few fundamentally novel ideas, attempting instead the combination of diverse, often supposedly conflicting, conceptions from sociology's stock of long standing doctrines: consider the Grand social theories of Habermas, Giddens and Bourdieu. Whilst these 'theoretical' schemes are almost invariably offered with an avowedly ecumenical intention (their *spirit* is perhaps less ecumenical than is advertised) they do not really achieve much in the way of the sought-for integration across social science, but only add to the

Babel-like situation, each acquiring their own enthusiasts, but failing to attract more than a few of those dissidents who, purportedly, should be ready and grateful to be drawn into their big tent. The very ambition for 'Sociological theory proper' is, however, one which has now been demoted, often out of disillusionment with and consequent opposition to the very idea of science generally and, thus, with the 'scientific sociology'.

However, it is not our view that the move away from 'scientific sociology' is to be welcomed as a move away from 'science', for, as we discussed above, the thought which forms Peter Winch's doubts about 'the idea of a social science' is that 'scientific sociology' had much more to do with philosophy (both metaphysics and epistemology) than it had to do with anything genuinely scientific at all. The idea of *opposition* to science seems supernumerary. The ostensible 'move away from science' is not actually that at all, it is much more a repositioning *within philosophy.* Winch has not, in our view, lost much relevance because things have changed a great deal within the 'social and human sciences' since 1958—*plus ca change*, after all.

As we noted above, Winch's main argument, in short, was that 'sociology' (and similarly much of anthropology, psychology, economics, linguistics …) in its then main tendencies, was really philosophy presented in a form which could only mislead both those who might be considered customers for its promised deliverances, but also those who practiced its arcane and often shambolic arts. Not only did Winch see 'sociology' as a species of philosophy, hc saw it as the wrong kind of philosophy, one which attempted to be, can we call it constructive, in ways that are not compatible with its character as philosophy. Winch's call to 'social scientists' was not then to give up science, but to give up (the wrong kind of) philosophy, and rather to philosophise in a spirit that they would actually find satisfying, instead. To philosophise—that is, to reflect, to think, and to look—in such a way that would actually deal with their intellectual needs, rather than always leaving them with the sense that 'more research is needed', because no real progress had been made with resolving or dissolving the philosophical needs that underlay their inchoate effort to empirically-or-theoretically-research their way out of them.

In some ways, the passage of time has done much to vindicate Winch's point about the quintessentially philosophical concerns of social sciences. Since Winch wrote there has been, across a whole range of disciplines, a very noticeable 'turn to the social' which, to some degree Winch himself inadvertently inspired, a change which has been so extensive and influential that it is often necessary to talk about 'social thought' rather than about 'sociological theory' to avoid misrepresenting the situation as the sole vehicle of theorising about the nature of social reality. A massive change during this period has been in the vastly increased receptiveness of Anglo-Saxon thought to 'Continental' and, especially, French, thought. The simple fact is that the most prominent figures in such thought—Althusser, Levi-Strauss, Foucault, Derrida, Deleuze et al., have only rarely been sociologists by profession, and have much more commonly been philosophers, openly engaging with philosophical problems and without much of the concern for investigative empirical scruple present in Anglo-American sociology. The explicit recognition of the philosophical nature of the problems at issue is not, from Winch's point of view, a satisfactory one, for, from his point of view, the wrong kind of philosophy is still involved.

Insofar as Winch was paid much attention, it was usually on the assumption that if science was surrendered, then it was alright to continue with the *philosophy*— with, roughly, sociological theory, with philosophical theories of the phenomena in question (e.g. 'rule-following')—on the assumption that the possibility of a new basis for the 'social sciences' should be considered: did Winch point to the right way forward for what he would call 'social studies' or did his own views about what ought to be done fail the test? But the idea of 'a right way forward' is one which is meaningless to Winch's thought, since the notion of philosophy *proper* which he inherits from Wittgenstein is of a philosophy that, in important ways, makes no attempt to go anywhere, for philosophy is not in such business. Hence, there is no right way of going there, though there is the possibility of an illusion that there *is* somewhere to go (see Kevin Moore's (2000) attempt to communicate this lesson about Wittgenstein's thought to psychology). Thus *insofar* as Winch was given attention, that attention was overwhelmingly negative, often completely dismissive, and in those comparatively rare cases in which he was given favourable assessment, this was often based on seeing him as a representative of an alternative *approach within sociology*, a hermeneutic kind. Negatively, Winch was/is set aside as incipiently idealist, and thus profoundly out of tune with a sociology that insists on becoming ever more relentlessly materialist, one where, having seen through Cartesian mentalism, the need is to focus on *the body* instead of *the mind*. Positively, Winch was/is considered as offering a new methodology for sociology.

Both these, the negative and the positive responses remained entangled with issues that Winch thought were philosophical in nature, and thereby ultimately pseudo-problems, problems of our own making, borne of our own confusions. Mostly left out of play in sociology itself, Winch has received considerable and continuing attention in the 'philosophy of social science', though for Winch himself the idea of a distinct branch of sociology that specialised in its philosophical problems, acting as an auxiliary to sociology itself would itself be a nonsense, a manifestation of the view of philosophy as an under-labourer to empirical/scientific inquiries that Winch repudiates at the very beginning of *ISS*.

In 'the philosophy of social science', Winch has been the focus of the long-running, and still continuing, debates about rationality, whether 'rationality' is a general idea which might be used to assess different societies and their practices comparatively, or whether each culture or practice must have its own inherent and potentially distinctive rationality. In this context, Winch is seen as advocating that reality is grasped through concepts, that different communities have to be understood in terms of their own concepts, and that, therefore, each community must confront its own distinctive reality—this makes him out as a 'relativist'. This line of thought is often identical to or runs parallel with the ascription to Winch of a doctrine about the inherent limits of cross-cultural understanding, implying, if not explicitly asserting, that only those who belong to a culture can really understand it, and that it is impossible *really* to understand another culture except from 'inside it'.

Winch's work remains a focus of live discussion even into the present, though interest in it is mainly confined to the ghetto of 'philosophy of social science', and is much more often the target of critical devaluation than of approving support—and still less often is such approving support, support of the true Winch, for it is more often approval of an alleged 'Winchian' methodology for social science, or of a 'Winchian' relativism, *both* of which are dire contradictions in terms, unhappy sides of the same unhappy coin. Unfortunately, the Winch that comes in for criticism, like the Winch(s) that come(s) in for praise, never existed. As we will try to explain, in different ways, and at some length, Winch never supposed that there was a 'social science' problem about the possibility of 'understanding another culture', that there were any *inherent* difficulties—bordering on impossibilities—in understanding another culture (after all, it is only 'another culture' by virtue of exigencies of birth and biography), only reminding us, instead, that there are familiar and practical difficulties that we all encounter at points in our lives in understanding other people and their ways—e.g. 'I'm completely out of sympathy with them', 'I can't get the knack', 'I don't see the point of it', 'I haven't got the time to spend finding out' and the like. *Insofar* (not far!) as Winch is 'to blame' for reigniting the controversies over rationality and alien cultures after the 1960s, then much of the further discussion has been a waste of time, faulting Winch's supposed solutions to problems that he did not accept *were* problems.

If Winch's arguments are rescued from their ghetto confinement, then they are seen to be arguments about central features of the *whole* discipline—features of the very idea of 'social science'—ones inviting scepticism about *how far* the innumerable ventures being pursued in the name of 'sociology' (or its spin offs such as 'cultural studies' and 'media studies') are engaged in truly empirical inquiries, and *how far* they remain motivated and bemused by philosophical—or, as Winch would sometimes call them, 'conceptual'—problems. In these connections Winch's views are deeply dissident for they imply that

a. the difference between 'conceptual' and 'empirical' problems is not well understood in 'social science';
b. that the division between the 'conceptual' problems and the empirical inquiries reaches much further into the supposedly 'empirical' parts than most sociologists imagine, and is certainly not remotely captured by the difference between 'sociology' on the one hand and 'philosophy of social science' on the other; and
c. that very often the appearance of being an effort to solve an empirical problem, one with genuine factual content, is only superficial and is seriously misleading, to those engaged in the problem-solving, fact-finding effort as well as to onlookers.

Winch did not—and did not need to—hold that 'social science' has *no* empirical content, only that many of its significant and central concerns do not hinge upon, and will not be resolved by, factual investigations. That it has some empirical content does not bring it significantly close to the natural sciences, nor even mean that its main business is finding out hitherto unknown facts. Winch was insisting that the problems he was talking about were problems *in sociology* (anthropology, politics, etc.), in the sense of being problems that are present in sociology's main efforts at theorising and explaining, and *not* just problems to be debated in the marginalised literature of 'philosophy of social science': the very fact that it could seem otherwise is surely symptomatic of the problem his diagnosis identifies.

Winch may have been side-lined in sociology subsequent to his key contributions. This does not, however, mean that his arguments are irrelevant, even less that they have been proven wrong by subsequent developments; only that their character and implications *still* await proper recognition. *If* we are right in our presentation of Winch, and *if* Winch is right in what he argues, *then* what he says is not only continuingly relevant to 'social science' but it invites a fundamental rethink (*in* would-be social science disciplines). Rather than just assert that this is so, let us—necessarily briefly—point to two very prominent areas of recent social thought which illustrate the case that Winch developed.

Recent sociological thought has involved a largely unresolved struggle over the necessity for sociological theory, and it is the two 'sides' to that struggle that we treat as the material of our final introductory illustration. 'Postmodern' views subsume the fate of 'sociological theory' under that of 'science', holding that generalised doctrines about the totality have lost credibility in the modern world, not least as a result of the reflexive application of favoured social science ideas to social science's own doctrines. Sociology has often presupposed a difference between itself—scientific or at least empirical—and ideology, and the stock form of a huge proportion of its work has become: people *think* they know what they are doing, but we sociologists (psychologists, anthropologists, 'cognitive scientists', etc.), will show (through employment of our methodology or through theoretical reconstruction), that they do not. The pre-eminence of this form of procedure owes much to general scientistic prejudice in the academic etc. world, but also owes much, slightly more specifically, to the concepts of 'ideology' (which can be traced back to Marx) and 'the unconscious' (derived from Freud, latterly via Lacan). But if the Marxist and Freudian lineages are credited with showing that the language is irreducibly saturated by ideology and unconscious determinations, then what about 'social science' discourse itself? Such a simple turn can yield a strongly negative assessment—such discourse *can only be* itself an expression of ideology and the unconscious. It is not that everyday discourse does not—because it cannot—represent reality, whilst 'social science' discourse can, but that the very possibility of representation itself goes into crisis. The impulse toward general theory becomes a discreditable form of the will to power, and the aspiration for positive representation gives way to a drive at the perpetual destabilisation of all purported representations (with the notion of 'theory' being redefined into a very different form than structures of logically arrayed general structures, not least because the idea of 'logic' has itself become suspect).

Rather than concede to such sceptics, sociological theorists have sought to reassert the need for old-style theorising, a scheme of comprehensive generalities that can encompass the order of the social totality (on behalf of, at least in some cases, rounding off the 'unfinished project of modernity'). The principle form which the 'return to Grand theory'[25] or, alternatively, the move 'back to sociological theory'[26] have taken is that of synthesising pre-existing sociological doctrines. This involves

25 cf. Skinner (1985).
26 cf. Mouzelis (1995).

identifying the central problem of sociology as a false polarising of doctrines, ones which set up a dichotomy between 'structure' and 'agency', 'objectivism' and 'subjectivism', 'idealism' and 'materialism' among other dualisms. In other words, the project of sociological theory as such has become rather generically known as the agency-structure problem, one of treating the supposed polarities as two sides of the same coin, and incorporating them within a single over-arching scheme which will 'explain' how societies maintain their unity ('soft' rather than overtly coercive power is the simple answer often given).

The need for these unificatory schemes results from disputes between rival schools of sociologists who—at least allegedly—affiliated themselves with one or other poles of the polarity that the above—purported—dichotomies constitute, where an assault from those positioning themselves on the 'agency' or 'subjective' extremes on the legacy of classical sociological theory seemed to threaten the whole tradition spawned by, especially, Marx. Sociology's founders, such as Marx and Durkheim, had been adamant that society is more than just an ensemble of individuals, and that complex forms of social organisation which *take precedence* over individuals arise, 'structures', that are the proper subject matter of sociology. If society—in some sense—consists only of individuals, then there are no 'structures' to be studied, let alone that can be appealed to in explanation of the actions of individuals, since it is the fact that structures 'precede' individuals that means that they are explanatory of what individuals do. The desire for unification arose, then, from the need to defend the need for 'structure' in sociological theory, whilst making concession to those who advocated the indispensability of agency. Up until the attempts at structure-and-agency synthesis, theorists of 'structure' were as misguidedly one-sided as those who commend agency, for they had excluded agency from the account.

What kind of problem does the contrast of 'structure' and 'agency involve? In reality, it is nothing but a continuation of the metaphysical debate over 'determinism' and 'autonomy'. How far are individuals *made* to do what they do, and how far are they exempt from any kind of compulsion?

The exercise is conducted as if it were an issue in ontology. The argument is whether 'social structures' really exist as well as 'individuals' (to which structuralists had traditionally responded with the views that 'individuals' have no real existence but are merely products of social structures). Thus, the need for a concept of 'structure' calls for a demonstration that 'social' and not just 'individual' facts are real. However, the argument is not just about whether it can be established that structures *are* real, but involves the ploy of arguing that the idea that they are not would put sociology in a completely implausible position. The idea of 'agency' threatens the prospect of extreme—incredible—voluntarism. Individuals would be completely free to do anything that they wanted. There would be nothing, save the laws of physics, to limit their actions. That people should be free in such a way is just not a conceivable state of affairs, which, as the 'structure' and 'agency' confrontation segues into a combination, shows the need for something to set a limit to such extreme voluntarism—and what would or could be more suitable than a concept of 'structure'.

But surely there is no need for the doctrines of a sociological theory to establish that we are not free in this—somewhat ridiculous—sense. If social scientists think that we, as ordinary persons, imagine ourselves as either omniscient or omnipotent then they are surely the ones who have the utterly implausible conception—if there *are* sociological theorists who envisage individual action as free in this extraordinary fashion, they surely need correcting, but this does not prove they need a notion of 'social structure' to save them from folly, but, and only, a healthy reminder that they do not, in their own real lives, imagine that actions are like this at all.

The *problem* is really a result of thinking that our participation as individuals *in society* need be thought of as a relation of causal determination. The idea that we, as members of the society, are not *really* doing what we think (i.e. imagine) that we are doing feeds on the idea that our intentions and purposes are not what make us do what we—think that we—want to do. Some think this must be so because intentions and purposes are non-material, mental phenomena i.e. epiphenomena, and therefore cannot qualify as real, material, causes. The *real* causes of our behaviour are essentially unknown to us, and so it is society, not ourselves, that makes us do what we do. Sometimes, the argument is phrased in terms of 'constraint' rather than causation, where social structures are seen as restricting what individuals can do, preventing them from acting in ways which they might personally prefer in favour of ways that the social order requires of them.

Since what people have in mind is a general theory it is all too easy to suppose that the idea that *something* makes us do the things we do identifies the explanatory form for actions—actions result from causes. From that springs the idea that *everything* we do we are made to do. For some people, this thought brings a *frisson*, or is somewhat uncanny—we never really know what we are doing, our actions are the mere effects of unknown causes. Such ideas are not ones that come after empirical inquires, but ones that go before them, and do not themselves constitute hypotheses that will be tested but provide a basis on which hypotheses might be constructed and thus determine how the results of any inquiry will be permissibly understood.

The idea that we are *always made to act as we do* would be in conflict with the idea—presumably that of extreme voluntarism—that we are *never made to act,* being always free to do absolutely whatever we want. We opened this *Introduction* with J.L. Austin's maxim about philosophers, that there is always the bit where they say it, and then the bit where they take it back; well, it is as well to bear this in mind here, for we are not saying that it is easy to convict *any* real sociologist of holding such unrelentingly determinist conceptions, at least with any consistency, but there are, for example, 'anti-humanists' who want to argue that individual human beings are, *as individuals*, virtually insignificant for social science, which is essentially about 'structures' and not about 'individuals' at all. (Such 'anti-humanism' is present for instance at key moments in the thought of Lacan and some of his followers, of Althusser, of Foucault in his 'archaeological' phase, and perhaps also of Levi-Strauss.)

The idea of individuals as mere puppets of social structures (if that is what determinism in the sociological context means) may draw some but it repels others—it is too much to believe that *everything* that we do is something that we are *made* to do, and it is perhaps this that gives a toe-hold for the idea of a synthesis. If we cannot deny that some things we do are things we *are* made to do, and others are cases in which we *are* indeed quite free to do just what we want, then the two seemingly polar extremes can be brought together.

A synthesis premised in such preconceptions must surely lead to the idea that people engage in two kinds of behaviour, that which is determined by the social structure and that which is autonomous or free. There are 'margins of freedom' within the limits of determination, it is said, sometimes allowing people to 'break out' of the control that the structure imposes on them.

We should now note that the notion of structural determination is as often and as much wound up with the idea of political regulation as it is of causal determination, though these are rather different issues in truth. Thus, social structures are thought of not as simply causes which produce whatever effects they produce ... they are thought of as machineries of control which seek (in a metaphoric sense) to control *all* our behaviour, in which objective they are seen as being very largely successful.[27] Thus, individual autonomy, agency, is that behaviour which escapes the control of the social structure, and which can only be behaviour which defies or escapes the dictates of the structure.

We have been treating the attempt to reassert sociological theory by way of syntheses, as mainly defensively motivated, responding to one line of threat, which was that of eliminating the notion of 'social structure' from sociological discourse. Another line of threat, as already-intimated, is that arising from what we have called 'postmodern' conceptions, ones that have become critical of the idea that an all embracing theory of society is possible, ones which have, in important ways, attacked the possibility of determinate meaning in the context of theoretical reason.[28] One basis given for thinking this is that society is too diversified to be brought under any *single* theoretical scheme; another is, as mentioned, that in any case such a scheme will not be an objective representation of social reality, but only a disguised means by which one part of society seeks to impose its conceptions and needs on all the rest. A general theoretical scheme simply cannot be an objective portrayal of society because it is an attempt at representations, and all representations, as mentioned above, are pervaded by unconscious psychological and ideological impulses and do not really capture anything beyond themselves, but provide—for those of us who make naïve use of them in our daily affairs—only an 'effect' of representation, but not the real thing[29] itself. In other words, language possesses only partial meaning, in the sense both that it only captures part of the picture, and in the sense that the picture it paints is on somebody's side.

The attempted subversion of the idea of general theory is, however, itself a product of *theoretical* deduction, one which initially accepts the idea of a language as

---

27 John McGowan (1991) writes, "postmodern theory, I argue, is driven by the simultaneous fear that a monolithic social order shapes contemporary life and hope that a strategy of preserving pluralism (difference) can be found".

28 We do not make any attempt at a thorough treatment of postmodernism or post-structuralism, here. For a reasonably detailed critical engagement with Derrida on deconstruction see Hutchinson *Shame and Philosophy*, chapter 2, section 5.

29 The preservation of the very idea of the real thing itself here makes clear already that postmodernists are merely sceptics in a new guise. They have not fundamentally shifted the debate, as Wittgenstein does; they are merely disappointed Realists.

a self-contained system, whereby the meaning of expressions is *entirely* determined by the internal relations between the elements—the signs—of the language. (One can blame Saussure for kicking this off.) From this, it follows that the relationship of language to anything outside it must be arbitrary, and also entirely so, for any part of the language is shaped by its place in the language system as a whole. But if the aim of a general theory—amongst other representations—is to (re-)present things as they are in themselves, then this idea of language erodes that possibility, for the way things are in themselves plays—by definition—no part in fixing the forms of language, leaving the language without any intrinsic connection to that which it purportedly represents. Take this line of thought—often dubbed a 'structuralist' one, owing to its affiliation with 'structuralist linguistics'—a step further, and suppose that language is not so tightly closed a system as had been presumed. Without withdrawing from the idea that language is a system of arbitrary signs, allow that the language is not quite so systematic as the original theory held. Admit, that is, that there is some 'play' in the relations between the signs in the system and the idea that the definite meaning of expressions is fixed entirely by the internal relations of the system—the signs are defined in relation to each other, but now only comparatively loosely, meaning that if there is to be any fixity of meaning it must be supplied from some source other than the relations of the language itself (this is a move from 'structuralism' to 'post-structuralism'). The necessity to fix meanings in actual instances calls for the intervention of power, the imposition of a definiteness on relations that are not intrinsically definite, and such power will be driven by the unconscious psychological and ideological impulses already mentioned. In simple terms, language cannot say anything definite about the nature of things because language itself is not itself definite. Hence, language cannot *really definitively* be about anything other than itself, since what can be said in the language is a product of the language structure itself plus the unconsciously operating needs to portray things in one way rather than another. 'What there really is' (such that such talk might be allowed at all) is not only outside language but necessarily beyond any possibility of—cognitive—contact.

Arguments like these can again seem either quite thrilling or deeply perturbing or, just plainly and obviously wrong. Whichever of these reactions they elicit in their readers they seem to leave no one feeling indifferent! Should one embrace such arguments, one can have the sense that one has (finally!) seen through all the delusions that human beings have lived by for millennia, that *one* has understood that nothing is what it seems. It is in this sense that one can see the strong affinity with scientism and grand social theory; all of them—be it McIntyre's attempted rehabilitation of Hempelian deductive-nomological scientism, Habermasian grand social theory, or Derridean deconstruction—claim to provide the methodological lens which will enable us to identify and thus break free of prejudice, whether that be conferred by ideology or the unconscious.

In the case of post-modernism however, there is, as already implied, a further implication ... At the same time as we unmask unconscious prejudice, we have also grasped that there is no point in trying to say what things really are in contrast to what they appear to be. The exercise can only be one of exposing illusions without attempting to set up new ones in their place (and this makes the status of 'postmodern theory' itself a kind of imponderable). 'Reality' is now merely a delusional outward projection created by the workings of the language and of power relations that jointly hold us in their unwitting thrall, leaving us all in the same boat, and unable to say, with any validity, that one thing is better than the other, simply reducing all disputes to disputes of taste. Within the last three decades there has been an intense, ferocious and bitter struggle—called, in some contexts, 'the Culture Wars', and in others 'the Science Wars' and ranging across many different disciplines, including historical and literary studies—between those who embraced some version of these ideas and those who vigorously resisted them (the conflict peaked and has died down, but this does not mean that the divisions that produced it have ceased to exist).

The first point to make is that the two sides of the Culture and Science Wars is that many of their disagreements can be crystallised as being over whether language has a necessary or an arbitrary connection with reality, and in that respect they, so to speak, take in each others washing. Those on the one side, often calling themselves Realists, insist that language does *and must* have a necessary relationship with a reality external to and constitutively independent of it if it is to count as providing 'successful' representations. Our language is, in important respects, the way that it is because of the conditions that things in themselves, external reality, create for representation—if we're not going to be making mistakes all the time (and if we did we would soon be extinct) then the way we represent the world to ourselves and each other *must* at crucial points fit with the way the world is, must correspond to the intrinsic properties of whatever it is that it *does* represent. For those, the persistence and success of our way of life testifies to the truth of the arguments. Their opponents, though, show that if one accepts their—the opponents'—picture of what makes language meaningful, then there *just can't* be anything necessary about the relationship between language and anything external to it. The organisation of language is arbitrary which means, in the end, that language only 'represents', it never really represents at all.

This disagreement is not an *empirical*, but very much a philosophical, dispute, one which proceeds as many philosophical disputes do. That is, both sides can be seen to share certain fundamental premises. The (postmodern, etc.) critics do not dispute the initial premise that the idea of a representation is of something that represents the intrinsic nature of reality as it independently is. Rather, they leave that idea in place and then ask whether anything can possibly satisfy this requirement, going on to prove—to themselves at least—that *nothing can* meet this requirement because (as we have put it in this condensation and simplification of very complex controversy) a true representation would be entirely culture-free, unaffected by all ideological distortion, but all signs are contingent, and can therefore stand in only an arbitrary relationship to anything outside the language, meaning that *no* signs are culture free, and consequently that there are no *true* representations, only things that have the false, deceiving appearance of representing things. Rather than putting the initial premise in question, that 'representation of reality' requires a necessary correspondence, the critics accept this, and thus 'find' that the very idea of representation is thrown into doubt. One can, however, equally well put that premise into question, wonder whether this is a good characterisation of things that we would ordinarily call representations, and thus find out that one could consider that 'being arbitrary' and 'being a representation' are not antithetical notions—as though we were to take the fact that some measures operate in feet and inches and others in metres and centimetres as proving that there is no such thing as measuring the length of anything. Neither 'feet' nor 'metres' offer themselves as intrinsic properties of objects, but only as units of measurement which can—and manifestly are—used to determine the degree to which different objects might be the same as or some different length from each other …

The Continued Need to Read Peter Winch

To return then to our title; one would be mistaken if one thought that the claim that there is 'no such thing as a social science' implied that we are in some—inchoate and incoherent—sense anti-science. We are anti-scientism, yes, but even that doesn't capture what we really mean to get at in what follows. We are anti the driving-thought of much of what passes as social science and philosophy of social science today (and dating back to when Winch authored *ISS*). For Grand Social Theory—as propounded in various guises by Bhaskar, Bourdieu, Giddens, Habermas, and so on—deconstruction as a methodology in the social studies—as exemplified in exercises in the deconstruction of textual authority pioneered by Derrida (e.g. Clifford 1986, Ashmore 1989)—and scientism—as propounded in positivist guise by authors such as McIntyre and in realist guise by authors such as Manicas—all claim to provide, by way of furnishing us with a methodology, a lens through we will finally be able to see the ideologically-driven or unconsciously-driven prejudice about our status as social actors, the way we relate to our social institutions and norms, and the identity of our actions: what we are really doing. Ours is not an attempt to say that no-one (social actors, members of a society: *people*) can be mistaken about these things, but that people being mistaken about what they are doing and how social institutions impact upon them does not imply that what is required is a methodology of social science, or a theoretical framework, so that we might apprehend what it is they are really doing or see how a person's relation to a social institution must be.

The analogy between a methodology (or theory) and a lens, which we invoked above, can be briefly explored in a little more depth, here. The fact that you might mistake a coiled rope in the corner of your garden for a snake on a dark night, or that you just missed the typos in the paper you wrote despite three read-throughs does not mean that you need spectacles. Similarly, a person might act in a manner that they only later, following a discussion with a colleague, identify as motivated by envy, or, a person only late in life might come to see that many of their moral beliefs, that they now consider to have negatively constrained the choices they've made, stemmed from their relationship to the institutions of the Church and the way this unconsciously structured their beliefs.

It does not *follow*, in the former cases, that we need a pair of spectacles: that is settled by a visit to the optician. The mistakes in question are due perhaps to similarities and poor conditions in the case of the snake/rope and to carelessness (not being attentive enough) in the case of the missed typos. Spectacles will not make a room lighter and will not make one more attentive. Similarly, coming to see that my action was motivated by envy is a matter of honesty with oneself (sometimes, a colleague's honesty forces one to acknowledge such things and be honest with oneself), and coming to recognise the influence the church has exercised over the choices one has made is a matter of seeing the contingent nature of those choices (that there were other possibilities) and that the Church's teaching does not allow (denies) that the choices it recommends are contingent (denies other possible choices if one is to be a good person).[30] But even this analogy doesn't quite get to the nub of the issue we want to draw out here. For methodologies are not thought to operate in a manner analogous to spectacles, correcting deficiency in vision, bringing our (ideologically or unconsciously restricted) vision back to 20-20 vision. No the analogy would be better between the role claimed for methodology in the social sciences and the X-ray spectacles of science fiction (with the rider that what they enable one to see—below the surface—is what is most significant; is what is real).

In short, there are a couple of themes that recur again and again and again, throughout this book, and we make no apology for this repetition. These are the themes of the identity of an action and of the everydayness of understanding. They recur because so many of the misunderstandings and criticisms of Winch, and therefore also of those of us who believe his teachings to be as (if not more) relevant now as they were 50 years ago, are based on a failure to grasp these points in full. So, whether we be explicating Winch (Chapter 1) explaining why he is not an Idealist (Chapter 2), demonstrating the affinities and differences with Ethnomethodology and other 'qualitative' sociologists, such as Erving Goffman (Chapter 3), or defending Winch against the charge of conservatism (Chapter 4) we find ourselves returned to the same issues: understanding what a person is doing is a perfectly mundane and everyday affair; where it is difficult, as when we—as *occasionally* happens—come upon a people who seemingly do things in a very different way to us, then we need to make more of an effort, just as we do when we are reading a book we find hard going, *not* leap to supposing that a pair of spectacles (i.e. a sociological method/ theory) is what would help us. Our difficulties in reading are with what's in the book, not with the eyes we use to do the reading.

What they are doing, the identity of their action, is simply what the action means for the actors in the social setting: that identifying this is sometimes hard, and involves sometimes (e.g.) lateral thinking, does not equate to there being any need whatsoever for a social theory/social science.

In subsequent chapters we go into many of the issues we have introduced here in more depth. We have sought—in outline here, and in depth in the body of our book—to defend Winch from what we see as almost ritualistic misunderstanding. 'Ritualistic', in something akin to the pejorative sense used of that word in the likes of Frazer and Evans-Pritchard, rather than in the more open-minded sense present in the work of Wittgenstein and Winch ... Unthinking, *functionalistically* beneficial to group-solidarity, and positively superstitious ... The superstition being that of scientism (and, by extension, grand social theory and post modernism) making it impossible to see room for an alternative way of thinking that could threaten the imperium of the only Method permitted any viability and importance ...

---

30 What one, therefore, comes to see in this case is the contingency of is the Church's conception of the good.

The social studies, unlike the 'social sciences', not only begin but also end with non-academics, with (competent) members of a community. Social study is above all something that we do most of the time, we humans. It will be evident throughout that this is a thoroughly *Wittgensteinian* interpretation of Winch. We believe that much of the (rampant) misunderstanding of Winch's project is a result of a failure to understand the centrality for Winch's 'philosophy of social science' of Wittgenstein('s)—or at best a failure to understand Wittgenstein himself. We take seriously Winch's Wittgensteinian (therapeutic) heritage, and suggest that a Winch read after the fashion of Wittgenstein (read aright)[31] is immune to the main charges against him. Wittgenstein is no Idealist or Relativist, and just so, Winch is not; etc.

There are not that many books that become legends in their own authors' lifetimes. *The Idea of a Social Science and its Relation to Philosophy* is such a book; we mean, in *this* book, to dispel the legend. Peter Winch was a very fine philosopher indeed, but 'the legendary' Peter Winch, the Winch hated or despised[32] by his many 'foes' and loved by his few 'fans' is a lesser, fictional, character. The true Winch was more radical than foes or fans allowed. He was a (Wittgensteinian) philosopher who for the first time made it fully possible to see that 'social science' not only had no clothes, but that there isn't an emperor at all, either, and no need for one. There is no 'there' there. There is and can be no such thing as social science, in the sense in which advocates of a science (or even grand theory) of society have wanted there to be. Winch did not give us a new way of doing social science, a 'Wittgensteinian, rule-governed' way. To echo his supposed nemesis, Donald Davidson (2001 [1974]), and the only partially sympathetic A.R. Louch (1963, p. 273), he intimated the absurdity of *the very idea of* social science ... The legendary Peter Winch is a fictional character[33]— the true Winch was far more important and far more radical in teaching that 'social science' is a quintessential modern myth. But myths in the would-be form of science are the worst kind of myths—for, far more extremely than magic or religion, they cannot *bear* to admit their own nature, not even through a glass darkly ...

---

31 See Hutchinson (2007), and Hutchinson and Read (2008).

32 This might strike our readers as a little hyperbolic. See Gellner op cit., if one wishes to confirm that it is not hyperbolic.

33 For an example in this regard see Winch's review of James Bohman's (1992), *New Philosophy of Social Science*; Winch writes of Bohman's book, "The second of the introductory chapters is particularly difficult for me to discuss, since a great deal of the argument hinges on criticism and rejection of views I am alleged to have held in my 1958 book *The Idea of a Social Science*. My difficulty is that I recognize as mine hardly any of the views discussed; indeed, most of them are views which I *criticized*. To substantiate this in detail would quite inappropriately take up the remainder of the space I am allowed for this review, but there is one, as it were scholarly, point that I fear I must make. Not merely does Bohman nowhere take account of, or even mention the existence of, a number of other papers by me which are certainly relevant to the interpretation of my position; he even describes approvingly some criticisms made by Alasdair MacIntyre of my paper 'Understanding a Primitive Society' without finding it necessary actually to refer to that paper, even to the extent of including it in his bibliography. So much for the 'virtual dialogue' between interpreter and interpretee on which Bohman later rests so much theoretical weight" (Winch 1995, p. 473).

It falls to us at this point to add only that much of what we have said already and much of what we say in what follows *should already be clear* if one reads or has read carefully Winch's *ISS* and a few subsequent papers: i.e. "Understanding a Primitive Society", "Trying to Make Sense", "Can We Understand Ourselves", and the *Preface* to the 2nd edition of *ISS*, and maybe add Rai Gaita's short but very insightful introduction to the 50th anniversary edition. However, the last 50 years since the publication of Winch's book demonstrate that careful reading has not been in abundance when it comes to Winch's work. We dare to hope that the present text might go some way to reversing this trend.

Chapter 1

Beyond Pluralism, Monism, Relativism, Realism etc.: Reassessing Peter Winch

The Legend

Peter Winch's work has been hugely influential in the philosophy of the social sciences. But wait; is that actually true? Many sociologists and philosophers of the sciences at least know Winch's name. If they know more than that it will be his work in the philosophy of the social sciences (rather than in, say, ethics or the study of Simone Weil). Do they get Winch's ideas right? Or has his 'influence' mostly been the spawning of some 'followers' who he would largely repudiate and of many 'foes' who actually fail to engage with (and thus in a key sense fail to disagree with) what he meant? Has Winch unfortunately been 'influential' in the philosophy of the social sciences only in creating an argument between friends who are not his real friends and foes who misunderstand, rather than rebut, him?[1]

For anyone who admires Peter Winch's work sufficiently to read it carefully, reviewing the secondary literature on him is a depressing experience. One not infrequently encounters bowdlerised versions and crude caricatures of what he thought[2]—and here we talk about many of his would-be friends ... With his 'foes' the situation is far worse still. They attack with much zeal theses which Winch

---

1   The all-too-predictable irony of this if, as we shall suggest, the latter is so, this would in a sense be exactly what Winch's own thinking would predict: that there has been an insufficiently serious effort to understand Winch, among those who would wish to criticise him. That, if one wants to criticise, one has first to understand, and this first base is all-too-rarely attained. That, in order to have a shot at understanding the strange, one sometimes first has to put it at a *greater* remove from one, from the kind of thing one is used to thinking about a theory being (indeed, in this case (of Winch), as in that of the Azande: one has to be prepared to consider the possibility that what one is trying to understand is not a theory at all. One has to be ready to open one's mind beyond scientism and beyond theoryism). In sum: the primitive misunderstandings of Winch that one generally encounters mirror closely the primitive misunderstandings of the Azande etc., that Winch sought explicitly to overcome!

2   We are thinking here, for instance, of certain moments in the work of B.D. Lerner and of Patrick Phillips. Lerner's (1995) paper, 'Winch and Instrumental Pluralism' purports to be a development of Winch's views in a desirable direction, toward an 'instrumental pluralist' rendition of cultures very different from ours; Phillips's (1997) reply, 'Winch's Pluralist Tree and the Roots of Relativism' argues that Winch's views do not need developing in that direction, because they already *are* 'instrumentally pluralist'—but Phillips thinks this is not desirable, because it leads to 'relativism'. We argue below that with interpreters like these, who needs enemies ... (but we thank them, for at least inspiring the title of this chapter).

supposedly held. These 'foes' rail against Winch's philosophical or political(!) 'conservatism', or against his 'revisionism' concerning the practice of social science; one finds seemingly-endless criticisms of Winch for being too slavish a follower of Wittgenstein—*and* sometimes also for having failed to follow Wittgenstein faithfully enough. Above all, there are endless and repetitive assaults on (or, among Winch's 'followers', sometimes endorsements of) Winch's alleged 'relativism'.

Winch died in 1997, and some reassessment of his work has been going on for the last decade. Colin Lyas's (1999) useful book, *Peter Winch*, was a welcome step forward, as was the 50th anniversary reissue of the second edition of *ISS*, with a helpful introduction by Rai Gaita. Our hope is that there will be a real and thorough rethinking over the coming years, and would like this book to be (part of) and to provoke this. Such an assessment needs more than a re-reading of *The Idea of a Social Science and its Relation to Philosophy*, a work whose 50th anniversary is upon us as we write, in 2008. Here we undertake the following task(s):

I. Illuminating Winch's (Wittgensteinian) conception of philosophy, which informs everything he wrote (this is the main burden of the current chapter);
II. Rebutting central misunderstandings of Winch, particularly those which have emerged in recent years (we begin this task in the current chapter, and complete it in a couple of our subsequent chapters, those on idealism and on conservatism).

Before beginning these tasks, we outline now some key elements present in any genuine understanding of what remains Winch's central work in the philosophy of the social sciences. We try to generate a 'picture' of Winch that, even if the reader is not entirely convinced, might at least work as a corrective to the 'received view' of Winch's philosophy, the ruling 'picture' of his thought.

What is Winch's 'Picture' of the Understanding of Human Action?

A word of warning: this question already risks presupposing much too much, as our scare-quoting hints. *Does* Winch have a picture of the understanding of human action? Or does he only guard against various natural/frequent misunderstandings that are produced by attempting general accounts of action? The social sciences are supposed to explain 'human action', give new understandings of 'human behaviour'. But *is there any such general task that really needs doing*?

We might note some occasions on which—and ways in which—an expression like "understanding other people" is used in everyday speech which is its home. This expression has a variety of specific uses, outside theoretical 'social science'. It might be used by someone in distress at their lack of social skills; "I have trouble understanding other people". Used in a positive sense, it would probably be heard as self-satisfied: "I know how to understand people. Let me tell you what makes people tick …". But social theorists apparently want to provide a foundation, or a general *method*, for understanding people (almost as if we were all about to start from scratch in doing this and now, in year zero, require a general formula for understanding). In this, theorists don't just envisage surveying the myriad techniques all members of human societies have for finding each other comprehensible. They mean, instead, something like a *single* general, teachable method, one that can be mechanically applied and understanding automatically read off.

In everyday discourse, much more often than invoking any supposed need for or realisation of methods of general understanding, one speaks in more specific ways than those mentioned above: "I understand you perfectly", "I don't *understand* why my mother always does that", "D'you understand the game of Chess; can you teach me?" It would be best to give up the notion that there is an intelligible general thing, "*the* understanding of other people". If one is to talk of this at all, if one is to talk of enhancing our state of understanding of others, or indeed of ourselves, then we think that one must resist the temptation to think of 'understanding' as one kind of thing, and, consequently, to over-generalize, to unnecessarily 'theorise', to fantasise a 'method' ('social research method(s)', and a 'theory' of society) for achieving it.

Winch argues in his *ISS* that the social sciences are programmatic, that they have been designed with philosophical purposes latently or blatantly in mind. They have been designed, in various different ways, on the model(s) of certain conceptions of natural science; or, even as they retreat from allegiance to 'science' the idea that they are *empirical* enterprises remains central to their identity. They ask, "How can we bring human life under the heading, under the concept, of 'science'", or, in post-scientific mode, "How will empirical—or theoretical—investigation transform our understanding of human life; how will it serve to disabuse us of certain prevalent illusions?" But, Winch asks: what are their—the social sciences'—problems, their puzzles? What problems do they actually have? Or, what problems do they 'investigate'? And what could possibly be the justification for the assumption that human life in general can be effectively and profitably brought under the scientific or of some other form of empirically generalised concept?

Most readers just do not take Winch's—full—title seriously enough. Just as Wittgenstein was a 'complete Bolshevik' in the philosophy of mathematics, so is Winch in the philosophy of the social sciences. People tend to read Winch and think that the issue now confronting them must be, "How, if at all, could we incorporate Winch into the way we now do social science?" But Winch's title is best unpacked as "On the Very Idea of 'Social Science', on how philosophy can dissolve it, and on how philosophy can do this in part by taking back to itself what was stolen by 'social scientists'".[3] Winch is not trying to put 'social science' right, but to say that the *whole idea* is wrong-headed. Hence, no "Here's how to do (and not to do) social science aright", nor "here's a better method for social scientists". Winch is pressing questions on would-be social scientists as much as making proposals to them: "*What are you trying to do? What genuine empirical problems are you trying to solve? Is there any clear idea of this? How does the idea that a 'social science' is needed get a hold in the first place?*"

That this was the central nexus of Winch's concerns we think becomes much clearer in writings of his that followed the publication of *ISS* when he is writing for

---

3 Compare Louch's interesting writings on Winch and 'social science'.

those readers who do not presuppose the aims and ambitions of social theory or the concept of philosophy-as-a-primarily-theoretical-discipline. (Thus we will spend a fair amount of time with those subsequent writings of his.)

Having raised a concern that any attempt to extract a methodology for social science, or a theory of it, will be alien to Winch, for argument's sake we take the risk of outlining a tentative answer to the question raised above, the question of what 'picture' of human action we may usefully—for purposes of at least displacing one's compulsive attachment to other, more culturally-dominant pictures—find in Winch, by drawing attention to two distinctions present in Wittgenstein's writings, and drawn upon by Winch in *ISS*.

(I) Between *understanding* and *explaining*

Donald Davidson, in reply to the Routledge published series of "little red books" of philosophy, which included *ISS*, insisted[4] that giving reasons involves causal explanation. However, we, like Winch, deny that this need be so (*ISS*, p. 45). The assumption of much social science is that all explanations are causal, so that either (a) reason-giving explanations are not causal and therefore do not give explanations of human actions, and will not feature in social science (save as expressions of ideology) or (b) that reasons do explain, but they do so in a causal fashion.[5] Winch thinks that reasons do play a pervasive and important role(s) in our practices, some of which are of course 'explanatory', but to give a reason is not *ipso facto* to postulate a cause. Understanding human action in terms of its reasons is, for Winch, what—at its best—social study/human 'science' can do.

What is it to understand human action? Need it (normally) involve interpretation/ explanation, or is this an overly intellectualised starting-point? Can it instead simply involve description[6] and taken-for-granted understanding(s), understandings-in-practice? Winch writes:

---

4   It is interesting to note that Davidson's claim that reasons are causes is just affirmed, not argued for, in this founding article of his, and the wide acceptance this claim has since met perhaps suggests how strongly the wish to believe that actions need explaining—and that explaining means *causally* explaining—has a hold on contemporary culture.

5   Our questioning of this assumption will be tantamount to modern heresy to many. Our point is as follows: understanding X (where X is an act token) is facilitated by grasping a person's reasons for X-ing. One does not need to subsume X under a causal law, or see it as a manifestation of an underlying causal mechanism in order that it be understood.

6   cf. the instructive title of Nigel Pleasants's paper, 'Winch and Wittgenstein on Understanding Ourselves Critically: Descriptive, not Metaphysical'. Though we must dissent from some of Pleasants's criticisms of Winch in his *Wittgenstein and the Idea of a Critical Social Theory: A Critique of Giddens, Habermas and Bhaskar* (London: Routledge, 1999)—there, despite the homage to Winch in the title, Pleasants makes some of the moves we are critiquing in this essay: he treats Winch as a covert metaphysician—specifically a transcendentalist about rules—with definite assertions to make and theses and theories to convince us of. These reservations aside, Pleasants' book comprises a devastating critiques of Giddens, Habermas and Bhaskar.

Understanding is the goal of explanation and the end-product of successful explanation. But … [u]nless there is a form of understanding that is not the result of explanation, no such thing as explanation would be possible. An explanation is called for only where there is, or is at least thought to be, a deficiency in understanding. But there has to be some standard against which such a deficiency is to be measured: and that standard can only be an understanding that we already have. Furthermore, the understanding we already have is expressed in the concepts which constitute that form of the subject matter we are concerned with. These concepts on the other hand also express certain aspects of the life characteristic of those who apply them (Winch 1990, p. x).

These lines come from the (Preface to the) revised edition of *ISS*. Regrettably, few of Winch's latter-day critics take full account of how different Winch's *ISS* looks when re-read in the light of the Preface to the 2nd edition.[7] Several of the most frequent criticisms of the book are there either rebutted or conceded in a way which clarifies Winch's more mature understanding without involving fundamental revision. Why, then, has the Preface to the 2nd edition been largely ignored (by those writers to whom it has been available)? One of our subsidiary aims in the present work is to use as and where needs be an understanding of the totality of Winch's work on the philosophy of the social sciences, not just upon what he wrote on the subject up until the early 1960s.[8] Any reckoning with the point of view of Winch on the philosophy of the social sciences must in particular go by way of the 1990 Preface, which in turn should be placed in the broader context of Winch's plainly-Wittgensteinian later *corpus* as a whole. *ISS* was not only a young man's book, and a polemical work, it was also a *short* one, unadvisedly taken to task for omissions, or for overly concise statements susceptible of misinterpretation. Winch's later comments, and his broader corpus, provide bulwarks against hasty (mis)interpretation.

What, then, are the implications of the passage quoted above for thinking about understanding human beings?

---

7   Has Winch then substantively modified his 'views'? Has he actually abandoned his early 'bold' views? No; in some respects, he never held the 'bold' views attributed to him (e.g. like Kuhn, he was never in any useful sense of the word a 'relativist'); in other respects, his 'views' are just as 'bold' as they ever were. Only he has reformulated his expression of them to lessen (one hopes!) the chances of his being misinterpreted (As he puts it on page xi, 'I should now want to *express* myself differently …' (our italics)—most (though not all) of his concessions to his 'opponents' say only that he expressed himself badly before (though in philosophy, that is of importance)). Finally, as we endeavour to explain below, there is a key respect in which it is misleading even to describe him as having 'views' at all. *Qua* philosopher (or *qua* social student), he is we think often best described as having no views at all, as making no assertions, as not claiming anything whatsoever. (Whereas *qua* layperson, he has for instance the view that the poison oracle is not to be trusted, that it just isn't something by which he would want to conduct his life, etc.)

8   As we quoted in our *Introduction* (above, footnote 33), Winch writing of one of his critics, James Bohman, notes that while drawing approvingly on criticisms of some of his writing that followed *ISS*, Bohman does not himself go to those writings. The evidence strongly suggests that Bohman does not even read Winch's writing beyond the 1958 publication of *ISS*.

[E]ven if it is legitimate to speak of one's understanding of a mode of social activity as consisting in a knowledge of regularities, the nature of this knowledge must be very different from the nature of knowledge of physical regularities ... If we are going to compare the social student to an engineer, we shall do better to compare him to an apprentice engineer ... His understanding of social phenomena is more like the engineer's understanding of his colleagues' activities than it is like the engineer's understanding of the mechanical systems which he studies [...] I do not wish to maintain that we must stop at the unreflective kind of understanding of which I gave as an instance the engineer's understanding of the activities of his colleagues. But I do want to say that any more reflective understanding must necessarily presuppose, if it is to count as genuine understanding at all, the participant's unreflective understanding. And this in itself makes it misleading to compare it with the natural scientist's understanding of his scientific data (*ISS*, pp. 88-89).

The closing two sentences are crucial for our purposes. Winch is reminding us that, so long as one is not blinded by philosophical preconceptions (of, say, 'Relativist'— *or* Scientific 'Rationalist'—hues), social actors can gradually be understood in their actions, without imposition or irony. Furthermore, insofar as there is or might be any project of *understanding* human being(s), that is going to have to proceed by cases—considering mindful human beings in action, engaged in specific human practices—and courts failure if it doesn't begin by engaging with the 'order' inherent in/reconstructed by those practices. Here Winch writes almost as if he had read Harold Garfinkel, and (of course) interpreted him (as the 'Manchester school' of ethnomethodology do) after Wittgenstein.

   We tentatively suggest that liberation from the endlessly frustrated conviction that a 'human science' is forthcoming will begin (and, in a sense, end) by assembling a careful and un-imperialistic/un-impositional description of, roughly speaking, the self-understandings-in-action of the person or people in question.[9] i.e. Simply of ordinary people, ourselves and others. They are not baffled or confused all the time, many of their practical projects satisfy them as successful, they are evidently not (by and large) enigmas to themselves, endlessly puzzled by what goes on in their cultural environs. Whatever else one might have in mind to do as a 'social scientist' one needs to ensure that one *understands* those one proposes to 'theorise' *first*, for unless one understands what their activities are *for them* one cannot even begin to address their lives, and potentially re-characterise or criticise. A first thing to remember is that in many cases *we* the social scientists are *them*, the supposedly naïve dwellers in the society, that our 'research' doings draw heavily upon. It needs to be borne in mind that discussion of Winch on 'understanding' has been heavily weighted, and thereby distorted, by the focus on 'Understanding a primitive society' and therefore upon a case—oracular magic—that can be puzzling and calls for some kind of explanation. (That was *why* Winch chose the case as one to examine—*because* of its

---

9   As is made clear below, stressing how people understand themselves *in action* is not equatable with substantive social theorizing, e.g. of the kind favoured by Charles Taylor or the Symbolic Interactionists. Winch's 'picture' isn't intellectualistic or rationalistic: for detail, consult Winch's tellingly-titled paper, *Im Anfang war die Tat*, in his (1987), *Trying to Make Sense*, and p. 170f. of Lyas (1999).

being unusual, genuinely and persistently puzzling! It gets his intent horribly wrong, to turn it into a paradigm case of ordinary social understanding, as if every time we get to understand someone we have to put together an Evans-Pritchard-plus-Winch type of enterprise!)

But (A) the fact that sociologists are characteristically studying people with whom they share many understandings-in-practice does not obviate the problems of misrepresentation and imposition since those understandings in and of practice are commonly subjugated to the impulse to theorise and the demands of preconceived methodologies. The problem, in many areas of sociology, is not that of finding a better method or theory for understanding of co-members'[10] practices but of clearing the theoretical and methodological detritus out of the way, allowing a more lucid appreciation of what, in one way or another, one *already* understands. And (B) even though sociologists are engaged with those in the same society, this of course does not eliminate all problems of understanding, only the idea that there is *a single, unified* problem, which is that of the professional researcher understanding the naïve natives of the same society. There *are* problems of understanding, but they are not problems between a (sort of) scientist and a scientifically lay person, but of the sort that arise amongst members of the society themselves, where different kinds of people and different ways of doing things themselves present assorted problems of intelligibility. The kinds of problems that arise, very roughly, between people who have a disagreement about something …

In those cases where we are dealing with people—whether from an 'alien' culture or from 'our own'—whose activities really puzzle us, *one* (and only one) useful way of doing this is to compare them with *whatever* actually helps us understand them. We don't impose a standard on them from our own practices, but we look for comparisons which will help to see them right. Such comparisons need of course to be apt—and may need to be surprising/unsettling to us.[11] Thus, Winch suggests, the advantages of comparing what the Azande do with their poison-oracles to what Christians do with prayer—provided that one hasn't already got a wrong-headed idea of what Christians are doing when they pray (e.g. praying to God is not like calling a taxi, God is not required to give us what we ask for so whether prayers come true is not a test of predictive capacity but is, or ought to be, instructive for us). We can also sometimes profitably compare and contrast their attitudes to their practices and 'contradictions' within those practices to those of our own philosophers and mathematicians.[12] Or we can look at our own 'superstitious' attitude toward

---

10 'Co-members'—Those who inhabit society along with us, who are members of the community/communities that we are.

11 Saying this does not force us back into a Realist/Literalist account of description and understanding, both because the weaknesses of any comparison are at least as important as its strengths (see below), and because a comparison's 'aptness' may be quite uncashable in any 'correspondence' terms. For full argument as to why, on the latter point, see Read's writing on schizophrenia and Faulkner in *The Literary Wittgenstein* (London: Routledge, 2004) or in his (2007a).

12 H.O. Mounce (1973), goes into detail on this comparison in his mostly illuminating paper, 'Understanding a Primitive Society', *Philosophy*, 48(1973), pp. 347-362. Mounce rightly insists that it is not enough for Winch to say, 'The Azande's practices are not profitably

certain pieces of metal and pieces of paper (i.e. money).[13] Or we can compare and contrast the Zande 'witches' with 'witches' as those are known to us from our own society and history—Winch stresses that this comparison is particularly fraught, and it may be unwise to translate the Zande words as 'witch', for it is a quite different case to our own. ... In sum, we can cast some positive light on others if we open-mindedly look for ways of repairing breaches in *our* understanding; and, more important still, when we look at the 'game' or 'games' which they play, we can and must note carefully what's *wrong* with various appealing analogies we might want to make to help 'interpret' them, and thus we can see—or learn to see—how to avoid misunderstanding them.

Apart from the 'problem' of understanding another society or practice, it is Winch's remarks on rule-following that have been most seriously challenged. These remarks, however, will themselves be misunderstood unless it is recognised that they fit the general pattern outlined and, rather than recommending 'rule-following' as the model social science explanation, Winch's direction is quite contrary to the idea that rule-following is a candidate form of theoretical explanation for people's conduct, one that sociologists could be urged to adopt. Winch's point is that rule-following 'explanations' are already in place and in operation, for they are, *inter alia*, the kinds of explanations that, as ordinary persons, we give to one another. Sociologists need no urging to adopt 'rule-following' understanding for they are up to their necks in understanding what they themselves and others do as rule-following both in their personal lives and as sociologists, though in the latter case largely on an extra-mural basis without regard for their official theories.

To reiterate, the first thing one needs to think about in developing a 'social study/ studies' are some genuine problems, instances of things that we do not understand ('alien' practices are the main/typical examples).[14] But, most of social life is not a problem for anyone, which is why (a) sociologists have to try to create problems by proposing strange ways in which we might view familiar things so that, then, we will see that we (allegedly) do not understand them: e.g. if we look at what we do from the vantage point of history-as-a-whole or the standpoint of the totality or through the lenses of Marxism, functionalism, structuralism, poststructuralism etc.; or if we actively forget what we socially-know, and pretend that we are looking

---

compared with our science'; he needs to look at the similarities (for example, there does appear to be a predictive element in Zande practice, as in science) as well as the differences. What Mounce is doing is taking seriously Winch's remarks, and endeavouring to learn from them in a way more nuanced than Winch himself. Thus Mounce is largely exempt from our criticism of most readers of Winch in this chapter. For, like Pleasants (1999), he doesn't misunderstand the character of what Winch is doing, but makes only an internal critique of certain points within it.

13 This is Pleasants's approach in his (op cit.); and his work, like for instance some of Chomsky's on linguistic propaganda, can be usefully seen as exemplifying not social or critical *theory*, but critical *description*—the describing of society with a view to bringing out ways in which it needs to change.

14 Things that are before our eyes so much—are such second-nature to us—that we cannot even see them are another such class, that we will discuss from time to time, and that are central to enthnomethodology and 'Conversation Analysis'.

at ourselves or at some of our institutions as if we were looking at a strange tribe (think e.g. of some of Goffmann, or of Latour and Woolgar); and (b) the notion of 'understanding' is typically totally wedded to the idea of having a theory, and it is enough to point out that we—ordinary folk—do not have a theory of something (or, worse, have a wrong theory, a mere ideology), and therefore cannot be said to understand it, and therefore need the sociologist to explain it to us ... Sociologists just don't have genuine empirical problems—in the way that Keynes at least had the occurrence of the business cycle to explain[15]—of the sort that would motivate a genuinely explanatory venture on their part. Their 'problems' are mostly artefacts of the prior possession of their theories (or as much 'sociological' research is, are addressed to administrative, quasi-administrative or frankly political problems—is there an 'underclass', what stops people rising up in revolt, etc.). Their theories do not originate as genuine responses to things that puzzle us. In fact, we are inclined to hold that sociology is overwhelmingly driven by a preoccupation with the form of explanation, not with giving any actual explanations.

This is arguably what the vast majority of 'human science' *is*: simply misbegotten epistemology and metaphysics.[16] Winch's main role is *not* a methodologist's, one who enables one to understand better what 'the methodology of social study' is and must be; his treatment of 'social science' is reflective and clarificatory, an attempt

---

15 Compare also Read (2007a).

16 Some of the small minority is genuinely empirical and or fully political 'policy studies'. A full exposition of this point would be the topic of a further chapter, one we do not include here. In brief: Some of social science is harmless quasi-bureaucratic local 'policy studies'-type work. e.g. What proportion of the population have home access to inside toilets? Such factual enquiries, important in some administrative and political contexts, are like another portion of 'social science' which is similarly 'local': enquiries into social *history*. Both such enquiries, let it be noted, run serious risks of being methodologically unsophisticated in ways which can turn out to be problematic. But these risks are almost insignificant compared to the far more intense risks that arise when it comes to 'the big questions' of social science, the questions which set the social sciences apart from or 'above' 'mere' history or 'mere' policy studies, questions such as 'What is the structure of Modern society?', or 'Does "society" really exist?', or 'Who *really* holds power?', 'How obedient are human beings?', even 'What is human nature?' These questions are—where they are not just matters of common sense— philosophical questions, at best, Winch suggests. Social theorists want to choose how to live, and to understand what it makes sense to say ... in short, to do philosophy (including here ethics and political philosophy), *by other means*—but the means are singularly ill-chosen, and while the conceptual confusion that results from them perhaps 'makes us think we have the means of solving the problems which trouble us ...', whereas, in fact '... problem and method pass one another by.' (*PI*, Part II section xiv, p. 233). For Wittgenstein, to quote this key passage once again, "The confusion and barrenness of [e.g.] psychology is not to be explained by calling it a 'young science'; its state is not comparable with that of physics, for instance, in its beginnings". The dreadful mistake of the programmatic approach to the foundations of human science is to suppose—to hope—otherwise. All that is properly left to 'human science'—to social study—is, for Winch, specific questions arising in specific circumstances concerning the understanding of things that we find hard to understand, concerning coming to terms with persons who we don't naturally 'get'. This non-systematic endeavour is best pursued with a sound philosophical sensibility, an open mind.

to locate some of the roots of confusion in such plain, non technical expressions as 'understand', 'explain', 'rule', 'reason', 'cause', 'rational'. He insists especially that any instance of genuinely explanatory social study must be premised upon the existence of a puzzle (since there can only be explanation where this is misunderstanding or puzzlement), something where there is a deficit in our understanding or which tends to confuse us or others. Where there is manifestly room for explanatory questions, there is no reason to assume that the kind of explanation required *must* be the sort that involves some professionally developed general theory. Winch does not rule out all possibility of theory playing a role; rather, he puts the onus on would-be theorists to establish where 'derived from a theory' is the appropriate species of explanation in relation to the issues to be understood.

(II) Between *acting-on-a-rule*[17] and *interpreting a rule*

This is the *key* distinction made in section 201 of Wittgenstein's *Philosophical Investigations*: "[T]here is a way of grasping a rule which is not an interpretation, but which is exhibited in what we call 'obeying the rule' and 'going against it' in actual cases." When one acts on a rule, one normally does no interpreting. One grasps the rule.[18]

Thinking about (II) naturally connects with thinking about (I), above, in the following way: If one is interested in accurately *describing* human behaviour for the purpose of *reporting* it—a large part of which, though by no means all is action-according-to-a-rule—then one will need, much as Wittgenstein says, to 'grasp' the rule actually being followed by the person(s) one is describing, and will manifest that grasp in (for example) how one goes on to see the rule being applied in new examples of that person's action(s) which one encounters. One will want to avoid *interpreting* the rule being followed in such action *if* that can be avoided, on pain of otherwise risking missing just exactly what rule truly was being followed—acted upon, acted 'from'—in any given instance. One will want rather just to look, and see it. And then probably to describe it. Indeed, this, we contend, is what ethnomethodologists—and, in general, good ethnographers—typically do. Some of their work is an 'existence proof' of the possibility of sometimes doing what Wittgenstein invites us to do: roughly, simply looking and seeing, rather than always thinking (in the sense of intellectualising or theorising).

This move contravenes the 'conventional (philosophical) wisdom'—common, albeit under different guises, to philosophers as otherwise divergent as Nietzsche,

---

17 For detail, see Read and Guetti (1996). D.Z. Phillips's (2000) paper, 'Beyond Rules', partially defends and elaborates Winch, and points in the same pro- and post-Winchian direction. For papers which explicate Wittgenstein on rule-following with which we are in agreement and which we recommend to our readers, see Warren Goldfarb (1985) 'Kripke on Wittgenstein on Rules' and John McDowell's (1998a) pair of papers 'Non-Cognitivsm and Rule-Following' (pp. 198-218) and 'Wittgenstein on Following a Rule' (pp. 221-262).

18 See, again, John McDowell's paper 'Wittgenstein on Following a Rule' (op cit.) which is most informative on this point. See also Hutchinson (2008), *Shame and Philosophy* on world-taking (chapters 3 and 4).

Gadamer, Habermas and Donald Davidson, and just as common among a very wide spectrum of contemporary human and 'cognitive' scientists—*the dogma that it cannot be meaningful to speak of a description of some human behaviour that is not already an interpretation of that behaviour.* Gadamer, for example, for all his many philosophical virtues, continually risks over-intellectualizing ordinary human action by means of investing it all within an *interpretive* horizon; whilst Davidson assimilates 'understanding' of language to 'radical' interpretation, which is in turn unfortunately not clearly distinguished from explanation. Such an approach is overly—narrowly—scientific and risks mechanising human being.

The 'non-interpretivism', the grasping, which by contrast we are recommending here is not Positivistic, for it does not imagine description as an isolated and purely object-oriented/fact-gathering phenomenon. Rather, after Wittgenstein, J.L. Austin, and Harold Garfinkel—and, of course, after Winch—it allows indeed that there is what we call description[19] (which is not best assimilated to interpretation), and that it is important, but does not imagine that it prescinds from one's grasp, as a participant in a practice, of that practice as a lived activity. (One can see here already what we will gradually focus in on below: that in the philosophy of the social sciences, one is (or ought to be) always in the business of looking for judicious, perspicuous, modes of presentation: for 'reminders', for truisms. One is looking not for discoveries, but simply for ways of making perspicuous presentations of the terrain of what it makes sense for us to say.)

None of this implies that there is only ever one 'true description' available of any given piece of (e.g.) rule-following—there can be several or even indefinitely many true descriptions of same; what this means is only that an action is such under a description, following G.E.M. Anscombe (2000 [1957]). But it does preserve a role for the notion of descriptions which are not *ipso facto* interpretations. For example, as one sits at one's desk and writes, or reads, the description of one of the objects in front of one on the desk as 'a glass' is not an interpretation. And the description of the activity we are currently engaged in as 'writing' is not an interpretation either. These are ways in which we *take* what is before us on the desk to be such and *take* what we are doing to just be such-and-such, respectively. We simply *take* there to be a glass in seeing the glass, we do not interpret what is before us as a glass—other possibilities of what 'the glass' might be said to be do not arise only to be eliminated in favour of the best interpretation, 'a glass'; they do not arise at all. The insistence that all perception is interpretation is an example of the craving for explanation, where explanation involves comprehensively general propositions, and where, therefore, something which is an *occasional* feature of our activities—there are times when we need to interpret—is converted into a general/universal characteristic. The important point is, one might say, procedural as opposed to ontological.[20] For, if we call all apprehendings of our world interpretations then we lose clarity regarding the way in

---

19 And, of course, understanding.

20 In that it is not a claim grounded on a commitment as to what is taking place (or not taking place) in the brain. It is merely a claim designed to make our relationship to our world, to phenomena, perspicuous. It is a 'grammatical' claim regarding the 'grammar'—meaning— of 'to interpret' and/or 'to see'.

which we meet our world. We over-generalise; we give into the scientistic craving; we fail to see and to teach *differences*.

One way such a lack of clarity can lead to obscurantism is that clearly illustrated by J.L. Austin's (1962) pig example in *Sense and Sensibilia*, which we invoked in our 'Introduction' and we draw upon again here. Austin, in response to sense data theorists, wants to make perspicuous a distinction: that between having evidence for something (evidence of greater or lesser weight for a pig being in the vicinity) and apprehending something (taking something to be, *seeing it: there being a pig before us*). Evidence is only relevant when our apprehending of the 'thing' is in question—sight of the pig is not—further—evidence of its presence. What *we* are doing then is no more (and no less) than offering a reminder to our readers that ordinarily they distinguish between interpreting that *x* and apprehending—or taking there to be—*x*.

If one not only avoids explaining but (more important) avoids interpreting, then *one avoids a hermeneutic*. One sees no need to add *anything* to people's practices as they understand them (both explicitly—if interpretation is actually called for, for example, and—the usual case—'implicitly', in practice).[21] One hopes to capture the terms of the rules which they are following—always bearing in mind that this, too, is no single affair, that there are all sorts of rules, and all sorts of problems in acting according to those rules, as well as to being able to tell that someone is so doing.

The objection, frequently made against Winch over the years, runs roughly thus: 'Why so much talk about *rules*? Surely it is absurd to think of human behaviour as literally rule-governed—surely that removes its spontaneity, and over-intellectualises it, at one and the same time! That's got to be un-Wittgensteinian—Wittgenstein didn't believe that human beings are profitably-described as rule-following animals—*and* in any case it's wrong-headed. Winch errs, on this view, in centring his philosophical picture on rules. We would do better to focus, not on rules, but on norms, or on practices'.

An initial response would be this: *Insofar* as Winch speaks of "rule-governedness", then this is best heard, to avoid putting Winch in the undesirable position of mimicking the social theorizing that he (rightly) critiques in others, as a picture that Winch himself employs, for the purpose of re-reorienting his readers to their subject matter: the study (*where* such is called for) of society. Our worry here is that the objection assumes that Winch's conception of philosophy is substantive and theoretical; in particular, that Winch is an advocate of a particular implicit (rule-centred) 'social theory', where 'rule-following' will be called upon to meet the requirements that any other purported social theory is expected to meet. Rule-following does not ask for

---

21 This need not be politically conservative, as explicated in subsequent chapters. To anticipate: To describe is not yet to evaluate; to get what people are doing is not yet to criticise. Evaluation and criticism comes later—but sometimes it will surely come! And generally, and crucially, such criticism will take the form roughly of indicating to the people one has described how they themselves should be able to come to understand what they are doing as problematic: the self-understanding of people can be extended/changed/improved, by means of bringing descriptions that they themselves can be brought to accept back to haunt them … But all of this is a more complicated affair—more of a fraught, human undertaking—than the elitist dictations-to the lay-people that are the subject-matter of conventional, crude 'social science'.

exemption from those requirements; rather it tries to show that they are inappropriate. Whereas we should want to claim that Winch is successfully read as having *no* social theory, *no* substantive philosophical anthropology. Even to speak of Winch having a 'picture' of human action, as we did earlier is, as suggested there, to court misunderstanding. Such a picture, we are now suggesting, will only be necessary, helpful and relevant if it is designed to prevent one from making *particular* kinds of mistakes, falling into the habit of generating *particular* kinds of misunderstanding. It will not be Winch's place rather to give us a picture which aims to reflect the 'general metaphysical truth' as to the nature of persons.

Winch is not asserting, "Rule-following is the essence of human nature or human action". Of course, as Winch concedes in the Preface to the 2nd edition of *ISS*, his imperfect mode of expression at times in that book led to that interpretation of his words. But in acknowledging this he is at one and the same time clarifying that this is *not* what he was *advocating*. Winch's remarks on rule-following form no part of any theory of human nature. Winch is not a social theorist and the talk of rule-following is best-heard as an analogy.[22] Alternatively, we might say learning about other people is to some extent *like* learning the rules of a game. (Rules are an *object of comparison* that Winch is suggesting for us; that is their central role in his text.) In important respects, Winch brings in rules to point out that in many areas of activity the notion of doing things 'correctly' and 'making mistakes' are involved, and this could not be so if those activities were to be causally explained (though Winch does over-generalise a little in making the notion of rule and mistake interwoven, since the notion of rule is, in other contexts, internally related to 'violation', and in yet others to 'validity').

Games come in many varieties, and thus how we understand the nature of rules should be equally varied. Some games have strict rules to the extent that failure to act in accordance with those rules is a failure to simply play the game: Chess, for example. Some games have rules which we operate within, but which don't so much dictate our movements as invoke limits to the sort of movements it is legitimate to make in pursuit of the goals of the game (if there are any): Association football, or boxing, for example. Some games are more like a dance, more free-form, if you like; the goal (should it make sense to talk of such games as having goals) of the game being merely pleasure (or a tolerable way to pass a few hours, maybe) for the participants. Here the rules are dynamic and are not so much followed as made up as the game is played: 'catch', for example.[23] The claim that Winch *seems* to make, that "meaningful action is rule-governed action", is (rather) part of the 'elucidation' he is engaged in, emphasising that there are often—not always—standards that determine what constitutes an activity of that kind, whether the activity has been performed correctly and so on. Over-archingly, for the purposes of de-mythologizing (i.e. de-scientising) sociology—this is an 'elucidation' that Winch famously engages in on pp. 42-3 of *ISS*. The point of this elucidation is again to point one away from the

---

22 Likewise, his talk of 'conversation'; see *ISS*, pp. xvii-xviii, and below. (For Winch's last words on the potentially misleading nature of focussing on rules, see *ISS*, p. xiii.)

23 For an informative discussion, see again D.Z. Phillips 'Beyond Rules'. See also *PI*, sections 83 and 66.

idea that one is working through these issues in order to decide what is the best way to start building a social science, whether one should opt e.g. for a rule-following model rather than a causal one. Winch's is very importantly an attempt to place a limit on the idea that all explanation is causal in nature (see Alasdair MacIntyre's (1962) "A Mistake about Causality" as another very telling attempt to achieve the same effect). The truism that many actions are actions-according-to-a-rule, and the 'grammatical' point that explanation by rule is not of the same form as causal explanation, establishes that not all explanation is causal.

Thus, the 'argument' for rule-following emphasises that one is engaged in *reflection* on the practices that are found amongst the ways of people living their lives (including ourselves in the/our social studies) and that establishing, applying and appealing to rules is a commonplace amongst these.

So, once one is clear on all this, it becomes clear that to formulate a social theory based on norms or practices rather than rules would be a step *backwards*, not a step forwards: the point about any of these terms, for 'we Winchians', is precisely NOT to fall back into formulating a social theory around them or on the basis of them! To try to improve/repair/perfect one's social theory or social metaphysics is a profitless and counterproductive exercise, taking one deeper into this disease of the intellect. Notions such as 'rule', 'norm' and 'practice' are first and foremost part and parcel of our social life already; and what Winch is urging upon one is to return to the understanding of social life that one always already has, *before* the inclination to 'social science' gets in the way. Foregrounding 'rules' is a way of becoming clear about what one has grasped already in its fundaments, just by virtue of being a competent social actor. Insofar as it starts to look like more than that, it is becoming problem, and not solution.

Winch's Critics: The Case of Theodor Schatzki

Let us review Winch on rules by means of dealing with the objections Theodore Schatzki makes to Winch on behalf of what he, Schatzki, takes to be a properly 'Wittgensteinian' point of view. We choose Schaztki because he is no fool … Schatzki is not a *crude* misinterpreter of Winch; if he misinterprets, it is at least worth paying serious attention to where and why he does so, though he is in quite direct conflict with Winch in that he thinks that Wittgenstein's philosophy can be put to something like sociological theory-developing purposes.

Schatzki refers extensively to *Wittgenstein* in an effort to support his case, but, in a pattern with which we are all-too-familiar, fails to cite more than a minimum of *Winch's* words to support his case. Schatzki argues as follows: "In Winch's account, understanding a practice requires a grasp of the usually nonexplicit rules governing it … In Winch's view … understanding a given surface phenomena (sic.) (a practice) requires a grasp of something below the surface which governs it (non-explicit rules)" (Schatzki 1991, p. 324).[24]

The metaphor of surface and depth here is liable to mislead. As there is no direct quotation from Winch at this point in Schatzki's paper, it is hard to know precisely from where he gets it; but it could not possibly be Winch's account.[25] For the 'account' of which Schatzki writes is exactly the kind of picture that we find in (say) Chomsky, and that any Wittgensteinian who takes seriously that "nothing is hidden" must resist.

It is worth quoting extensively from Winch, to see what he actually says, at the point in his monograph to which Schatzki refers:

> In the course of his investigation the scientist applies and develops the concepts germane to his particular field of study. This application and modification are "influenced" both by the phenomena to which they are applied and also by the fellow-workers *in participation with* whom they are applied. But the two kinds of "influence" are different. Whereas it is on the basis of his observation of the phenomena ... that he develops his concepts as he does, he is able to do this only in virtue of his participation in an established form of activity with his fellow-scientists. When I speak of "participation" here I do not necessarily imply any direct communication between fellow-participants. What is important is that they are all taking part in the same general kind of activity, which they have *learned* in similar ways; that they are, therefore, *capable* of communicating with each other about what they are doing; that what any one of them is doing is in principle intelligible to the others ...

> [I]f the position of the sociological investigator (in a broad sense) can be regarded as comparable, in its main logical outlines, with that of the natural scientist, the following must be the case. The concepts and criteria according to which the sociologist judges that, in two situations, the same thing has happened, or the same action performed, must be understood *in relation to the rules governing sociological investigation*. But here we run against a difficulty; for whereas in the case of the natural scientist we have to deal with only one set of rules, namely those governing the scientist's investigation itself, here what the sociologist is studying, as well as his study of it, is a human activity and is therefore carried on according to rules. And it is these rules, rather than those which govern the sociologist's investigation, which specify what is to count as "doing the same kind of thing' in relation to that kind of activity" (*ISS*, pp. 85–87, emphasis in original).

Winch is here attempting to teach us differences.[26] He is, we would suggest, onto the thought, much exploited by ethnomethodologists, that what 'social scientists'

---

24 Again, Schatzki is a useful commentator to focus on here partly *because* of his undoubted Wittgensteinian leanings. If even he gets Winch wrong, things are in a bad way—as we fear they are.

25 We suspect it stems from Schatzki having a standard social science conception of a rule as a kind of theoretical mechanism, rather than looking to see what count as rules in Winch's own text: how are the rules of counting in sequence not explicit—counting in this sequence just *is* the rule.

26 Michael Nedo, of the Cambridge Wittgenstein Archive, tells us that Wittgenstein had originally thought of using as a motto [for *PI*] a quotation from Shakespeare's *King Lear*: 'I'll teach you differences'. The precise way in which Winch saw the differences in this case is well-explicated on p. 61 of Lyas (1999): '[A]n explanation in the natural sciences does not

typically present to us as 'data' are already pre-digested; that the true data of social study ought to be, and in fact must be, typically what is observably present and observably underway in interactions between persons.[27] He is not using the notion of 'rules' in any doctrinaire fashion, for the 'rules' he does mention can readily be pointed to, such as those which call for a change of regime after an election, which regulate the consultation of the poison oracle, which require the washing of hands prior to a religious ceremonial (and those that instruct a washing of hands for reasons of hygiene). There are even rules about how UK postage stamps should be positioned on the envelope with respect to the orientation of the monarch's head.

Put another way: the word 'rule' is not a theoretical term, it is a perfectly ordinary English word, and Winch uses it as such: there are innumerable activities—such as the spelling of words in English which are obeyed many times on every line of this book—that are extensively or in some aspects rule governed. To state this is not to offer any theory of writing or of English spelling; it is merely to describe, state a truism about, writing. It would be a deep mistake to treat such an observation as providing a basis for a general account of action, especially as an interpretation of someone who does not believe that such an account is needed! Winch's invocation of rules does not require him to push through the idea that action is rule-following— action = rule-following—into a general truth, but only to point out that, given that

---

remind us of something … We are not reminded about sub-atomic particles: we find things out about them'. Whereas, strange as it might sound, a large part of the activity of sociologists consists simply in reminding us—unfortunately, often *in very misleading* (e.g. reductionistic, impoverished, or highly-abstract) *terms*—of things about ourselves and others which we were not ignorant of to begin with.

27 For detail, see for example, Mike Lynch's work. Lynch, unlike some influenced by certain strands in Garfinkel and especially by the later Harvey Sacks, avoids falling into a quasi-scientific rendition of ethnomethodology as the *general uncovering* of the 'hidden truth' of (the constitution of) social order, and sticks to an appropriately Winchian rendition of the (piecemeal) tasks of philosophically-sensitive social study. As Lynch (2000) argues in his paper 'Against Reflexivity', to speak and work as the best ethnomethodologists do, in a manner attempting to escape as much as possible from abstraction (e.g. terms like 'observable', 'reflexive', 'indexical') in favour of the concretion of actual social settings, is far less liable to be misleading than are the alternative modes of writing more commonly found in the social sciences, which even imagine that they are following Wittgenstein when they speak for instance of a 'double hermeneutic' as characteristic of social behaviour and (especially) of social science. As we emphasize more or less throughout this chapter, the use of the word 'interpretation' is often much more perilous and misleading than has generally been realized—and this we think is why Winch uses it far less frequently than do those (e.g. Geertz, and 'interpretivists' in the '*Verstehen*' tradition) to whom he is often assimilated. Winch generally avoids the intellectualism which 'interpretivists' typically fall into. Crucially, he agrees with Wittgenstein that what matters is *both* to understand humans as engaged in ordered practices etc., *and* to understand that stressing the deed, not the word or the thought, is usually least liable to mislead philosophically. We act, we obey rules blindly, and 'as a matter of course'—see pp. 30-31 of *ISS*. (Our own brief diagnosis of the persistence of the intellectual temptation to intellectualism among intellectuals is … perhaps so obvious after the use of the word-root 'intellect' three times in one sentence that we won't bother giving it here.)

rule-following and causal explanations *are* different kinds of explanations, the patent presence of innumerable rules in social life simply *blocks* the ambition to erect a general, causal theory. Schatzki is quite right insofar as what he is doing is suggesting that any 'individualist' or (more generally) theoreticist attempt to render rules as a foundation for the explanation of human behaviour—as for example in Chomskian linguistics, and in much of Cognitive Science—is bound to fail. But this point is not appropriately directed against Winch.

Schatzki's other main argument against Winch opens as follows: "Winch begins from the assumption that each society has its own concept of (or rules for) the intelligibility of human proceedings" (p. 318). Schatzki's mistake here is again to interpret a propadeutic strategy as though it were a general theory—it is plain that there are differences amongst human practices in standards of intelligibility, differences to be found both within a society and across them, the truth of which mundane observation blocks the idea that there are universal standards of intelligibility worth speaking of or that there is a universal method for understanding all practices. However, it is unwise to translate this into grossly generalised claims such as that 'each society has its own concept of ...' when Winch's effort is directed against the *whole idea* that we need to engage in some comprehensively systematic comparison of societies' respective concepts of intelligibility.

Winch's concern is with sensitivity to particulars, involving restricted, detailed and careful comparison of instances of conceptual variation, all of which will be lost in gross, sweeping, indiscriminate generalities of Schatzki's kind. Winch doesn't argue that 'we' (the English) have one concept of intelligibility and the Azande another completely different one, as though 'ours' is a scientific mode and 'theirs' their oracular system. He surely proposes, instead, that scientific concepts are not general standards of intelligibility even in our own society, and as a result are an irrelevant comparison to 'their' oracular practices. The oracular practices are different from, but not entirely unlike, some religious practices in our society, and the former can be made more intelligible to us by noting that they are akin to practices current amongst us. One doesn't even have to be religious to grasp the cogency of Winch's linking of oracular consultation to prayer (in certain respects). Schatzki's is also a bad translation of Winch in that it suggests that Winch can accept only *difference* —each society has 'its own' concept of intelligibility which is different from every other's. Nothing of this dogmatic sort is involved in Winch, for there are surely both differences and similarities between—even within—practices, let alone societies, in criteria of intelligibility, and the point is to warn against obliterating important differences—Winch's is, in other words, an attempt to point out the vaunting/ o'er-vaulting ambition often attached to the idea of giving sweepingly synoptic summations of diverse and internally varied practices in face of the multiplicity of similarities and differences involved. To the question: does a society have 'its own' concepts of intelligibility, the best *a priori* answer is—they do and they don't ... Which means *in practice* that the question, if it is to be asked at all, needs to be raised in respect of particular cases, and points of comparison ... but Schatzki thinks Wittgenstein can be converted into input for sociological theory.

So, *contra* Schatzki, Winch only claims that it will be useful when presented with a rendition of a 'primitive' society as essentially having the same concept of intelligibility as ours (as for example Frazer seems to think: he appears to think, as Wittgnstein says, that those he is studying are essentially English parsons, only stupid ones)[28] to consider alternative ways of putting things. *Provided we don't think we are stating a metaphysical thesis when we do so*, there will then be no harm in saying, e.g., "The Azande have a somewhat different concept of [say] 'prediction' (or 'contradiction') than we do (but not, apparently, of 'empirical cause')".[29] Alternatively, one might fruitfully cast it as a negative point: we shouldn't presume that other people, especially ones whose ways differ from ours, must have, or really need, the same concepts as ours. It is not an *a priori* matter to specify which concepts any specified collection of people must have, and since Winch was concerned with *a priori* matters any attempt to make substantive claims about the extent of uniformity or variety across cultures and practices other than those he/one had looked at would be a wholly invalid generalisation of his argument.

The underlying problem then is an intellectualist tradition thinking of understanding as the product of a universal method. Such a tradition is frustrated by Winch and Wittgenstein's emphasis on understanding as a highly personalised matter, conditional upon, e.g., one's efforts and one's sensibilities and associated reactions and willingness to rethink—one isn't willing to acquire a vocational commitment to being a monk, to put the time, effort, sacrifice in or one simply *can't* respond in this way to (say) the Bible in the way that devout Christians do, etc. There is no theoretical shortcut here, but practitioners in the 'social sciences' want to be assured that there is such a shortcut; that they can impartially, impersonally and with only the effort of learning a method and applying it to the phenomena, understand anyone, and therefore *everyone*.

Winch's important (1992) paper, 'Persuasion', seemingly unread by the vast majority of his critics, draws extensively upon Wittgenstein's writings,[30] to argue that one must both realize the radical nature of Wittgenstein's efforts to get one to question pictures that hold one captive, and simultaneously acknowledge that there is no such thing as finding a place outside all pictures from which to assess them apodictically.[31] Nigel Pleasants puts the moral of Winch's discussions of anthropology etc. strikingly-similarly:

---

28 Whereas Wittgenstein is struck by the profound sensibility of many of the people(s) portrayed in *The Golden Bough*—while he suspects that many English parsons lack such a (religious) sensibility!

29 See p. 101 of Goldstein (1999) for a useful rendition of Wittgenstein's thinking on the family-resemblance-ness of 'contradiction'.

30 See *PI*, p. 227; and *Culture and Value* (edited by von Wright, transl. Winch; Oxford: Blackwell, 1980), p. 87: 'God may say to me: "I am judging you out of your own mouth. You have shuddered with disgust at your own actions, when you have seen others do them"'.

31 See Winch (1992) pp. 129-130. (Again, this may sound like trying to have it both ways. We can hear the Analytic critics now: 'But you're not *saying* anything! Your Winch is not giving us any hard philosophical assertions to get our teeth into!' The critics are right. Only they fail to understand that this is inevitable, and exactly what the philosopher *should* be doing. Enabling us to see our language etc., aright—not giving us 'tinpot' theories and theses to knock down and put up again, endlessly.)

The central message of Winch ... —which has often been overlooked, or ignored—is the suggestion that in studying a so-called "primitive society" we might, if we engage in the task sensitively and imaginatively, learn something important about our own taken-for-granted form of life. I ... seek to follow Winch's advice that the very point of trying to learn about some apparently incoherent way of life is just as much to do with striving for an enhanced conception of one's own social conditions of existence, as it is with understanding that other way of life (Pleasants 1999, p. 2).

And surely this is right for those who are struggling to understand 'spiritual' matters, though it would not apply (at least, not in anything like the same way) to someone trying to get up to speed in mathematical physics.[32] Those who have thought deeply about these matters—for example, Martin Buber and the traditions he has influenced and which have tried to work these matters out practically (e.g. Gestalt Therapy, with its concept of 'contact')—have held that truly to *meet* someone—to *acknowledge* them as they are themselves—is part of what must be involved in understanding them, and that this must involve a readiness to open oneself up. To open oneself up to the other, part of what it is to *engage* with another person, is to have at least a *readiness* to change in response to them, and to the encounter. To understand another, to treat another as a 'thou', is not to treat them as an isolated ego which one is inspecting and 'interpreting'—*contra* Davidson and Cognitive Science, alike.[33] As any but the most scientistically deluded psychotherapists and travellers (e.g. field anthropologists) have long been aware, one cannot just study other people, if one would understand them. One must be ready to learn from them; to learn from them about them—and also about oneself, and about 'ourselves'; to learn 'the rules' (both in a loose sense

---

32 And this is what Wittgenstein was about in 'Remarks on Frazer's *Golden Bough*' when he pointed to things we do (e.g. kissing photos of loved ones) which somewhat resemble things 'primitive peoples' do. The point is not, as Schatzki would have it (and as Lerner thinks Winch himself thinks—see p. 183f. of his (op.cit.)), that we can understand them because they are really just like us; the point is that thinking about them enables us to notice things about us *which we forget, and whose nature is unclear to us.* Wittgenstein intends his point about our activity (in the photo-kissing) to surprise us—rather than having us absorb seamlessly a supposed item of knowledge about others; namely, that they are just like ourselves. It is thinking exactly *that* that Wittgenstein accuses Frazer of! (Thus, in the cause of our understanding others while remaining ourselves, Schatzki turns Wittgenstein into Frazer! What we *should* be doing by contrast is what Winch does: noting how openness to understanding others requires readiness to rework one's self-understanding.)

33 Are we lapsing here back into metaphysical humanism in a way which undercuts our argument and our reading of Winch? No, for two reasons: first, this is very much a supplementary point, which our main argument could easily stand without, for those readers who are uncomfortable with talking about therapy, *meeting* people, and so on; and second, this point is, we would maintain, still a genuinely Winchian/Wittgensteinian one (and though we cannot justify the claim here, a tremendous extant justification is to be found in Stanley Cavell's (1976) 'Knowing and Acknowledging' in his *Must we Mean What We Say?*, which in brilliant detail makes the tie between knowing the other ('epistomology') and actually acknowledging their reality as a person). We think that a substantial part of what Buber et al. do is *remind* us of features of our form of life—specifically, of the grammar of 'meet', 'understand', etc.—which we frequently forget in philosophy or 'cognitive' or 'social' science.

and in a tighter sense in specific instances) according to which they 'work', and order their lives. If we treat them as people at all, we use the unacknowledged resource of most sociology etc.—that is, our easy grasp of most of what most fellow humans do. Then our ability where necessary to focus on making sense of those elements of their lives which are mysterious to us can come into play–in a decidedly supplementary fashion.

So, to take a diagnostic step back for a moment: there appears to be an interesting fantasy at work somewhere deep in Schatzki's version of Wittgenstein, a fantasy which we suspect is widely shared among Anglo-American philosophers: a fantasy that one can learn all about the world and about other people without oneself changing, without changing oneself. Compare Schatzki's words: "To state Wittgenstein's views[34] baldly: there is either sufficient commonality and hence understanding or insufficient commonality and, as a result, no understanding" (p. 319). There is no place here for response to the other, for change. And yet Wittgenstein thought that the growth of one's own understanding, and the overcoming of one's 'ignorance' of one's own language etc., in part through one's grasp of the other, was of central importance. Thus witness his famous remark to his student Norman Malcolm:

> … what is the use of studying philosophy if all that it does for you is enable you to talk with some plausibility about some abstruse questions of logic, etc., and if it does not improve your thinking about the important questions of everyday life, if it does not make you more conscientious than any … journalist in the use of DANGEROUS phrases [Malcolm had used the expression, "the British national character"] such people use for their own ends. You see, I know that it's difficult to think well about 'certainty', 'probability', 'perception', etc. But it is, if possible, still more difficult to think … really honestly about your life and other people's lives (cited in Monk 1990, pp. 474-475).[35]

Or consider Wittgenstein's thought, used as an epigraph by Winch for his late paper "Persuasion", that "I ought to be no more than a mirror, in which my reader can see his own thinking with all its deformities so that, helped in this way, he can put it right". Winch, seemingly unlike Schatzki, and certainly unlike some of his other critics, such as Keita and Patrick Phillips, preserves and expands upon this role for "putting one's thinking right". Philosophy may be 'uncommitted enquiry'—but it is not without normative consequences.

Now, there's a danger that we might here be taken still to be writing as if 'understanding' was a philosophical problem, not a personal one, and we are, here, talking about certain sorts of 'understanding' where prejudice toward others may intervene: to reiterate, philosophy—or social scientific method—does not provide us with means of achieving understanding. Philosophy sure is uncommitted inquiry in that we are not committed—in our reflections—to the greater desirability of any one set of concepts we reflect on, but real problems of understanding arise in our

---

34 See our discussion of Winch's or Wittgenstein's having views in philosophy at all, above: Winch is (on our reading) a serious Wittgensteinian, in aiming *not to have* philosophical views.

35 cf. also Wittgenstein's preference for *change in the way people lived* over *explicit adoption of his philosophy.*

lives and have to be addressed through our personal efforts. Studying 'other cultures' is not a philosophical job, for that (the latter) is rather the clearing up of confused ideas like 'it is impossible to understand other cultures' or 'human thought processes are everywhere the same' etc. 'Understanding other cultures' in the relevant sense is something that sociologists adventitiously get involved in because their work brings them in contact with unfamiliar groups, ways of life, and practices, but 'understanding' these new contacts is not something that confronts sociologists distinctively. Rather, it is just the same order of problem—a practical one—that affects anyone who finds themselves in a new setting (e.g. an atheist amongst the religious, and so on).

Schatzki seems deeply attached to the idea of understanding as something that is done at a distance and can be considered in formulaic terms—as if there are specifiable conditions for understanding. His construal sounds rather like Chomsky or Fodor: you can't really learn anything, you can only really understand what you are already capable of understanding—there is no room for expanding your capabilities of understanding, of moving onto things that you really couldn't understand before and now you find you can. To reiterate our point: there is no formula for understanding, there are multiple ways of trying to understand, and one can make repeated and various efforts to understand something, and fail, before finding that one can succeed/has succeeded. Sometimes one small thing can make all the difference, sometimes one's understanding can change by degrees—light dawns slowly over the whole, as Wittgenstein (quoting Göethe) wrote—or one can experience a conversion, suddenly, abruptly a complete switch. Imagination can be involved and changes of aspect can play an important role too; furthermore, this is not to be thought of as a solo effort, for other people can help you understand, try to persuade you, teach you, put you through various experiences/practices etc. *So*, how much and what kind of effort one puts in, what sorts of imaginative exercises are employed, what kind of connection can be made between where you are and where you might want to be are all central to Wittgenstein's remarks on understanding but absent from, and thus unavailable to, Schatzki's version.

Perhaps the above will be seen as a little unfair to Schatzki. Perhaps he would accept that one can and sometimes does learn from others and transform oneself, in the encounter with other cultures, if one lets it be a genuine encounter, rather than being like the encounter of a biologist with a laboratory specimen. We contend nevertheless that Schatzki is thinking of the problem, with 'social science' ambitions and standards in place, wondering how Winch bears upon that problematic; but Winch is not concerned with that problematic because it is only a problematic if one ignores what Winch is saying about the nature of social studies. In the remarks from Schatzki that we have quoted, one can see that he makes it sound as if Wittgenstein thinks that it makes sense quite literally to assess—to quantify—the degree of commonality which human beings have with one another.[36] To repeat, here is his summation of Wittgenstein's supposed 'position':

---

36 Keita's (1997) position (in his 'Winch and Instrumental Pluralism: A reply to B.D.Lerner') is similar, only more scientistic. Keita thinks that 'the structure of the human brain is such that seemingly incompatible intercultural systems of ratiocination should really be understood within the context of how humans actually think' (p. 80). Wow,

To state Wittgenstein's views baldly: there is either sufficient commonality and hence understanding or insufficient commonality and, as a result, no understanding (p. 319).[37]

But we shall go on to show more fully both that it is already usually a misunderstanding to speak of 'understanding' as if it were a positive state to be achieved—and that it is already a misunderstanding to speak of Wittgenstein as having philosophical views at all.[38]

Schatzki immediately goes on from the remark just quoted to say something which indicates that he appears to think that Wittgenstein's 'views' are truth-evaluable, and he values them as true: "Wittgenstein's claim about insufficient commonality is obvious". We shall shortly query this notion, both exegetically and (more important) philosophically. Let us do so somewhat indirectly, by focussing first on a closely-related aspect of Schatzki's argument, as it affects Winch.

Schatzki's assumption that Winch thinks that different human communities may as a matter of substantive fact have very few commonalities to them is quite unwarranted. Let us ask the following: How could we determine whether as a matter of fact two human communities have 'many' or 'few' commonalities?

As soon as one asks the question, one realizes that it is, as things stand, a somewhat ill-formed question. There is no such thing as a substantive fact of the matter about whether two communities are deeply different from one another, independently of some specific standard of comparison. Whether something is 'deeply different' is a matter of nuance, and of context. One needs to understand in order to then make the claim as to commonality and difference. Schatzki puts the cart before the horse as it were in claiming that communities are deeply different to one another. Someone can at one time find a strange novel practice of a faraway tribe very reasonable or understandable; and at another one can be quite bemused by what one oneself did five seconds ago.

All we can do here (and all we need to do here) is assemble reminders. We can stop ourselves being confused. For example, as already mentioned (and this is discussed more fully below), sometimes it is useful to be reminded that what

---

a philosopher who can apparently read off from observable (?) brain structure 'how humans actually think!....'.

37 We find the way 'understanding' is treated as a yes/no matter pretty astonishing—as if there aren't inordinately many forms and degrees of understanding: for example, do you understand French? A few words, enough to read with, I can carry on a simple conversation. Who understands French the best? The French Grammarian, Rimbaud, a native Parisian? What is it to not understand French? To know no French words, to not be able to participate in a conversation in French, to not recognise French as French when it is being spoken?

38 See Wittgenstein's pointed insistence, in his debates on the philosophy of maths with Turing (see Monk (1990), pp. 419-420; though Monk himself misses the 'metaphilosophical' point here), that he, Wittgenstein, must not have any views or opinions. Otherwise, he would be (A) hostage to mathematical fortune, and (B) betraying his philosophical mission, as expressed e.g. in *PI*, sections 108-134. It is also pertinent to note that when Schatzki talks of stating Wittgenstein's views 'baldly', he means to state Wittgenstein's views in a way quite other than that in which Wittgenstein carefully chose to state 'them'—and other than Wittgenstein's text licenses 'them' to be taken. In this regard, see Hutchinson (2007) and Baker (2004) chapter 11 and his (2002).

counts as a contradiction can be very different in different places in different times. This is part of what Wittgenstein meant when he famously remarked that philosophy leaves everything as it is (this remark is cited approvingly by Winch on p. 103 of *ISS*, and we give it some discussion in Chapter 4). It is also part of what he means in a remark that is at the very heart of his so-called 'metaphilosophical' discussions in *PI*, but a remark almost universally ignored: "The civil status of a contradiction, or its status in civil life: there is the philosophical problem".[39] And it is precisely this that Winch brings out with his discussion of the 'contradictions' which Western observers find in Azande practice, where the issue is precisely Wittgenstein's point, that it is philosophers' *attitude* to contradiction that is the problem—their (formal logic-inspired) supposition that the presence of a contradiction must bring a practice to a halt. You have to look at the practice in context, says Winch, to see whether it is a good idea to say, "They have a different concept of 'contradiction' from us", or "What looked like contradictions turn out on closer acquaintance not to be so", or what-have-you. (Some such statements will be, at a given point in a particular 'conversation', much less liable to mislead than others.) If there is a contradiction in oracular magic, it surely does not bring the practice to a halt. And then that point has to be taken on board henceforth.

And there is not even, of course, a substantive fact of the matter about how to individuate communities in the first place—hence notice Winch's emphasis on the cultural independence of the Azande tradition from Western Christianity. Winch believes that 'social sciences' are somewhat (though only somewhat) less misleadingly described as social studies. (This description must not of course be allowed to lead one to think that Winch is an armchair sociologist, competing with sociology on its own turf. For this is a point *about* social science/studies, not a point *in* them, we discuss this further below.) Winch believes that, unless one is clear that a 'social science' is at best not just a science which happens to have as its subject-matter human society, but that the word 'social' decisively alters the character of the investigation in the study (studies) in question, one is likely to become philosophically confused. Of course, there is no substantive fact of the matter about *these* things either! Winch is *not* saying, "It's a scientific fact that you cut up the universe wrong if you classify (e.g.) sociology as a science". It doesn't even matter if the various social studies are grouped together under the heading of 'social science'—so long as one keeps a clear view of what is thus named, and what its character is. But that is almost impossible to do, even in the best of circumstances. Furthermore, Winch believes, with the ethnomethodologists and with Wittgenstein, that 'sociology' as a lay activity is ubiquitous, but, *for that very reason*, as a professional activity is only infrequently necessary.

Perhaps Schatzki himself, speaking in his own voice, would in the end not disagree with what we have said above. But he *follows* the standard reading of Winch, in accusing the latter of having the idea that communities are cleanly separable entities.

---

39 *PI*, section 125. This sentence is succeeded by the following famous passage: "Philosophy simply puts everything before us, and neither explains nor deduces anything. Since everything lies open to view there is nothing to explain. For what is hidden, for example, is of no interest to us".

This idea was suggested by some of Winch's incautious formulations in the first edition of *ISS*. He very clearly distances himself from this interpretation of his work, in the 1990 Preface to the 2nd edition. Let us explain this point further ...

Winch does not think that any 'social scientist' or 'social theorist'—still less himself—is in a position even to claim or argue that it is a matter of hard fact that the Azande is one community and ours is a totally separate one.[40] It's rather that it will sometimes be ethnographically (or indeed philosophically) helpful to distinguish between communities of people which are of course to some significant extent self-identifying. That's the important criterion, if a criterion we need: whatever one says about the social world must be responsible to social actors, in a manner having no parallel in the physical sciences. However, as just hinted, all this may have been somewhat obscured in Winch's original presentation of *The Idea of a Social Science*, by his sometimes appearing to grant the notion that we can definitively identify communities, and indeed that they are definitively separate and homogenous. But (a) there is nowhere in—his follow-up paper— "Understanding a Primitive Society" where Winch makes any similarly potentially-misleading remarks, nor in the various other papers in which Winch subsequently to *ISS* spoke of sociology, anthropology etc.; and (b) those who criticise Winch for having left the door open for 'relativism' in *ISS* have failed to appreciate his clarificatory remarks in the new Preface to *The Idea of a Social Science*. Here (especially on p. xiii), Winch specifically remarked that he had sometimes expressed himself in a manner that might mislead in the first edition of *ISS* on crucial issues connected with that nature of rules, and thus unnecessarily exposed himself to the kind of misunderstanding we see in (for instance) Schatzki. Indeed, in the Preface to the 2nd edition, Winch goes on immediately to say that, if he had paid closer attention to passages such as sections 81-82 (on rules) in *Philosophical Investigations*, then he

> ... might have avoided the impression sometimes given in this book of social practices, traditions, institutions etc. as more or less self-contained and each going its own, fairly autonomous way ... Again, and connectedly, the suggestion that modes of social life are autonomous with respect to each other was insufficiently counteracted by [the] qualifying remark ... about "the overlapping character of different modes of social life". Different modes of social life do not merely "overlap"; they are frequently internally related in such a way that one cannot even be intelligibly conceived as existing in isolation from others (*ISS*, pp. xiv-xv).

Winch here evidently regrets some of his phrasings and possibly some more substantial aspects of his project in the first edition of *ISS*, and this is what he sought to redress in his 1990 preface. When read in light of that preface, Winch can be seen

---

40 And see again *ISS* (2nd edition) pp. xiv-xvi. (Winch points out the importance of the lack of a shared religious tradition between us and the Azande, in making it important to get the degree of cultural distance between us and them sufficiently *wide*, before attempting to understand. But this distance is not quantifiable, and total philosophical confusion is close at hand, if it is claimed to be 'total' (*Contra* Relativist interpretations of Winch).)

as interested above all in what it makes sense to say.[41] But of course, self-evidently, things are always said by people, in contexts. Philosophers tend to ignore this simple 'fact', fail to remind themselves of it, at their philosophic peril. So: what one says in one conversation, speaking as a philosopher with colleagues, may be very different from what one says in another conversation, speaking say with a foreigner from an extremely different background, or with an opinion pollster, or with a popularising scientist. To one, one might say that the Azande are very different from us; to another, that they are much the same; to a third, that they practice a peculiar and unattractive form of magic; to a fourth, that they have a way of life whose categories are hard to mesh in any successful way with our own. There would be no contradiction in one's saying all of these, and more, at different times and places, to different people. Winch is looking for ways of rendering helpfully the concept of 'society', and is reaching for formulations which will be least likely to confuse and most likely to productively assist his audience; he is not stating or trying to state once and for all The Truth about social life, for the 'substantive truths' found in his writings are, as they must be in any properly Wittgensteinian exercise, banalities.

To further support our thought about the non-assertoric, non-constative nature of Winch's thought hereabouts, note the use of the notion of 'internal relation' in the above quote. This term is explicated in the *Tractatus*, and, in the relatively rare contexts of use it has in Wittgenstein's later work,[42] it has much the same sense as it did there (Winch emphasizes the continuities in Wittgenstein's philosophy far more than is usually appreciated—for some detail, see below). The term 'internal relation' cannot be used faithfully to Wittgenstein in a way which provides a general account of 'metaphysical glue' between rule and application: indeed, that idea does deserve the kind of criticism which Schatzki (inappropriately) levels against *Winch* on rules.

So, what sense *does* 'internal relation' have in Wittgenstein's work? Well, crucial to it, as Winch was extremely well aware, is that internal relations cannot, strictly speaking, be spoken of at all. 'They' are not genuinely relations. (Thus there is of course an air of paradox to our discussion too. Talk of internal relations is thorough-goingly *transitional*.)[43] Only 'external' relations are actually relations, between separate things. And there have to be separate things, if there are to be relations

---

41 See the discussion later of Winch's account of the importance but oft-misunderstood nature of the role of language in a sound conception of philosophy. (In a longer presentation, we should of course reckon with the increasing influence of Rhees on Winch's mature thought (and others such R.F. Holland and Raimond Gaita). But this would certainly require an entire paper to itself, to discuss adequately.)

42 See Read (1997), where he points out that Wittgenstein only rarely speaks of 'internal relations' after c.1939. (It is also to be noted that Winch came to think that speaking of social relations as internal relations may foster the unwarranted impression that social relations are always 'cosy', whereas Winch remarks on p. xviii of *ISS*, once again pre-empting his 1990s critics, that one needs to take account of 'what role in [a conversational interchange] is played by strategies of deceit, blackmail ..., punches on the nose, etc.')

43 For explication, see Cora Diamond's work on the *Tractatus*, most of it collected in her (1992), *The Realistic Spirit*. Also see the discussion of 'internal relations' in Denis McManus (2007), *The Enchantment of Words*.

(between thing*s*). To say that there holds an internal relation between 'things' is to say that on inspection one might well find that what one was taking to be things related are not discrete items at all; that so much as one can talk of two—internally related—things one is talking of 'one' carrying with it the other: such as to grasp the concept of 'fire' is to have grasped the concept of 'to burn'; or, one might simply emphasise, more humdrumly, that they utterly and obviously 'go together' as the notion of 'fire' and 'burning' do.[44]

It follows that when Winch speaks above of different 'parts' of social life as 'internally related',[45] or similarly of humans as 'internally related' to each other, and of social relations as *being* 'internal relations', what he is really saying is usefully put as follows: that they are not causal, or external, relations at all. The notion of 'internal relations' as Winch employs it is a wholistic notion that can be understood in contrast with the 'external' relations of causal connections. In the causal case, two things that can be identified independently of each other and one can be the cause of the other—it is an empirical question whether one thing is the cause or effect of the other. With respect to something like a rule, though, the rule and the action which follows the rule cannot be identified independently of each other, since the rule is a rule prescribing the action and the action is properly identified as an action according to the rule—it is not an *empirical* question as to which kind of action follows from obedience to a rule since the identity of the action type is given in the sense of the rule. I.e. understanding a rule is in many cases knowing what to do—'driving on the left' is the action that corresponds to the rule 'drive on the left'. It may be an empirical question as to whether one can find an instance of someone obeying that rule and performing the action, but the connection between the rule and the action comes from *understanding the rule* not relating empirical occurrences. Therefore, characterizing them as relations can, riskily, lead to society being thought of in nonsensical atomistic ways. For example, when we pick up the notion of 'internal relation' for a while we see that, though it cannot be ultimately satisfactory, and though it can risk leading us to say things which sound awfully like (nonsensical) metaphysical 'theses' about the social world, it at least usefully closes down the unprofitable avenue of thinking of different practices as being (metaphysically) hermetically sealed off from one another, and furthermore intimates instead an alternative picture which may help to point up the *absurdity* (not falsity) of the atomism and ontological individualism which so often turn up in social theory.

Having got somewhat clearer on Winch's observations on the concept of 'society' and 'social relations', we are finally in a position to turn directly to the following

---

44 In this regard see *PI*, section 474. One also should hold in mind the thought that internal relations are not invoked in the sense in which they were by the British idealists. They are themselves radically contextual. Whether one concept is internally related to another— whether grasping one entails the grasping of the other—is itself very likely a contextual matter. Here again one should look and see. In *TL-P*, Wittgenstein illustrates the notion of internal relations by referring to a story by the Brothers Grimm, 'The Golden Kids'.

45 Giving the lie to the common (Norman Malcolm's) 'autonomous communities' interpretation of Winch's thinking discussed earlier.

question: Is There a Genuine Question Concerning How Strong the Commonalities Between Persons Must be in Order For Them to be Mutually Comprehensible?

Our remarks about the absurdity of thinking that philosophers (or 'social scientists') are in a position proprietarily to individuate communities and pronounce upon their openness and closedness to one another lead naturally into a thought of even more importance for comprehending what Winch, after Wittgenstein, is up to in his philosophy of social science. We are thinking of the allegations of 'relativism' and 'incommensurabilism' made against Winch (we will examine the related allegation of 'idealism' explicitly in the next chapter). Sometimes these are prosecuted by self-proclaimed rationalists (e.g. Martin Hollis) who think Winch is defeasible on quasi-empirical grounds—we need, Hollis, argued, a 'bridgehead' of shared beliefs in order to comprehend people from other cultures, and that bridgehead is to be found in our shared human rationality. Sometimes, this idea becomes more explicitly quasi-Kantian in nature, as in Davidson, who at points suggests that his ultimate grounds for his notions of 'charity' and 'humanity' are 'transcendental'. *Such* an idea can seem related to Wittgenstein's thoughts about 'form of life', especially to the famous passage in *PI* on 'agreement', sections 240-2.[46]

But these remarks of Wittgenstein's are not quasi-empirical, nor even about transcendental conditions of possibility. They are grammatical 'reminders', pointers away from certain specific philosophical confusions in which it is extremely easy to find oneself embroiled; confusions even of 'the grammatical' with 'the empirical', for example. Thoughts such as 'We must presuppose massive agreement in order for there to be able to be disagreement at all' are not therefore truth-evaluable, are not quasi-empirical claims nor even transcendental truths. Just as it is absurd to imagine that philosophers or their kin can individuate communities by means of determining the facts of the matter as to what communities there really (irrespective of how people take themselves to be 'communed') are, so it is absurd to imagine that philosophers can enunciate true statements, 'assertions', 'theses', which (would) settle the debate of 'rationalism against relativism', or decide whether claims of incommensurability are true or not. It is *absurd*, as we suggested above in discussing Schatzki, to suppose that there is a substantive philosophical or anthropological *fact of the matter* about whether the Azande are 'really very different' from us or not. Or even about whether they are incomprehensible in 'our categories' or not. The would-be point is deflated by the recognition that questions like this can only be asked in the environment—context—of some standard which gives 'in what respect' we and they are to be compared. Otherwise, the answer will always be: they are and they aren't.

One clear and helpful way of putting this point is perhaps as follows: 'incommensurability' is itself *not measurable.* One can't measure 'loads of agreement', 'very different', 'necessarily partial understanding', and so on. For it

---

46 On which, see Read and Guetti (1999), 'Meaningful Consequences', a paper which sets out concretely how 'form of life' is … not something stateable. To avoid particularly crude relativistic misreading of Wittgenstein here, it is crucial to bear in mind that the agreement in question is of course 'agreement' *not in opinions but in form of life.* (Agreement as Davidson and Hollis have it, by contrast, seems to be pretty much agreement in opinions.)

raises the obvious question as to, do they agree with us: about what exactly? Thus if one stands by or contradicts the *thesis* of incommensurability one sounds as if one is ruling something in and something else out; but when the 'thesis' is unpacked there are no clear determinations of what is being ruled in or excluded. The only theses there can actually *be* are sheer banalities and tautologies, such as perhaps: "When two scientific disciplinary matrices seem very different to one another, *beware* of conflating them and assuming that one can be actually expressed in terms of the other." This Kuhn-inspired propadeutical remark is pretty much tautologous. It is helpfully phrased explicitly as a warning rather than as an assertion. It should *not* be seen as a substantive doctrine.

The whole debate of "rationality *vs.* relativism", the whole debate of those who imagine themselves to be arguing for or against Kuhn and/or Winch, fails to gain purchase, simply fails to get off the ground. There is nothing to be said on the 'question' supposedly at issue, the question in Kuhn's case of whether as a matter of fact (say) pre-Einstienian physics is incommensurable with post-Einsteinian physics. Kuhn's deep message is not "The truth is that there have been scientific revolutions which render scientists unable to understand each other, and us unable to understand old science/scientists". His message is not well-put as the truth of a pluralised Kantianism, as Hoyningen-Huene (1993) has claimed it is, nor really as any kind of relativism. His message, rather, is something like, "If you're really interested in the nature of the sciences, if you want (as any serious student of science should) to understand what the sciences are and how they work, then try looking at science differently from how Whig historians of science and formalistic philosophers of science have taught you to. Try taking seriously the differences between old and new science (rather than seeing the old through the lens of the new). Use my 'new concepts', such as 'revolution' and 'paradigm', if they help you (*Sometimes* I, Kuhn, find them helpful, but I wrote a whole book on the transition to quantum physics without using the *words* that I initially used to pick out those concepts). But, be ready to abandon them instantly if they stand in the way of a sound grasp of the actual concretion of scientific practice in its historicity and in its contexts". His message is philosophical, in an important sense;[47] but we think it is not helpfully-described as epistemological or metaphysical. Those words carry much too much baggage. (If we re-read Winch's *ISS* in light of his later thought, we think that we can see that Winch himself would have been less likely to have employed those words, in his own voice—though they were not even then intended to be understood in the more usual ways they are used in philosophy.)

Likewise, there is simply nothing finally definitive or fact-like to be said about whether Azande thought is incommensurable with ours. Winch's deepest message is something like, "If you're really interested in the nature of lay and professional social inquiry, then try looking at culture(s) differently from how scientistic 'social scientists' and rationalistic philosophers have encouraged you to. Try taking seriously the differences between us and them (rather than using the readiest-to-hand aspect of our own culture as a lens through which to view them). Use Wittgenstein's terms to do so, *if* those help free up your mental cramps".

---

47   For detail on all this, see Sharrock and Read (2002).

Winch was (and became increasingly) well-aware of the risk that he would be *read* as saying something more substantive and theoretical than this, as was Wittgenstein. But he *had* no theory of how society is, of how humans are, nor even of how sociologists ought to conduct themselves.[48] He investigated the concept of 'society', the concept of 'social science', and the concept of 'philosophy', and found that certain oft-made methodological and philosophical 'mistakes' were less likely if one attended to the results of such investigations, which were, after all, intended to put us back in touch with things which in our everyday practice we all of us already understand perfectly well. *He had no theory.*

One way of seeing the logic of our argument is as follows: try taking seriously the idea that there is a debate, a debate heavily constrained by and even settle-able by the invocation of facts, a debate which philosophy can hope then to have settled and to pronounce assertorically and definitively upon, a debate concerning (say) how different the Zande are from us. If there is such a debate, then let us hear the 'evidence' from the sides to it. Well, for example, we have Davidson opposing 'conceptual scheme relativism', a 'relativism' often associated (largely wrongly, we are suggesting) with Winch and Kuhn. One of Davidson's key claims is that there must be massive agreement in order for there to be disagreement. That we must presuppose that anyone we are 'interpreting' shares a vast number of beliefs with us; otherwise, we cannot go so far as to treat them as a person or their language as a language.

But has it ever been explained what this presupposition—if heard as quasi-factual, rather than 'merely' as a situation-relative grammatical reminder—amounts to?

We can make perfectly good sense of the project of enumerating (say) the number of tigers still alive in the wild in India; or even of the project of enumerating the hairs on one's head; or even conceivably, given certain 'border' constraints, the number of grains of sand on a given beach.

Matters become rather less clear when it comes to enumerating the number of dialects spoken in a country. Criteria for individuation of dialects are rather less clear, more purpose-relative, exposed to philosophical debate, beset by the special features of any of the objects of the 'human sciences'. And this is not the same as holding that the criteria are difficult to agree upon, in a similar way in which the criteria for counting how many lakes there are in Finland are so difficult. In the case of Finnish lakes the problem is agreeing in advance what counts as where a lake ends: how narrow and how long the channel must be between it and the next lake for us to be able to say there are two lakes linked by a channel, rather than saying there is one lake which narrows significantly in the middle. The point about dialects is not so much that we find it difficult to agree prior to counting but that what counts as a dialect is purpose-relative and dynamic. This has parallels with Wittgenstein's self-posed question in the early remarks on the 'builders', in *Philosophical Investigations.* Here Wittgenstein explores the question as to whether the primitive language-game of the 'builders' could be—might count for us as—the *whole* language of the two 'builders'. In some contexts the answer would be "No": The builders are merely employing words as signals, they are doing no more than "giving voice". In other contexts,

---

48 For support, see Sharrock and Anderson (1985) "Understanding Peter Winch".

for other purposes, we might be inclined to answer "Yes": the builders are clearly employing words (iterable signs, in Derrida's terminology) to communicate. They are manifesting the human "power of speech". The point of which Wittgenstein's imaginary scenario avails us, read-aright, is that what we count as a language is dependent upon the purpose of our counting. Similarly, enumerating the number of people one has truly loved is a project perhaps as intrinsically important as it is fuzzy and desperately difficult (and potentially life-changing), if taken seriously.

When it comes to enumerating the number of beliefs one has, or the number of beliefs two people share, do we really have any idea how to *begin* the process? Is there really a 'process' here which we can begin at all? Can Davidson's notion of 'massive agreement' be 'operationalised', *at all?*

More specifically:

- How are we to count beliefs whose referents are identified differently by the believer than by ourselves?
- How are we to count beliefs in the puzzle-cases of belief which philosophers are so fond of?
- And, crucially, all the different forms/cases of belief investigated for example by Wittgensteinian etc., philosophers, by philosophers of religion, indeed by philosophers of anthropology (e.g. 'belief-that' *vs.* 'belief-in'; 'belief' as *trust*; belief-in-practice as discussed by Winch, Pleasants, etc.)?
- What about meta-beliefs?
- Concatenations of beliefs?
- 'Unconscious beliefs'?
- What about degrees of belief, and gradations of belief (e.g. 'I believe x with about 75 per cent probability')?
- Do we only count propositional beliefs (as opposed to, say, my belief that my keys were in my pocket, that though I didn't manifestly hold the belief, my surprise at finding my keys not to be there on arriving at my office implies I was 'holding' such a belief)?

And so on—the list could easily be extended.[49]

We suggest that one can have no clear—in the abstract—notion of what it is to enumerate one's beliefs, and that the idea of such, which appeared to be a way of introducing order to the interminable debates around relativism (and 'refuting' relativism), debates in which Winch and Kuhn supposedly figure on the side of the relativists, gains no purpose. One could of course invent some way of enumerating our beliefs—religious authorities have occasionally attempted to do so in restricted contexts for purposes of establishing whether one is a heretic or not—but how could something which one thus *invented* solve a philosophical problem?!

The only tenable thing to say is as follows. It may sometimes, for certain 'practical' philosophical purposes, be useful to say:

---

49 Compare here J.F.M. Hunter's (1973) work on belief as not a 'phenomenon'.

i. 'We must share lots of things—e.g. beliefs—in common with others in order to be even treating them as human beings, as susceptible of understanding, at all'.

And it may sometimes be useful, for the same kind of purposes, but in *different* local circumstances, where the discourse in one's area has taken a *different* kind of illusionary turning, to say:

ii. 'People can have different world-views/paradigms, which make them partially impenetrable to one another.[50] One has to be ready to see others as deeply different from oneself'.[51]

But neither 'saying' should be heard as an empirical assertion or anything like one.

Winch and Kuhn had cause to say the latter kind of thing (ii) more often than the former (i), *because they were largely combatting inherited traditions of 'Whiggism', 'rationalism', and 'Realism'.* They look to some as if they were 'relativists', because of their concern, owing to the cultural situation they were placed in—to the dominant cultural trends of their time and context (in later times, they would have been (and in fact were!) more concerned to combat 'postmodern' relativism)—, to combat certain particular kinds of confusions more than others. Their looking a bit like relativists is not a matter of their beliefs or 'doctrines'; it is a function of the *audience* that they were most concerned, therapeutically, to aid and exorcise. If they were truly irrationalists, they wouldn't have been bothered by helping out such an audience. Indeed, if anything, the concern of Kuhn and Winch to combat excess tendencies toward 'Realism' or 'rationalism' *is a mark of the degree to which they were themselves temperamentally and intellectually close to just those traditions!* This is obvious to anyone who has cared to understand Kuhn, who himself cared intensely about science and its image and its difference from non-science disciplines, though not about astrology or post-modernism or 'dream catchers'. In Winch's case too, something similar is true, when one looks closely: Winch wanted academic inquiries to be respectable and sound, not pseudo-scientific; he was concerned that 'social science' was giving the seeking of knowledge a bad name, and wanted apposite social study to occur (and for proper recognition of where it already occurs), instead. He wanted philosophy and its analytical rigour to reign in its full domain. He wanted thinking people to take seriously the quest for (and presupposition of) Reality in which all of us in different ways are engaged. He had no desire to promote irrational

---

50 See p. 199 of Winch 1997, '[T]here is *a kind of understanding* of [Zande] practice that we ... do not have. I will try to express this by saying that we cannot imagine what it would be like for us to behave as the Azande do and make the kind of sense of what we were doing as the Azande, we assume, do make of what they do; or perhaps: we cannot imagine taking the consultation of the oracle *seriously*, as the Azande do'. See, similarly, p. 223 of *PI*; and p. 32 of Lyas (1999).

51 Again, against the foolish claim that Winch thought of communities (nonsensically) as apodictically identifiable and hermetically-sealed one from another, we should note Winch's fascinating late discussion of difficulties which can arise (in) understanding members of our *own* culture. See again his (1997) 'Can we Understand Ourselves'.

ways of living or to give any harbour to such ways of thinking. On the contrary; Winch wanted to place us in a position where we can properly criticise social practices that we do not believe in, and was irked by intellectual doctrines that prevent this from actually being able to happen.

Both thinkers, Kuhn and Winch, were, in this crucial regard, the truest of children of the Enlightenment.

So: we should not thus fall into the trap of thinking that Kuhn and Winch *believed* (ii), and disbelieved (i), simply and assertorically, permanently. No; not at all. They did not wish to hold, to argue for, the theses often attributed to them by Davidsonians and others; they only wished to remind us all of how we might best avoid saying nonsensical things about the history of science, about the understanding of persons and cultures, etc. They had, they have, no views, they make no assertions. Winch is no more a pluralist (as Lerner wishes he was, and Patrick Phillips thinks he might actually be) than a monist (as Lerner thinks he is). He just isn't in that kind of game.

To be fair to Schatzki, his line of thought is subtler than that of (e.g.) Hollis, in that Schatzki not only emphasises that commonality is needed in beliefs, but also in emotions, needs, physical environment, primitive reactions, interests, and so on (see p. 316 of his essay). There needs to be, says Schatzki, 'agreement' in much of the whole warp and weft of form of life (and compare *Investigations*, section 206). And there is of course something right about this. But the same argument that we ran above could be applied to each of these in turn: there can be no such thing as quantifying the degree of commonality; there is no *fact* of the matter as to how much commonality is required; and the claims about the need for a 'shared form of life' do *not* in the end amount to assertions. They are not claims that could be contradicted, or theses that are controversial. They are—they can only be—efforts to return us all to our actual life with language, no longer deluded by nonsenses that masquerade as science-like claims.

Why Then, Given the Above, are Kuhn and Winch so Misunderstood?

We have already indicated that the answer to this question is multiple. But it must be said that it is only certain incautious remarks that Kuhn made that gave his interpreters *any genuine* reason for foisting this issue onto him. Winch was if anything slightly *more* careful and circumspect than Kuhn, and certainly more cautiously faithful to Wittgenstein in his approach; but as mentioned above, certain incautious remarks in the first edition of *The Idea of a Social Science* did unfortunately offer hostages to fortune, but, even so, only if one considered those expressions in isolation and overlooked the places where Winch did distance himself from or offer a different understanding than those that his critics seized on—Winch, as we have remarked throughout, suffers from *partial* reading probably as much as anyone does. (We give a slightly fuller account toward the end of this chapter as to why Winch has been as badly misunderstood as he has.)

Against Interpretation

To recap: If we are to risk generalizing at all, we shall say that the production of descriptions or presentations of human action/behaviour which are not interpretations, let alone explanations, is the only way to avoid grossly failing to 'capture' that behaviour, given that such rule-following etc. behaviour is utterly unlike what we call the 'behaviour' of inanimate objects, is active, deed-like—though, again, largely in a non-interpretative fashion. Most human behaviour does not involve interpretation, so its understanding *need* not normally be interpretive either. *Contra* the claims of Charles Taylor and other critics of Winch, even self-understanding or self-description need not be self-interpretation (or theory-laden, or necessarily draw upon tacit knowledge). It is an interpretivistic (or post-modernist) dogma, a piece of 'theoryism', to claim that linguistic articulation of wordless self-understandings is necessarily interpretive. (When we ask someone what they are doing, sometimes they simply tell us. Or: sometimes we can simply see, without needing to be told. That such seeing is defeasible does not force upon one the inference that it never happens; that something is *logically* open to being otherwise does not translate—social constructionists to the contrary—into 'therefore it might actually be otherwise'; i.e. being defeasible is a *logical* possibility, not a matter of being actually, in practice, open to refutation, let alone refuted!) "Self-understanding" etc. is, again, vital to understanding humans as human animals rather than as material objects or even as (the vast majority of non-human) animals—but it is not (necessarily) interpretation. One needs to think, not of someone viewing themselves from the standpoint of another and speculating on why they themselves have done something (a very unusual case), but rather of someone having the capability to alter what they are doing in response to social circumstances, say in response to a failure to make themselves understood, or in response to a surprising change in the physical environment (usual cases).[52] *Then* perhaps one will have the chance to see clearly how human action is, and what "self-understanding" (when understood in a properly non-intellectualist sense) amounts to.

Of course, the *terms* used in all this are not *in themselves* crucial (i.e. so long as one understands "explain" or "interpret" in a sound non-scientist fashion, etc. then one can happily use terms like "explaining/interpreting human action"—as Winch on occasion does. And somewhat similarly: if the word "description" seems somewhat forced, as we are employing it, then we will happily shift to another word that seems to you more felicitous, such as perhaps "presentation" or a "seeing"). We are not word-fetishists or language-policemen.

But distinctions at least along the lines that we have made are we think usefully correlated with the words (describing, understanding, explaining; acting-on-a-rule, interpreting a rule) discussed in (I) and (II), towards the start of the chapter—in common and intuitively useful senses (uses) of those words. Thus we take it that it is useful to say that Winch (1970 [1962]) hopes in his paper, "Understanding a

---

52 We need to think, that is, in the kind of ways suggested by Ethnomethodology, as explicated for instance by Mike Lynch (1993), pp. 14-17. Lynch and Winch are much happier in this regard than (say) Taylor, Weber, or Jaspers.

Primitive Society"—his critique of the great anthropologist, Evans-Pritchard—to be pointing the way toward a description or presentation of Azande practices which will not impose upon them.[53] And imposition will, he thinks, result from (and amount to) interpreting them or (worse) explaining them. Instead, Winch invites us to *look at* the language-game the Azande are actually playing: to see it, or grasp it:

> It might … appear as though we had clear grounds for speaking of the superior rationality of European over Zande thought, in so far as the latter involves a contradiction [over criteria for the attribution of "witch-hood"] which it makes no attempt to remove and does not even recognize: one, however, which is recognizable as such in the context of European ways of thinking. But does Zande thought on this matter really involve a contradiction? It appears from Evans-Pritchard's account that the Azande do not press their ways of thinking about witches to a point at which they would be involved in contradictions. Someone may now want to say that the irrationality of the Azande in relation to witchcraft shows itself in the fact that they do not press their thought about it "to its logical conclusion". To appraise this point we must consider whether the conclusion we are trying to force on them is indeed a logical one; or perhaps better, whether someone who does press this conclusion is being more rational than the Azande, who do not. Some light is thrown on this question by Wittgenstein's discussion of a game … (Winch 1970, p. 92).

Winch goes on to suggest that the Azande are 'playing a *different* game':

> It is noteworthy … that the Azande, when the possibility of this contradiction about the inheritance of witchcraft is pointed out to them, do *not* come to regard their old beliefs in witchcraft as obsolete. [According to Evans-Pritchard himself:] "They have no theoretical interest in the subject". This suggests strongly that the context from which the suggestion about the contradiction is made, the context of our scientific culture, is not on the same level as the context in which the beliefs about witchcraft operate. **Zande notions of witchcraft do not constitute a theoretical system in terms of which Azande try to gain a quasi-scientific understanding of the world.** This in turn suggests that it is the European, obsessed with pressing Zande thought where it would not go—to a contradiction—who is guilty of misunderstanding, not the Zande (ibid., p. 93, emboldened emphasis ours).

Winch's primary concern is, then, to avoid *mis*understanding[54] a radically different society (or misunderstanding religion; or art; etc.). He is not asserting, "Here is the truth on what these 'aliens' are", nor "Here is how to enter into the positive 'empathic'

---

53 Once more: one should take care not to suppose that Winch is trying to give us a superior piece of human scientific research as such—he is not setting himself up in competition with Evans-Pritchard and Co., but is rather only saying what must be going on in any 'human science'.

54 Putting the emphasis on '*(not) misunderstanding*' rather than on any alleged quasi-Collingwoodian empathy or imagination, or on some quasi-anthropological methodology that Winch is taken to recommend under the heading of '*Understanding*', could be couched in Austinian terms of shifting our view of which word around here is the 'trouser-word'. Perhaps more important is to note that this is one of the points where Winch is frequently misread; for example, by Schatzki, who suggests (on p. 319 of his op cit.) that Winch aims at a positive state of understanding, whereas for the most part all Winch aims at is the removal of mental cramps etc., which force us into ethnocentric etc. misunderstandings.

state of understanding them"; and what he is asserting is merely (thinking back now to our much earlier discussion of 'understanding') that one doesn't misunderstand some people but, *in the ordinary sense of the word*, understands them. If one doesn't misunderstand them, one does—in this straightforward sense rather than in some fantasised theoreticist sense—understand them. (Understanding and not misunderstanding, once we have become clear that 'understanding' is not something special or mystical, are of course 'internally related'.)

So, to a reader who might ask, why can't Winch, and we, say: So Winch does understand the Azande better than Evans-Pritchard does; Why is a concern to get understanding right not as legitimate as avoiding misunderstanding; indeed how is it different? And we can now see that one can say these things, provided that one does so with care and subtlety … This is very important, and helps make perspicuous another aspect of Winch's practice signally neglected by most of his 'friends' and 'foes'. Winch, to say it again, is trying to put us in a better position to avoid setting up a spurious problem—that's all. A bit like with Kuhn's recasting of scientific progress in terms of progress only *away* from past insoluble puzzles ('anomalies'), there is no teleological vision in Winch; and he is not setting up a rival methodology to that employed by field anthropologists either, not least because his whole understanding of the Azande comes from Evans-Pritchard's own book—it is not Evans-Pritchard, the ethnographer, who is being challenged, but Evans-Pritchard the reflective interpreter, and he is being challenged on the grounds that his interpretations don't fit with *his own* ethnographic report.

Here we arguably have an outline example of someone—Winch—being able quite successfully to "follow along with"—to make something of—an 'alien' discourse without *imposing* on it or *interpreting* it in terms other than its own. But, again, not through any theory, nor through a superior/rival piece of quasi-empirical sociology.

For, mostly Winch just accepts that Evans-Pritchard understood the Azande perfectly well as a result of living with them—it is to be remembered that Evans-Pritchard's account is rejected on only one point, albeit a key one, where he tries to say what their practice amounts to by comparison with ours. Winch's critics are as one in their failure to understand this aspect of Winch's disagreement with Evans-Pritchard. It certainly isn't an attempt to establish that there are inherent obstacles to understanding another society (this impression probably follows more from an over-reaction to the (very reasonable) strictures in *Idea of a Social Science* on being able to write a history of art without sensitivity to colour, shape etc., and is illicitly projected onto "Understanding a Primitive Society"). Winch's whole discussion concedes that, to a large extent, Evans-Pritchard has succeeded in understanding the oracular practices, for Winch uses Evans-Pritchard's account of those practices against Evans-Pritchard. Again: The disagreement is really on one point, though it is a central and profound one, which is when Evans-Pritchard comes to make a *synoptic* statement about how 'we' differ from 'them' (one which pertains to the point of their practices rather than to the specifics of them—which of our practices are they most like?). If you like, we could put it like this: Evans-Pritchard wants an overall evaluation—can a rational person believe these things? One can see plainly enough from Evans-Pritchard's very detailed story that they have the oracle, that they have such and such rattles, that such and such moves comprise curing rituals and all the rest—we can see, too, that all these are different from what we do. But the question that Evans-Pritchard is bothered by, inherited from the anthropological tradition, is: but do they think differently than we do? To which his answer is: in all their everyday affairs they are as practical and empirically minded as we are. But when it comes to their magical practices … It would be wise perhaps to recognise that the problem with the Azande isn't the possibility that their practices are possibly nonsensical in a Wittgensteinian sense i.e. examples of 'language on holiday', but that they are at risk of being *dismissed* in a parochial spirit as purveyors of nonsense, things that no self-respecting person could possibly believe. (Whereas the onus on the true Wittgensteinian is not to dismiss, not to police, but: to try to make sense. To practice therapy, from a stance of non-superiority.) The Wittgensteinian-type problem arises within Evans-Pritchard's own thought and his attachment to a metaphysical picture of the relationship between language and reality, which stands between him and what he has already pretty much and pretty well understood, with the result that the apparent problem in understanding a primitive society is a pseudo-problem.

So, we contend that one of the attractions of the Azande case for Winch is that 'here is an excerpt from the social studies where there is a real problem of understanding'—the anthropological tradition is puzzled about what to say about alien magical practices; but then the question is: what kind of problem in understanding is it? The problem which perhaps puzzles 'us' more generally is: how can they believe that stuff? That is the question that Evans-Pritchard tries to answer: they, like us, are sensible at the level of practical empirical doings, so why don't they, like us, see that their way of doing things can't possibly work? Evans-Pritchard then tries to answer this question by arguments about the parts of their belief system that explain away the failures of their practice to deliver the goods and so on, and it is just here that Winch intervenes, to argue that the problem in understanding does not arise from the Azande's witchcraft being any less sensible than are their practical/empirical matters, or *prima facie* any less sensible or plausible than ours are—the obstacle is one that Evans-Pritchard puts in his own way, by making metaphysical assumptions about the relation between language and reality, and by giving science an ostensibly culturally-neutral role in adjudicating between them and us. Winch's response to this is to rearrange some of the facts in Evans-Pritchard's own account, and to adopt more perspicuous standards of comparison with 'our' practices (Evans-Pritchard treats them as most like misfiring versions of our scientific practices; Winch says they are not much like these, but maybe more akin to some of our more 'ritualistic' practices, such as prayer), and, if we do that, then our problem, which is why they don't see through their practices, will go away, for it is no more a problem than: why don't we see through ours? The *obvious* implausibility of their ways are an artefact not of the obvious truth of our science but of the fact that its familiarity to us endows it with that obviousness (which *doesn't* obviate, of course, the difficulties that arise for those who are spiritually 'tone-deaf', so to speak).

None of what we say here entails, either, an incapacity to make judgements on other cultures. i.e. It doesn't require a "nice-bloke" supposition that everybody is basically a nice bloke like me—Winch is careful to position his own arguments on his evaluation that *Azande* culture is basically an affable one, so there is nothing really 'dark' about their witchcraft; but this is true (*if* it is true—animal-rights advocates might of course differ (pity the chickens); and compare here again Pleasants's intelligent *political* critique of Zande culture and witchcraft) of *Azande* culture, not of *all* 'alien' cultures. We are not bound to any moral relativism and can—and should—condemn another culture if it is 'dark', for it is perfectly natural, perfectly human, for us to combat someone else's world view, to damn them as heretics, fools etc. ... but we should be clear that when we do this, we are not doing so because we have rationally proven them to be mistaken in their ways or in their beliefs, but rather we have *rejected*—are viscerally opposed to—their way of doing things. Read this way, Winch remains close to Wittgenstein's remarks on the conflicts between religious believers, or between believers and non-believers—after all, having read and absorbed Winch we—the authors of this book—still can't possibly do what the Azande do,[55] their practice has no place in our lives (nor should we imagine their lives incomplete because there is no room for science in it). Perhaps we might state the point as: there are no guarantees in the business of understanding, and there are no guarantees that one can e.g. overcome one's repugnance toward or the fact that one is fundamentally out of tune with what others are doing.

Paraphrasing a Wittgensteinian 'slogan', then, one might try simplifying our line here as follows: Don't look for the interpretation, look for an adequate description. A description that will not evince/evoke failures to meet those one is encountering *as they are.*

Again, we must stress that our remarks above too are 'grammatical reminders' (see *PI*, section 127). They are not transcendental claims, nor gestures at ineffable truths, nor general contributions to a theory of society, nor any such. Winch, like Wittgenstein, gives us reminders, 'only'. He tries to judge the mythological errors we are likely to fall into, in part by looking at errors (e.g. Evans-Pritchard's, or similarly Frazer's, Pareto's, or Levy-Bruhl's) that actually have been influentially fallen into. (Take for instance the following disastrous confusion of perspectives within one sentence, to be found on p. 43 of the abridged (Oxford: Clarendon, 1976) edition of Evans-Pritchard's classic text; "We must remember that since witchcraft has no real existence a man does not know that he has bewitched another, even if he is aware that he bears him ill will".)

And it is perhaps important to reiterate that our reading of Winch resists assimilating his 'view' to that of most '*Verstehen*' theorists of the social sciences, and to Weber. Our view, based upon the letter of the kind of quotations from Winch given above, is that Winch's thought is falsified if one fails to recognize the difference he finds between descriptions on the one hand and interpretations/explanations on the other. Winch had a lot of time and sympathy for the Idealist tradition, for the work of Dilthey and Collingwood for example. He felt that they essentially grasped certain important philosophical points which eluded their Positivist foes, then and now. Likewise, Winch can be drawn close at various points to certain schools of

---

55 Though we may, as discussed earlier, be changed by genuine open-hearted exposure to the 'alien': for instance, one may feel able to be more attuned to a sense of sacredness of the Earth. Though not, presumably, a sense of the sacredness of only very specific bits of the Earth, as is the case for a number of indigenous peoples' 'belief'-systems.

conventional sociology, such as the *Verstehenlich* moments in Weber, and some classical Social Interactionism. But we want to insist again that in the main Winch resolutely refused to take up any position whatsoever *within* social theory. He is not advocating any positive picture of the human being, or of (the) human society[56]— though he sometimes recommends certain pictures for certain prophylactic purposes. He is not, for example, asserting the truth of a picture of human beings as 'rule-following animals'—it is not Winch's 'finding', or even 'conclusion', that people (sometimes, often though not always) follow rules, and always (in an empty, non-factive sense) can be said to be within the realm of the normative—*it is a complete banality*. Winch rather follows Wittgenstein in pointing out how easy it is to be confused in attempting to understand other human beings who are perhaps strange to us if instead of taking account of their practices as already having/making an order, we rather interpret them merely 'positivistically', as merely acting in accord with rules; or if we fail to understand how different (say) their understanding of the effects of an alleged contradiction within their practices is to what we might have expected. Thus we think it unwise and unhelpful to try to read Winch as (say) a philosophical social interactionist, with a particular theory of what human interaction is and of how important it is. If we are to associate Winch with any sociological 'school', it would have then to be, as already suggested, with the non-scientistic, Wittgenstein-influenced, resolutely local practices of 'ethnomethodology'. If Winch has an ally in sociology, it can we think only be Harold Garfinkel and his followers, who do not advocate a substantive theory of society. We might then think of ethnomethodological practice, in the work of Harold Garfinkel, Eric Livingston, Harvey Sacks, Jeff Coulter, Michael Lynch, Rod Watson and more besides, as being a fine-grained ethnographically-oriented non-fictional version of what Winch and Wittgenstein are up to with their examples, prophylactics and reminders.[57]

If Winch were aiming to describe a positive doctrine of understanding, then he would be an Idealist or a *Verstehen*-theorist. For all his affinities with these, he is neither. If it be responded, 'Well then, if he is not aiming to describe a positive doctrine of understanding, then why is the crucial section of ISS entitled "Understanding Social Institutions", and why is his great essay entitled "Understanding a Primitive Society?", then, to reiterate and sum up our arguments above, the answer is threefold:

1. The "understanding" in Winch's titles is better heard as denoting the ordinary *activities* of trying to understand and of understanding others, not as denoting a *state of understanding*. He is interested in reminding us of the ways in which we ordinarily come to understanding of others, interested, that is to say, in the '*grammar*' of understanding.

---

56 He is not for example directly following Collingwood's over-intellectualist vision of human society and history—see his careful words on p. 131 of *ISS* (and again at the close of the Preface).

57 See, for instance, Sharrock and Watson (1988), 'Autonomy Among Social Theories', which makes clear just how different the task of ethmethodology and, by—qualified (see chapter 3)—extension, Winch is from that of mainstream sociology or social theory.

2. Furthermore, Winch is writing *about* this activity (he emphasises that his inquiries are reflective), and not, except in the most schematic and illustrative of ways, actually *undertaking* it. He isn't to more than a very limited degree engaging in the activity *himself*; he is not an anthropologist, or a practicising ethnographer (he adds nothing in the way of empirical information to Evans-Pritchard's study, nor could he possibly have done so, given his not having done any field-work, etc.). This should be obvious.

3. Finally, the activity he is talking about is one that we think least likely to mislead, to encourage a wrong assimilation with philosophical approaches or with methodologies that were not his, if we put his endeavour in negative terms. He was chiefly concerned to prevent the creation of unnecessary misunderstandings, for the sake of better pursuit of the activity intimated in (1) and (2), above. ... He wants those engaging in the activity of would-be social science to appreciate better the extent to which their fieldwork needs to be informed by attention to our language, to meaning, rather than assuming the methods of the empirical natural sciences. This should be clear, in the case in which Winch goes into most detail: that of Evans-Pritchard. Winch offers tools for avoiding misunderstanding what Evans-Pritchard has actually given us, by way of an insight into the Azande; and these in turn yield conceptual tools which may be to other anthropologists' benefit. In short: while *ISS's* point could be signalled more clearly by shifting to a title such as "The Very Idea of a Social Science", "Understanding a Primitive Society" could be perspicuously retitled as "Avoiding Misunderstandings of Primitive Societies", or, better still perhaps, "On Primitive Misunderstandings of 'Primitive' Societies".

And so now we are justified in venturing that a key 'mistake' which Schatzki makes—and Patrick Phillips and Lerner after him—is to treat Winch as a social theorist, who put us in the alleged position of possessing an understanding either of particular societies or of society in general. Thus Schatzki in fact covertly treats Wittgenstein as a social theorist too, though not to the extent that someone like David Bloor attempts to do.[58] When we see clearly how the Winch/Wittgenstein approach eviscerates generalistic abstract questions such as for instance 'How great do the commonalities between persons need to be for understanding between them to be possible?' of content, we see, among other things, how futile the debates over Winch have tended to be.

To illustrate our meaning here, it is worth adding that salient and we think sensible support for distinguishing for prophylactic etc. purposes, as we have done above, after Winch, not just between description and explanation, but between description (and understanding) on the one hand and interpretation on the other, can be found in the Jeff Coulter's paper, "Is Contextualizing Necessarily Interpretive?":

---

58 The title of his (1983) book *Wittgenstein: A Social Theory of Knowledge* already says it all, really, in terms of making perspicuous the depth of Bloor's strong and wilful misreading of Wittgenstein.

It is undoubtedly true that some readings of texts ... are best construed as "interpretive", as (involving) the making of "interpretations", but this is not true for each and every facet of a reading of—or of reading-and-understanding—a text [for example] a psychiatric clinic record (1994, p. 692).[59]

And: if the reader continues to require further detail concerning how it is that it is 'possible' for there to be plain (self- etc.) description (or 'presentation'), and how interpretation is not ubiquitous, then the place to go is to the ethnomethodologists' concept of the "accounting" and "accountability" of human practices/actions. Winch is much closer to ethnomethodology than to 'symbolic interactionism', 'Verstehen'-theory or philosophical Idealism, in this regard.

In sum, rather than as usual assimilating interpretation to the description side of Wittgenstein's famous opposition between description and [theoretical] explanation,[60] thus risking concealing the important disanalogies between description and interpretation, *we might usefully try out assimilating it rather to the explanation side instead, and notice the similarities there.* This is, we think, the main moral of thinking through oppositions (I) and (II), with which we began the chapter, above. (Again, the terms themselves are not vital—and all these concepts are of course 'family-resemblance concepts', there being for example many 'kinds' of description[61]—but the *points* we are trying to make here, both therapeutic and prophylactic, are we think sound.)

If this is right, then the best one can do, one might say, is present (rather, one might say, than *re*-present) the thought and language of an 'alien'.[62] But, if it 'hangs together', in the way Winch suggested Azande thought in the final analysis does; if it can be made sense of without being imposed upon; if its character is such that one can come to describe it accurately, in important part through understanding it (at least initially) as they understand it: then one need not thereby falsify it—and then one really can present it. (And need not necessarily interpret it.) *And, in such cases, then this 'best' is quite clearly: wholly* good enough.

---

59 See also p. 442 of his (1996): '[One] ought to distinguish between "reading" a text and "having (or arriving at, etc.) a reading of a text", between ordinary cases of "understanding" what a text says or what it means and cases in which "interpreting" may be involved'.

60 See Wittgenstein's *PI*, section 109, and section 654.

61 See for instance *PI*, section 291; also *PI*, section 24 and p. 200.

62 Of course, in a trivial sense even this must be a recontextualisation—but the point is, it needn't be anything like a translation or an interpretation. 'Translation'—Quine's term; 'Interpretation'—Davidson's. Both risk leaving quite out of account the aspects of language, which James Guetti (1993) calls 'grammatical effects', which make all the difference between simply extracting one's own version of what someone is saying on the one hand, and doing what can justly be called 'understanding what they are saying' on the other (or at least understanding what one *can* of it and 'witnessing/letting be' the rest). Our point is that genuinely understanding even what one can of something strange, and letting its nuances and style and otherness be, is not well-subsumed under the heading even of 'interpretation' (let alone of 'translation').

A Provisional Conclusion

To reiterate: like Winch, like any good Wittgensteinian (or indeed any good 'human scientist'), we do not confront the task of 'understanding other people' as any kind of general project, and find that any difficulties that we meet in our studies do not arise from the impossibility of transcending conceptual disjunctions but from the substantive nature of the situations, practices, cultures etc., we are dealing with, as e.g. the difficulties of learning enough mathematics to follow advanced mathematical work or of not letting one's religious indifference get in the way, or of overcoming one's lack of facility with other languages etc. Like Winch, and many others, we are convinced that it is often the case that insufficient effort is taken by philosophers and psychiatrists and historians of science (and so on) to understand the strange.[63]

As we pointed out above, Winch's arguments being reflectively *a priori* cannot dictate empirical facts and certainly cannot determine that, as a matter of fact, the activities of human being must be found to be—*must* be—coherent and intelligible: whether or not difficulties in understanding can be overcome is to be found out in the attempt, and the determination as to whether the difficulty lies with 'us' or with 'them' likewise to be made in the same way.

So, we have argued that Winch's philosophical suggestions, his hints and reminders, are extremely effective. We see no grounds whatsoever for thinking that Winch's commitments involve any relativism. No more, though, do they involve any of the other 'isms' that have been reactively bandied about by Winch's 'commentators'.

We have here sketched a reading of Peter Winch's mature philosophy of the social sciences, according to which Winch is perhaps-surprisingly congenial to Wittgenstein (on a resolutely therapeutic reading of the latter), and to much ethnomethodology (on a Wittgensteinian reading of the latter, following 'the Manchester school' of ethnomethodology, particularly).

Those who would read ethnomethodology as advancing lots of positive theses about society and about structure/action, as having for instance a particular, controversial stance on the spectrum laid out in the standard "structure vs. agency" debate, will likely be unsympathetic. As will those who would read the later Wittgenstein "irresolutely"[64]—as having substantial things to say about the form of (bits of) language, etc. But any such readers need we think to reckon with the

---

63 But sometimes, after much trying, one ends up judging that it's not possible to do that; in which case one ends up instead noting the patterns in a discourse but concluding that nevertheless there is an *irrevocable* incoherence in that discourse. (For such a case, see Read 2003.) We here presuppose a roughly Cavellian rather than Rortian reading of Wittgenstein. That is, a non-absolute distinction for certain 'practical' purposes between speaking 'inside' and 'outside' language-games. For detail, see the papers by Crary, Cavell, and Conant in Crary and Read (eds), *The New Wittgenstein* (op cit.); and on the distinction's non-absoluteness, see Scheman's paper in Sluga and Stern (eds) (1996).

64 The term is due to Warren Goldfarb, who takes the Diamond/Conant reading of Wittgenstein, with which Winch was thoroughly if guardedly impressed (see his 'Persuasion' (op cit.) for detail) to involve in particular a 'resolute' understanding of the *Tractatus's* austere hard-line on the tendency toward nonsensicality of *all* philosophy. For discussion of

exegetical and 'substantive' argument that we have been making. An argument which attributes to Wittgenstein no theses or theories, and which suggests that followers of Wittgenstein such as Winch have been cruelly used by those who have taken them to have implicit social theories, philosophical anthropologies of the human, etc. There is no substance to the 'idea' that human beings are all essentially the same; nor to the 'idea' that they are fundamentally different, 'community by community'. Winch would not suggest that communities are as a matter of fact 'cognitively closed' to one another, the frequent attribution of such a view to him therefore is somewhat disappointing. (Nor of course would Winch suggest that as a happy happenstance of metaphysical fact there is enough commonality between communities for communication to be possible, etc.). We turn in the next chapter to specific examination of what is probably the most widespread misunderstanding of all of Winch: the claim, already implicitly-undermined above, but seemingly almost endlessly-tempting to Winch's readers, that he was a "linguistic idealist".

---

irresolutism in readings of Wittgenstein's later work, see Hutchinson (2007) 'What's the Point of Elucidation?'.

Chapter 2

Winch and Linguistic Idealism

Winch's Idealism…?

Was Peter Winch an idealist, specifically a linguistic idealist? Did he, following the Ludwig Wittgenstein of legend,[1] believe that ideas, expressed in language, determined the nature of reality? Many certainly paint such a picture of Winch (as many have of Wittgenstein). Is this picture of Winch fiction or reality? It is, we shall argue, the former. 'Winch-the-linguistic-idealist' exists only in the minds and writings of his detractors (and those would-be friends he would reject). The Winch that one finds constituted by his writings on social studies is not, we submit, committed to Idealism.

Winch, Wittgenstein and Philosophy as Therapy

Winch makes remarks which seem like hostages to such misfortune, proposing that 'concepts' are or ought to be the central focus of attention, saying that social relations are like the exchange of ideas in a conversation, and—perhaps even more suspect— that reality shows itself in the sense that language has. Treating these points as free standing, it would be possible to (critically) construe them as committing Winch to the view that studying our ideas about reality (concepts) is all that is needed to understand reality itself, that social relations are made up of people's ideas, and that what is real depends upon the language. The remarks we have identified are ones which hold an important position in *ISS*, and, if indeed central to Winch's thought, then at least strongly suggestive that linguistic idealism *is* the right name for his doctrines.

Such a construal depends upon focusing upon remarks considered in isolation, both from the text to which they belong, and the philosophy from which they come. It is a fundamental of Wittgenstein's thought (see Chapter 1, for Winch as a resolutely Wittgensteinian thinker) that philosophy does not consist in doctrines, which is why his own philosophy is more properly identified with a method—a method(s) of reflecting on, clarifying, and alleviating confusions—than it is with any substantive theses. Wittgenstein always took the view that philosophy did not consist in *any* doctrines.[2] It is rather an *activity* (that of achieving clarity in cases where the lack of it—particularly with respect to the workings of language—created troublesome

---

1   A legend which owes much—though not all—to the writing of Bernard Williams (1974). For detailed critical engagements with Williams's writing on Wittgenstein see Sharrock and Read (2002), pp. 158-161 and Dilman (2002), chapter 4.

2   His early 'doctrinal' interpreters notwithstanding; see Hutchinson (2007).

and persistent confusion). As Wittgenstein advised, if he seemed to be stating any controversial theses, saying anything factual that could be disputed, then that should be taken as a sign that—somewhere—he had gone wrong. Note, this does not mean that one could never say anything factual in philosophy, only that the things we could say *as a philosopher* would not and could not be factually informative, could not state empirical news, but could only state facts of the most 'trivial' kind: i.e. over which there is no dispute (e.g.; 'red' is a colour word in English). Wittgenstein's insistence that his own philosophy has—in the way of proprietorial, informative theses—nothing to say is no personal idiosyncrasy, but, an overt reflection of the general but obscured condition of philosophy. It is not only Wittgenstein but other philosophers too who, in the relevant sense, have nothing to say. Other philosophers' works may look as if they feature doctrines, but these are not—given the nature of philosophical practice, they could not possibly be—genuine doctrines. They mislead because of superficial exterior resemblances to the form of genuine doctrines. In reality, they are likely expressions of confusion, confusions which either lead to a combination of words for which we have not efficaciously designated a clear sense being mistaken for an intelligible proposition or to the wrongful identification of the form of some expression (where a linguistic stipulation is advocated as if it were a factual description). For Wittgenstein, the nature of a philosophical problem is: I can't find my way about.[3]

To expand on this a little: That philosophy has 'nothing to say' means that philosophy has *nothing factually informative* to say, that it is not in the business of telling—it has nothing to tell people that they do not already know. It cannot be informative, evidence bearing, because philosophers do not engage in information gathering activities. Philosophers have no methods for finding things out, they do not undertake investigative researches that would accumulate new information, and are not, therefore, in a position to know anything—to have any information—that is as yet unknown to others who do have fact-finding procedures of their own. Anything that philosophers know *as a factual matter* they know by other means than their philosophical understandings. This means that philosophical disagreements between philosophers have no empirical content—there is no point of information that could be appealed to in settlement of their differences. This explains also why Wittgenstein's method consists in 'assembling reminders' (*PI*, section 127): all that one needs to know to 'solve' (rather, 'dissolve') a philosophical problem is already known, and all that is lacking—not a lack that is necessarily easily remedied—is an appropriate taking stock of what is known. Done effectively, this will show that the real problem is absence of clarity rather than paucity of information, and is no result of ignorance.

Thus, on this ('our') method, philosophy forms no constructive programme but is occasioned by response to puzzlements that are created very often by the attempt to 'step back' from ongoing practices in which one is otherwise cognitively at home, with the intention to take a reflective view of them. In the transition from engagement in those practices to a standpoint imaginatively external to them, it is possible that a

---

3   For an explication of Wittgenstein's employment of such directional metaphors throughout his corpus see Hutchinson (2006), *Unsinnig*.

loss of right perspective takes place, and that the attention is focused on aspects of the existing practice in a way which isolates those aspects from their place amongst the circumstances which make up the practice to which they belong. Wittgenstein's own 'method', then, provides no means of finding out matters of fact but engages with the tricky business of recapturing a *clear* view of what is already understood as a matter of familiarity with the ways of practice (on both sides of philosophical disagreements).

The claim that language determines reality would be a doctrine, and a controversial one at that, meaning (a) that *if* Wittgenstein/Winch should advance that—controversial—doctrine it would call not for acceptance but for a review, in terms of Wittgenstein's own practice, of where he had gone wrong in his philosophical practice or (b) that this is a misleading conversion of Wittgenstein's methodic dissolutions of confusion into positive doctrines about the nature of reality. Of course, there can be no automatic assurance that Wittgenstein or Winch invariably stuck to their recommended approach, but the determination of whether in respect of issues about 'language and reality' either of them failed to do so is a matter primarily for and of more detailed examination of Wittgenstein's specific remarks, one which cannot take place here.[4]

Assuming, then, that Wittgenstein was consistent to his conception of how philosophy is to be done, and that therefore he has nothing other than the banal to say about what is factually the case, then saying what is factually the case is left to those who make empirical inquiries. To say that language determines or constitutes reality as some sort of factual assertion would make it a non-philosophical one— to insist that it *is* a philosophical claim would, by the same token, withdraw any suggestion of a factual status. Holding this, though, ostensibly opens the way to a no-win situation. So follows the standard complaint that Wittgenstein's philosophy can only concern itself with the language that we use to talk about reality, and cannot therefore satisfy those who want philosophy to concern itself with the reality that language is naïvely taken to be talking about: how is one to be assured that reality is as language represents it? Aren't there at least as good grounds for supposing that language does not represent reality as it is in itself? Trying to make Wittgenstein's philosophy satisfying to anyone asking those questions will mean that his work is read as proposing that the only way that (his) philosophy can talk about reality is by assuming that the given language of representation must be taken at face value such that the nature of reality can be read off from the existing language. The language is, so to speak, self sufficient, establishes its own correctness, and thus unilaterally dictates what it is to speak so as to represent reality. If language is a product of the human mind, and if it is wholly independent in *fixing* what can correctly be said to be the case in or with the world, then that seems to mean that reality itself makes no contribution to fixing how it is correctly to be formulated, which surely constitutes a species of idealism, a linguistic one.

---

4 Such examination is undertaken in Hutchinson and Read's (forthcoming), *Wittgenstein's Radically Therapeutic Method.* Preliminary work is undertaken in Hutchinson (2007); Hutchinson and Read (2008); and Read (2004a). Also, see Baker (2004), *passim.*

Taking these worries seriously shows, however, how very quickly the emphasis on the empirical emptiness—save for trivial and truistic assertions—of philosophical exchanges is forgotten, and Wittgenstein's philosophy is construed as what, by its own lights, it cannot be, a making of claims about how empirical states of affairs are of necessity.[5] The first of these charges, further, supposes that Wittgenstein's philosophy confesses its own distinctive situation—that it cannot 'talk about reality' in the way that some alternative and preferred philosophy can. However, in that respect Wittgenstein's philosophy is in no different situation than any other philosophy, potentially distinguished from these only in the extent of self-consciousness about the risk of writing as if one was saying something informative when one is, nonetheless, 'saying nothing', and in respect of the need to supply propadeutics for this. Additionally, such objections involve construing Wittgenstein's treatment of language as addressed to the issue of its truth, as though it was commending 'ordinary language' as speaking the truth about reality, when Wittgenstein's *whole* philosophy has as its most elementary insistence that the task of determining the truth of any empirical proposition is external to philosophy. (Ergo, Wittgenstein's philosophy is NOT an 'Ordinary Language Philosophy'.[6]) For Wittgenstein, the key differences that mattered in philosophy were not between factually true and factually false propositions but between expressions which were taken for empirical propositions when they were no such thing, especially when they are either (a) expressions that are taken to be intelligible propositions when they as yet lack any genuine intelligibility or (b) expressions that are taken as propositions though they are not (at least, not as yet) propositions at all, but, insofar as they are intelligible are, for example, prescriptions for linguistic innovation, recommending something rather than reporting anything, though being misunderstood as stating facts.

But, someone might ask us: Is Peter Winch actually working in such a philosophical context? The answer is: It is made quite plain in the book that *ISS* is a piece of philosophy, and that its central effort is to diagnose the sources of a confusion. The confusion is embodied in the idea of 'a social science', and it is—in Wittgensteinian terms—a canonical confusion: of non-factual inquiries for factual ones. The argument is focused on sociology as a would-be science (though the argument is also applied more briefly to other 'social/human science' disciplines such as psychology (especially psychoanalysis), to economics, and so forth), and is designed to show that the *central* problems that sociology addresses are not ones requiring empirical investigation, and certainly not the formation of distinctive methods of empirical inquiry. Notoriously, Winch claims that sociology is in large measure an offshoot of—a *branch* of, or (better) simply a *part* of—philosophy, imagining itself to have left philosophy behind by making its researches empirical, but here, too, as in the case of psychology, conceptual confusions and empirical methods pass one another by. Winch's is no attempt to recall sociology to philosophy, since his claim is that it

---

5   Wittgenstein was always deeply sceptical about philosophers' attempts to treat empirical relations as necessary, sometimes remarking (e.g. see 6.37 of the *Tractatus*) that the only necessities belong to logic.

6   Again, see Hutchinson (2007) for some detailing as to why Wittgenstein is not an ordinary language philosopher. See also Baker (2004), *passim.*

has never left it (and—perhaps most notoriously of all—that its concern with 'social reality' is a title only for misbegotten epistemology). Though these are the central platforms of *ISS* they are not usually taken seriously.

Empirical (and empirico-theoretical) Investigations and Conceptual Clarification

So, Winch's thought depends entirely upon the difference between empirical investigations and conceptual clarifications, and that he will therefore offer nothing except clarifications. The clarifications are primarily addressed to the confusion between empirically-based claims about social activities, institutions, and the like— e.g. that a practice such as the washing of hands is found across different social activities—and claims about what those facts signify—e.g. that the 'act of washing hands' is a constant throughout all those activities, to be dissociated from the 'rationalisations' that people give for that act in the different settings. Some people explain their washing of hands as an hygienic measure, others may give a religious explanation, but these are, empirically-speaking irrelevant, irrational responses to an activity that goes on regardless of how those doing it think about it: they are all manifestly, empirically-speaking, doing *the same thing*, though they each believe they are doing a distinctive and special activity.

This example, Winch took from Vilfredo Pareto, from a work first published in 1916, and, as such, it may be outdated, though the thought which it embodies has surely *not* disappeared from the social sciences, and is sufficiently persistent to provide a stumbling block to a commonality of understanding between Winch and his critics.

The fact that people do engage in washing of hands in different contexts of activity (practical, religious, legal etc.) is not in dispute, any more than is the claim that they would give different explanations of what they are doing in each context—the issues involved are not empirical. The explanations that the participants give are not empirically falsified i.e. they are doing exactly what they say they are doing, namely washing their hands, and their doing this is governed by its place in their respective practices—the child is made to wash its hands after using the toilet, not before; surgeons wash their hands (scrub-up) in preparation for surgery not when getting ready to dictate their notes; the Muslim washes his hands (performs *wudu*) before prayers not following, and so on. The idea that their explanations can be (collectively) contradicted arises from what we have argued is the driving preoccupation of so many social science manoeuvres, namely the form of explanation. Thus, inverted commas can be put around 'explanation' in respect of the different 'explanations' given for washing the hands, signifying that these are to be seen as (mere) rationalisations for an action which cannot be genuinely explained by these rationalisations. The obsession with the form of explanation drives the characterisation of the indigenous 'explanations' as rationalisations on the grounds that they differ from each other, while *genuine* explanation demands that the same explanation be given for the same phenomena. The same action (of preparatory handwashing) cannot be properly explained by three different explanations.

Pareto is exemplary of the problem Winch is attempting to raise in respect of both

a. illustrating how such factual materials as are presented in sociology are embedded in conceptions of explanation. Pareto is not seeking to find an explanation for an independently puzzling phenomenon, but is working from a conception of how things in general are to be explained, meaning that the empirical facts that are not otherwise problematic are puzzling from the point of view of applying his explanatory principle; and

b. *illustrating how much hinges on the designation of 'the same' with respect to people's actions.* Here Winch's gross argument is that Pareto disregards the fact that he has no especial privilege to say whether two activities are 'the same' and certainly none that overrules the judgement of those in those activities that, the washing of hands in an operating theatre is a different activity from Pontius Pilate's washing his hands. The former has a practical purpose, the latter is a political gesture. 'Social scientists' let us remember are self-appointed to their status as professional explainers, and there is no reason to accept that e.g. Pareto (or in contemporary terms, Jurgen Habermas or Anthony Giddens) is other than self-appointed to his elected task, and is therefore entitled to *overrule* the criteria that the indigenous practitioners of child rearing, surgery or politics employ to determine the identity of their actions. These self-appointed explainers are, of course, perfectly entitled to set up their own standards of explanation, and to develop their own preferred standards of explanation, but all-too-often the trouble with sociologists and many other 'social scientists' is that they cannot let the matter rest there. In part that is because to let the matter rest there would deprive their efforts of its sense of importance, of the idea that the 'social scientist' has a *special* role in society, one which makes it responsible for the general run of social affairs. 'Social Scientists' are not merely adopting different criteria from those that others use, but are adopting their criteria as purportedly general standards of correctness, reaching far beyond the concerns of their specific inquiries and thus being set out as ones that overrule and displace the standards applicable operative in other people's specialist practices.

One 'stumbling block' to the understanding of Winch, though not by any means Winch alone, that was mentioned above may be found in the example, which is chosen to show that the *appropriate* standard of identity for the things that people are doing is the context within which those things are done. So, consider: Here is a body that began its journey from the fifteenth floor of a hotel room, falling toward the car park; and here is another body falling from a bridge over a major river. Here are two events which are the same—bodies falling, subject to the law of physics. We do not deny that the events might be described as 'the same' from the point of view of the physics of motion, to which any falling body will e.g. accelerate according to the same laws.

However, there are surely respects in which the falling bodies are not the same—one began with the person being thrown off the bridge, the other one with the individual jumping from the hotel balcony. A homicide and a suicide are not by any means 'the same' event, and the fact that these terms would not feature in a physicist's description of the fallings to which we are witness does not mean that explanations in terms of 'homicide' and 'suicide' are irrelevant because they neither of them generalise over all falling bodies. What kind of event someone's falling from a great height might be is determined by the way in which it got started—did he jump or was he pushed?

Sociology's preoccupation with explanation presumes that explanation and description are distinctive activities. Hence, the fixation on forms of explanation whilst, by and large, leaving the business of description to take care of itself. Description is usually at best of secondary interest, explanation is the important thing, and, in any case, description will be a function of the explanatory system, once that has been identified—it will tell us what kind of phenomena there are, and how they differ, one from the other. Thus, to continue with the Pareto example, the phenomenon to be explained is the washing of hands. This can be identified and described independently of the explanations that hand-washers give. Their explanations fail the test of adequate explanation, and so can be set aside: some other explanation *must* be found.

However, the Pareto case can at least equally well be taken to show that the separation of explanation and description is not necessarily so sharp in cases of people's activities, and that the 'rationalisations' given of hand washing are not explanations but descriptions. It is not as if people in a surgical theatre wash their hands, and having done so are puzzled: why am I doing this? Searching through their thoughts they come up with this explanation: I wash my hands as a hygienic precaution. They might give this as an explanation to someone who, uninformed about their work, asks them why they wash their hands so assiduously, but that it is an explanation for others does not mean it is an explanation for them—they themselves need no explanation. Where washing one's hands preparatory to surgery is given to someone else as an account it is just as much description of what was done, as it is an explanation: it is an explanation by description. Indeed 'washing one's hands as a hygienic precaution' works as an explanation only because it reports what was done. 'Washing one's hands to absolve oneself of responsibility for Jesus' fate' would not be an explanation of what was done at the surgical sink since the surgeon was certainly not doing that, though most definitely that was what Pilate was doing. Pilate would have had *no idea* of what it would be to take hygienic precautions of the kind featured in modern surgery, and a modern surgeon just isn't in a position to do the ceremonial kind of washing that Pilate could. The washing of hands are *not* 'the same' actions at all, and 'washing one's hands as a surgical precaution' is a more expansive description of what is being done: in connection with the things that people do, giving a description often *is* providing an explanation.

It is not, first, for sociologists to decide what someone is properly said to be doing. The language they are using, after all, does not belong to them, but is one that they speak because they belong to the language communities about and within which they write: 'washing hands' isn't a description that any sociologist has contrived, and it is indisputable that, whether it is the correct thing to say or not should be decided by the way in which the language works, is used, within the activities to which it belongs (to domestic affairs: clean those dirty hands!; to medical situations: 'scrub-up before surgery'; or to affairs of state: washing hands as the ceremonial way to recuse oneself).

Now, what about the objection from, for example, cultural materialists, that these arguments play down, much too much, the underlying *instrumental* (or ends-means) rationality, in actions that are supposedly religious or ceremonial?[7] Is it not, thus, the case that hand washing is used in all these cases because of its effective practical connection with cleanliness? Could one not, perhaps, as evolutionary psychologists are wont to do say that 'hand washing' is a meme that disseminates because it is an adaptively functional practice, increasing survival chances by reducing the risk of infection? However, it is not being denied that hand-washing is indeed conceived as a cleansing activity in each instance, but the point that is being made is that the 'cleansing' involved is significantly different—cleansing one's hands of dirt so that one will not e.g. put dirty marks on the tablecloth is not the same as cleansing one's hands of dirt *because* dirt contains microbial life-forms, and these are quite different from washing off one's sins or responsibilities—there is a difference between a—perhaps unintended—by-product of an action, and the *point* of that action—and one is not explained by the other (the discussion of rendering actions in the following chapter, is relevant here).

Now, our evolutionary psychologist interlocutor might respond by arguing that his socio-biological characterisation of the action is the act-type and all other characterisations are token renderings of that act-type, some instances might even fail to qualify as tokens, being merely metaphorical 'instances' of the act-type. So, on such an understanding the child washing their hands before dinner, the surgeon washing their hands before surgery and the Muslim washing their hands before prayer are merely act-tokens of the act-type, evolutionarily explained—Pilate's washing of hands might be seen as metaphorical here. However, we submit that such an understanding as this rests on no more than stipulation of the act-type.

To stipulate that the evolutionary 'explanation' denotes the category—denotes the type—of action and other none-evolutionary 'explanations denote only instances or tokens of the category/type is just that, a stipulation; it simply begs the question of someone who argues—as do we—that each case—the case of the child, the case of the surgeon, the case of the muslim—has its own identity irreducible to the evolutionary explanation. Another way of putting this is that the dispute is over what is properly identified as the type of action under consideration: the evolutionary psychologist (for evolutionary reasons) insists that the type is identified as the physical act of 'hand washing' which is in all instances (in all contexts) something along the lines of a meme that disseminates because it is an adaptively functional practice, increasing survival chances by reducing the risk of infection; in contrast we argue that what our interlocutor relegates to the status of tokens (of his stipulated type) are types of action, and we argue this because an action is what it is given the meaning it has in the context in which it is undertaken.

---

7   See Marvin Harris (1974) for a monument to this kind of instrumentalist thinking in the name of cultural materialism.

But does this really give evolutionary theory its due? Will not our evolutionary psychologist interlocutor simply respond by insisting that e.g.: tribes that don't have hand-washing practices will tend to die out; so will tribes that fight a lot among themselves. What people think they are doing when they fight or when they wash their hands is only part of the point. The fact remains, our interlocutor will insist, that features of those practices which may or may not be perspicuous/accessible to their practitioners *do*, contra what we are saying, partly explain the persistence of the practices.

We can agree with our evolutionary psychologist interlocutor that the washing of hands can be said to have that as its role, while insisting that this does not mean that this role either exhausts or is even the dominant consideration in the action's identity. To insist that it is so is to be on the way to begging the question of us.

Evolutionary psychology is concerned to explain the commonality and persistence of certain practices—what it is about us as the animals we are that leads us to form households etc. Not necessarily an unreasonable question to ask, nor unreasonable to suppose this has to do with our evolutionary history—the objection to evolutionary psychology is an objection to its crudity, largely a result of it sharing the social sciences' fixation on the explanans without much care for or precision in specifying the explanandum. Thus, evolutionary psychologists would insist that the practice of handwashing is explained by e.g. natural selection through infection—but our point is that the explanation would just be incomplete because there is no 'one practice', handwashing, to be explained, but quite different practices which involve handwashing (is washing one's hands in water the same practice as washing them in medicalised liquids). For evolutionary psychology to persist in its line of argument, it then needs to adopt a philosophical position about the identity of actions, i.e. that physical movements of a particular species seen against the background of the evolutionary history of the species provide *all* the necessary criteria for 'the same'. All that we claim is that they fall (considerably) short of *this*.

What is and What is not Meant By: An Action is What it is—an Action—Only Under a Description

Another invitation to see idealism in the position we here defend might be found in 'conflating' an action and the description of that action. It may seem that the two are being said to be identified, that an action is identical with its description, meaning that a 'material' occurrence has been reduced to a 'linguistic' representation, and equally clear that talking about the one is not talking about the other. Are there not, further, intimations of incorrigibility? If the determination as to which descriptions of an action are the correct ones is to be left to the members of society then this is the same as removing the possibility that they could be wrong about this—since they decide what the correct description is, then correctness is settled by their decision, not by the facts about which they make the decision. The name 'Spot' and the dog 'Spot' are two distinct things, but there is no 'Spot the dog' independently of our pet-keeping and animal naming practices.

However, it is not that an action and its description relate through equivalence, so that an action is being taken for a description of it, or *vice versa* so that, alternately, the description becomes the action. The discussion above was about action and the way in which actions are individuated in the language, about how to specify *the identity* of the action that someone performed. 'Washing hands', after all, has to serve as the 'linguistic representation' which picks out the thing that religious, political and medical people allegedly all do. If there is to be discussion of the actions that people do, then the actions that are the reference for consideration have to be identified. 'Washing hands' does individuate those actions from other actions such as e.g. picking one's nose, scratching one's ear, washing the dishes, and so on, and Pareto is not being criticised for adopting that identification but because *that identification is incomplete*—it does not individuate the *actions* that can be done by washing one's hands. It is not that there are no ways to individuate those actions further: 'washing one's hands' is as far as any description needs to go, such that 'washing one's hands' must be the same activity in any and every case. There plainly are ways to individuate those actions further—the ones that Pareto has attempted to *take away* in order to insist that they are all one and the same action. Nonetheless, the fact remains, as is manifested in Pareto's attachment of the hand-washing to the assorted 'rationalisations', that the hand-washings *are* different, they differ in the social settings to which they belong, and, equally clearly, they play different parts in those social settings: washing hands in the medical setting is a means of removing infectious lifeforms, in the religious setting a matter of spiritual purification. No one would deny that the difference between idly kicking a football into an empty net and scoring a goal in the cup final could both be reduced to 'toeing a football' for there is no difference in respect of application of boot end to ball—the differences are, of course, in where the booting is done, and what results—at Wembley, the ball going past the opposing goalkeeper and all that follows from that, as opposed to on the recreation field in the absence of other players. Comparably, there is no reason to deny that the *identity* of the hand washings hinges on where they are done, i.e. which circumstances they belong to, and what their role is, i.e. what doing *that* comprises in these circumstances.

It is surely the case that what a goal (in professional football) is depends upon the felicitous circumstances specified in the governing association's rules, that the determination of whether a goal has been scored or not belongs to the sport of football—why would one invite the participation of chess players or physicists in deciding this? This does not mean that football's governing association is incorrigible. The rules of football do not feature *hypotheses* about the nature of goals, but stipulations of rules that define what a goal is. The footballer's governing body may be less than infallible in their judgements as to what rules regulative of goal-scoring are most conducive to entertaining or even uncomplicated football, but these are mistakes of judgement, not failures to apprehend evidence. The football example equally reminds us that individuals can be wrong about whether a goal is scored—spectators and commentators can be convinced there was a goal but the referee can disallow it—the ball did not cross the line, however it may have looked from the stands. It is referees who decide whether to allow a goal or not, and their decision is final, but even that does not make them infallible (as the sophisticated television replay machinery may make clear). However, there is a big difference between deciding that 'scoring a goal' is an altogether invalid species of description of what people do (such that nobody ever does, or has, 'really' scored a goal) and deciding that, never mind what the ref said, that really was not a goal. Setting up and running the game of football is no branch of empirical inquiry (though it may feature empirical inquiries and the nature of those e.g. conducted by official bodies under the oversight of lawyers, for example, or by the television panel using video replays, is determined by the practice).

There is no gap between 'the action' and 'its description' of the sort that critics worry about—as pointed out, identifying an action is no necessarily infallible affair, except insofar as one is invoking, as we are here, a tautology: *if* one has correctly said what action was done, *then* the act *is* the action so described. One is not going to be able to talk about *that* action at all if one does not have a correct identification of it (because one's commentary will be inaccurate)—there is no point in offering an explanation of why someone did something if what he did is incorrectly specified. Deciding what is to be put in place of those 'ifs' in any actual case is not the philosopher's or the sociologist's job.

The more expansive descriptions do not provide 'explanatory rationalisations' that are given *in addition* to the identification of the act to be explained, but provide more informative descriptions of the act—bringing out the intentions and understandings with which the deed was done, understandings of how the deed features in its setting (e.g. how much hangs on the toeing of the ball at this point in this game, which is, after all, no mere game, but the Cup Final etc.). More expansive descriptions elaborate or explicate what is contained in terser ones: the assertion 'checkmate' appeals to the state of play on the board, and to the fact that there is no further legitimate move that the checkmated player can make. 'Checkmate' will do for informed players, no more need be said. For a naïve onlooker, however, the description of the way in which the pieces are configured and the restraints that puts on their further movements may need to be spelled out. The explanation is achieved by pointing out what it is about the act—in relation to the rules of chess in this case—that gives it the identity that it has: a true checkmate.

The demands of sociological theorists for explanations can seem, from this point of view, rather spurious, based in artificially created problems rather than in general puzzlement. Specific cases that give cause for puzzlement *may* be a different matter. When 'primitive magic' is first described to us, or the behaviour of a 'cargo cult', for another example, it can be very puzzling to us as to what it is that these people are doing—how do their actions fit together, what is the point of doing this? In other words, we are not in a position where we are able to identify the actions of these people let alone give an explanation of them. We are, *as yet*, unable to *fully* identify their actions, to e.g. establish what they are hoping to achieve in burning up all their worldly goods. They are manifestly burning up their possessions, but to even call these 'worldly goods' is to invoke a possibly spiritual nature for their action—they are not just burning things, they are e.g. sacrificing them. An explanation can be given to us by describing what a cargo cult is, what part the Bible plays in it, what 'the cargo' refers to, what the leaders demand of their followers. We shall come to understand a great deal about what the cult members are doing *and why* they are doing it just by working to understand *what* they are doing. Further, if we are not bothering ourselves with hyperbolic worries about the relationship of language and reality we shall be happy to accept, on the basis of reading an anthropologist's telling, that we understand what their actions are *by having them described to us*. We will not feel that we cannot possibly understand what they are doing unless we go and see for ourselves—*if*, that is, we accept that the anthropologist has indeed described for us what they were doing.

This is not a model for *explaining social life in general*, for the point is that social life *in general* does not need explaining. There is no need for an explanation—of the kind offered by the anthropologist—to be given to those who practice 'primitive magic' or those involved in the cargo cult, just as there is no need for an explanation for competent chess players as to why this player has announced 'checkmate'.

From this point of view, much of the crucial effort in sociological theorising goes into trying to create the impression that there is something that needs to be explained (human action in general, perhaps) rather than into actually explaining anything (in the sense of removing a puzzlement that we already had about why people act in that *particular* way). There are no real surprises amongst the 'findings' of sociologists, psychologists or their ilk. The *understanding* of people's practices must inevitably go before any 'sociological' understanding of their actions to which those actions belong and, if the point about the real, philosophical, nature of sociology's problems is sound, this will forcibly and forcefully evaporate the need for 'explanation' of the sort that sociological theory is mostly designed to offer. Which is not to say that one cannot ask research questions about the origins of or conditions for certain sorts of practices, but it does suggest that there is no reason to suppose that such questions require or presuppose any unifying general theory, and certainly not one that will displace the relevant practice as the means of explanation of someone's actions under it.

The critique in terms of 'idealism' distracts attention from such questions as why, if Winch is wrong, are his critics *defending the possibility* of a general explanatory scheme rather than actually setting out some worked out, acknowledged scheme of that kind, this point reflecting the fact that sociological theories are characteristically manifestos for some highly general, empirically underspecified explanatory principles and descriptive categories. Why is it that sociology recycles through the confusions and self-contradictions of the sort that were catalogued by Pitirim A. Sorokin (1957) more than half a century ago?

However, reference to practices may not spare us from being caught in a closed conceptual circle, one which leaves us 'stranded' (so to speak) on this side of the language, cut off from the 'material world' on its far side. When *ISS* was first published, this was the real fear that accompanied many charges of idealism. Wittgenstein's philosophy—allegedly—gives no account of how we may be sure that 'our representations' reach out to the reality beyond them. Since then, of course, those with this anxiety have been pushed much more onto the defensive—they complain about a rising tide of irrationalism—by the prominence of postmodern convictions that language is self-contained, that, in a famous saying, there is nothing beyond the text.

But Wittgenstein *is not trying* to give us a correct picture of the relationship between language and reality. That desire is something for philosophical *treatment*. The contrasting conceptions of realism and idealism has them *both* starting off from the idea that the connection between language and reality shows itself in a correspondence relationship, one between the linguistic proposition and the extra linguistic reality, and then they differ only as to whether any such correspondence can, actually be established, or on how it is established (as it were, 'by the world', or 'by us'). The (linguistic) Idealist thinks that it can only be established, if it really can be said to be established at all, by means of turning the 'extra-linguistic reality' into something more or less linguistic. Wittgenstein may be seen as beginning in the same place as the Realist and Idealist, *in the particular sense* of trying to find where they are coming from, trying to understand them; but he steps back reflectively, at this juncture. Like everyone else, Wittgenstein supposes it is perfectly alright for someone to report (say) 'The wolf ate three sheep' and that it is equally alright for someone else to wonder if what is reported is indeed the case. Without worrying about whether someone who tried to establish whether what is reported actually happened is inevitably 'trapped in the realm of language' or can, at some point 'break through' it, let us ask instead how we are going to be able to tell whether the report is true or not. Which wolf, which sheep? **Those** sheep? But did the wolf really eat them or were they rustled? How will we be able to tell if the wolf did eat those sheep, some other sheep, no sheep at all etc? This is not Verificationism—this is turning our attention to the wor(l)dly ways in which the worries of the Realist and Idealist are overcome in everyday life. This turns our attention to the only way in which such matters are ever settled—*not* by reference to Reality, *nor* by reference to the contents of our minds, cultures, or words, but by reference to the facts and their descriptions and re-descriptions.

In short: Wittgenstein surely does not provide us with reasons to be confident that our representations 'reach out to reality', *but neither does he provide us with reasons to doubt that they do; and neither does he gerrymander reality such that our representations are bound to be able to reach it*. Rather, wholly consistently and entirely persistently, since his first work, he doubts that the question of the relationship of language to reality *as a general question* is *intelligible*. The key relationship for Wittgenstein is not between language and something external to it, but between language *in use* (at work) and language on 'holiday', cut off from its applications in (so to speak) the stream of life.

That one can ask and determine whether some statement is factual in the sense that it correctly states the facts, does not mean that one can then ask whether *the language* correctly states the facts. What is said *in* a language does not belong to the language, but to the practices within which the language is used, and the determination of whether what is said in the language does 'correspond to reality' belongs not to the language as such, but to those practices—the method for determining whether accusations of criminal guilt are true is the adversarial trial (in the UK), and the trial and conviction are conducted in English, but that does *not* make the evidence, the adversarial procedure or the defendant's proven guilt part of English (internal to the language). Contrastively, the method of determining whether claims about relations between rates of criminality and geographic neighbourhoods calls upon statistical techniques of sampling and analysis, that of connecting potential criminals to the scene of crime to methods from the biosciences, of responsibility for actions to the diagnostic techniques of psychiatry, and so on and on. It is not as if what can be intelligibly stated as a matter of fact and ways of checking what the facts are can be entirely independent of each other, for both are connected through the use of language in a practice (the play of a game and keeping the score). Again, this is not any kind of Verificationism. It is the priority of intelligibility over truth that is the basis for this line of argument—it is not that the truth of what is said comes from the language, but that an understanding of what would be the case if what is said were true derives from understanding of the language (and, thereby, how one might find out if what is said *is* true) where 'understands the language' *includes* understands at least aspects of the practice in which it is used.

Language—and language *in use*, at that—determines only what an expression says, and questions about the factual or empirical applicability of what is said can only be asked when what is said has an application in activity, a part to play in one practice or another.

Here another logical circle seems in the process of formation—this time, involving a practice as a self-confirming and therefore imperviously self-justifying operation. If we accept a practice's ways of determining matters of fact then are not we— Wittgensteinians—*endorsing* those practices, even though we may not explicitly be saying so. Are we not in fact endorsing them by saying that they 'determine matters of fact'? Only if saying 'they determine matters of fact' is taken as a substantive, rather than a 'grammatical' characterisation, and, in accord with all that has been said about the descriptive, grammatical character of 'conceptual inquiries' it is clearly the latter that is intended. In other words: some matters of fact get determined through the enactment of some particular practices. This is no thesis of linguistic Idealism. It is the merest grammatical remark; it is 'always already understood' by any competent human social actor who understands English. It doesn't actually *say* anything: it doesn't tell us anything about how things are as opposed to how they might else be.

Portraying the diagnostic techniques of psychiatry or the bioscientific methods of DNA evidence does not give support to those techniques—what do *philosophers* know independently of such techniques that would assure us that they work as advertised? Spelling them out portrays the content that the notion that the concept 'determination of facts' must have if it is to be of any use at all. The expression 'ways of determining the facts' is not a general expression which singles out some *completely general* ways of doing this, but—standing alone—an empty one, with meaningful application only when it is deployed discriminatingly within some practice. It is simply a fact that the question 'how are facts determined' needs to be asked as 'what instantiates "determining the facts" *here?*' e.g. in mathematics, in court, in beatifications, on the golf course *inter* innumerable *alia*. Descriptively, it is plainly–as illustrated by the examples just given—the case that 'determine the facts' has sense and *specific* application in a wide range of heterogeneous environments, and the attempt, to insist upon a single, unified application of it according to general principles enacts a very different approach to philosophical problems than that which any Wittgensteinian could take.

If there is no endorsement of linguistic Idealism, does this nonetheless leave us with a portrayal of practices which means that they are all of them equally self-justifying? (And thus, a kind of (practicistic) Relativism?) After all, if the justification of factual claims is 'internal' to the practice to which they belong, then does this not involve acceptance of that practice's procedures of determining what is a matter of fact? Whether or not those claims turn out, according to the ways of the practice, to be false ones, it normally remains impossible, from 'within' that practice, to call into question whether the ways of the practice which settle matters of fact really do anything of the sort. Witchcraft is almost invariably the example in mind. Blaming someone for witchcraft may sometimes be falsified by the procedures of witchcraft itself: the woman drowned, proving she was never a witch. However, those same procedures also succeed—women are convicted of witchcraft. But *we know* there is no such thing as witchcraft. There is no space within the Wittgensteinian story, it is *alleged*, for the possibility that people could possibly break out of the ways of witchcraft and accept *what we know to be the case.*

For a philosophy that eschews controversial factual theses, it would seem to put itself in the most monstrous contradiction: it is denying that we can be confident that there are no witches. Are we to adopt some desperately relativist measure, given that we can be no more certain that witches do not exist, than witchcraft practitioners are that they do, and say that the belief in witchcraft is just as true as our disbelief in it? Appalled at the idea of relativism, should we not resort to a realist insistence that there is a fact of the matter and that we know what it is? Are we not, that is, right to insist that they (the believers in witchcraft) do not, and that they are—demonstrably—wrong?

Again, the pertinent Wittgensteinian insistence that philosophy does not determine matters of fact is overlooked. If taken into account then it is clear that, insofar as the question 'Do witches exist?' is a factual question, it is by the very same token *not a philosophical* question, so it is not—see all the above—any philosopher's philosophical business to attempt to answer it. This does not put anyone in a relativistic situation, as though one were giving a default endorsement to both sides—any such 'endorsement' would be an empty form and a worthless move. If we cannot—*as philosophers*—say that they are *wrong* to believe in witchcraft, then are we not saying that they have just as much right to say they are correct as we do—but this is just to slip back into a substantive engagement when, *qua* philosopher, there is nothing to say about who might be right or wrong here (though there is, as the interminable debate over it and its frequent recurrence in this book makes clear, much to be said in the way of clarifying the different kinds of disagreements that there are over the issue of 'primitive magic').

The fact is that *we* the authors of this book are confident that there *are* no witches, but this is not a consequence of our having shown that the practice of witchcraft is factually in error. It is not so much even that we *do not* believe in witches as that *we cannot.* As we shall explain: *We* would not know how to *begin even trying* to go about believing that there are witches. The whole circumstances of our lives, the general scepticism about this—which was pressed on us from childhood on—and the widespread reliance on science, the protracted and saturatedly-intricate relationship with our culture, leave us in a position where we cannot ourselves take seriously the idea of witchcraft. This does not have to mean that we cannot acknowledge that others do take this seriously, or that we could not take seriously the task of understanding how they can do this when we cannot. It is not that we can see that witchcraft is mistaken and therefore cannot take it seriously, so much as that we do not even know how we could begin to take it seriously in our own lives. We are simply incapable of trying to consult the oracle or accusing the person in the next office of bewitching us. Our iron resistance to the reality of witchcraft does not come from evidence or from philosophical justification but comes prior to these—finding empirical or philosophical justifications that there are no witches could not make us any more confident that there are no witches (there *really* aren't) than we already are. It is not so difficult to see how people could do this when we see that in their lives the practice of witchcraft is as deeply and intricately embedded as disbelief is in ours (we take home-grown Satanists with a big pinch of salt, by contrast).

This might seem unsatisfactory to someone who wants to think that it is not so much that we have iron resistance to the existence of witches as that we have no rational basis for same. Shouldn't we ourselves be unsatisfied until we have a demonstration that we are right, justified, in *just refusing* it. If we are not wrong about witches, then are we not just prejudiced, and could that possibly be good enough for a rational person? Everything in our experience speaks against the idea that there really are witches, and *nothing* speaks for it. If this is a 'prejudice', it is so then only in roughly Gadamer's (value-neutral, non-pejorative) sense. It is not so much that we could consider that witches exist and then just decline to accept that they do, for, as explained, we just have no idea how we could begin to take truly seriously the thought that witches do (even *maybe*) exist. Anything that might be appealed to is just going to run up against the fact that we are unable—not necessarily unwilling—to take it seriously as a manifestation of witchcraft. We can give a host of reasons for thinking that supposed demonstrations of surpernatural powers are entirely fraudulent but these are *never* decisive against those who do believe—when proof of fraud is accepted in some case, the next question is: but does that explain all cases? Being able to give an endless supply of reasons for our inability to see how or where we could begin to be serious about witchcraft surely removes the disqualification that our resistance to the idea is irrational and (in the ordinary sense of the word) prejudiced, but doubtless it will not satisfy someone who wants to insist that a rational basis for disbelief in witchcraft would be a knock-out refutation of it: not just one that we would accept, but one that, so to speak, everyone would have to accept, their failure to do so being taken as proof of their own irrationality, as evidence that their failure to accept what we tell them is a result of their prejudices. This seems an unrealisable notion of rationality, and certainly not one that should be allowed to consign our confidence that witches are not amongst the furniture of the universe to the status of an irrational prejudice, nor that allows us to suppose that confidence in the damage they have done to the crops should be treated in that way either.

Can practices be criticised? Is it possible to criticise them either from within (they themselves set the standards of right and wrong) or from without (any outside assessment can only be made from within the traditions of some other practice, not some genuinely independent point of view)? A short answer to this question, if we were (as it were) forced to answer it, would be to say: Of *course*! Who could possibly think otherwise?[8] Our full answer to this question is to be found in our final chapter, on Conservatism. But we should also like to point out that there is an important sense in which such a question invites Wittgensteinians to a game they should not be playing. The question ought to be: does criticism take place? And once we have deflated the question into that, it answers itself. It is clear that practices can be given up, that confidence in them can erode or that people can become disillusioned. Resolute Western disbelievers in witchcraft are the successors of people who once believed in witchcraft but, in a complicated process the idea of witches lost its hold (just as the grip of religious traditions also weakened, sometimes leading to change of faith, sometimes to secularism). It is equally clear that practices are criticised 'from without', that a given practice is utterly condemned (clitoridectomy, capital punishment) or accused of major failings of a moral, policy or practical kind (or all three, as with the legal system, imprisonment, and probation—e.g. towards the close of 2007 a British judge attacked a police forensic method of DNA analysis leading to (at least temporary) withdrawal of it). Wittgenstein's *On Certainty* is all about how certainties can shift: the practical convictions that play the part of logical truths within a practice can become, in consequence of a progressive change in circumstance, testable hypotheses (Kuhn of course discusses similar processes at length, too).

The form that criticism often takes is not that which philosophers conceive of as rational criticism, which is that of a difference of opinion that can be settled by reference to the facts, brought to a point where the correctness of one and the falsity of the other would be self-evident. The form it often takes is that of disagreement about how the facts are to be decided, what states of affairs could comprise those facts and what sorts of procedures could determine their character—substantial agreement would have to be achieved before the disagreement could be brought to the facts i.e. where some facts can be taken as given. And such agreement is at least hard, if not impossible, to achieve. However, the absence of categorical proofs and disproofs does not prevent people from finding that their faith can withstand the severest tests, from keeping confidence in ways that have served them all their lives or, alternatively, becoming terminally disillusioned, disgusted or alienated.

It is not that Winch's arguments do not allow the possibility of 'conceptual change' for it is not their job to legislate possibilities but, as a descriptive enterprise to acknowledge the plain fact that conceptual change does take place. The idea that they 'exclude' the possibility of conceptual change amounts to the charge that Winch's arguments do not accept their critics' stipulation of what conceptual change should be and what form 'rational' change must take. Again, here is a key parallel with Kuhn: Kuhn and Winch are both above all concerned with the norm of major conceptual change not taking place *and with the nature and rationality of conceptual change when it does take place.* They are interested in the history and social nature of conceptual change, considered as a phenomenon that is in the main badly philosophically-misunderstood.

---

8   See again Crary's essay, chapter 6 of Crary and Read (2000), also see Pleasants's (2000a) and (2002).

Of Language and of Representation

It may be noticeable that 'language' has here been spoken of as a product of the *lives* of human beings, not of their minds, and that the languages that people have are tied up with, but not simple functions of, the lives that they live—one does not expect to find, in the language of an isolated hunter-gatherer group, the resources for reviewing and criticising television programmes or identifying the technical problems in getting cold fusion to work. The main argument has been cast in terms of a view of what philosophy can do, and of the things that such a conception allows can be said, given its reliance on language. That philosophy does not have a proprietary view of language, for the facts about language that it appeals to are ones that are available to pretty much anyone, such as the unsurprising fact that people who do not go in for sports and games would not have our overburdened sporting vocabulary, the equally unsurprising fact that people learn language relatively effortlessly and from others etc.[9]

It is equally plain that language—except in a very, no, extraordinarily stretched sense—is not a medium of representation *per se*. The word 'representation' is another ordinary word that can be added along with 'fact' to our catalogue, one of that sort of word that, Wittgenstein thought, needed to be treated less as a master category than as a ordinary word, no less humble than "tune", "Penguin" or "socket" (compare *PI* 108 and 116). The 'crisis of representation' is not an abandonment of metaphysics, but the disillusioned continuation of it, again mistaking the fact that 'representation' without application is empty, not a license to assume that general criteria are essential to the identification of a genuine or successful case of representation.

The fact that some paintings are representational does not mean we have to think that all of them must be *in a way* i.e. to rearrange the meaning of 'representational' in such a way as to include things that otherwise are counted as non-representational. Wittgenstein does not try to rule out such rejiggings of meaning but does ask whether the risk of confusion associated with them may be too great. Of those things that can be considered representational in the ordinary sense, then the criteria for determining what they represent and whether they do represent it are internal to the mode of representation—one cannot seriously assess a portrait as a representation without understanding something of painting, just as one cannot tell what, and how successfully a print out of some wavy lines might represent or fail to capture without knowing something of, variously, lie detection, medical diagnosis, or physics.

The idea that this highlights how representations are conventional in nature might be a fair way of putting it, but it would surely be foolish to suppose that this showed that they must be demoted from the status of representations. It just shows that representations apply conventions, that is what those things which are equally conventionally called representations are like. The continuation of metaphysics is to be found in the idea that representations fail to make contact with things-in-themselves, a thought which is, in the postmodern context, a context of Saussurean *assumptions* about language as a self-contained language system, one which

---

9   For explication of why this latter point need not be seen as surprising, see Part I of Read (2001).

determines meaning as a function of its formal relations. There is no connection between such a conception of language and Wittgenstein's repeated pointing toward the way in which parts of language are tied up with the needs of distinct activities, developing out of and through connections with the requirements arising in *the lives* of people, his highlighting of the fact that the language is not a system, let alone a self-contained one. Hence, the 'crisis of representation' is the product of a supposedly latter day realisation that real language cannot satisfy the traditional criteria for representation *sub specie aeternatatis*, associated with acceptance of the traditional criteria, producing the conviction that representation is impossible. As suggested here, it is the idea of a viewpoint *sub specie aeternitatis* that is mythological, not the array of endlessly assorted ways of doing things that, in their appropriate context, can be called representations.

Concluding ... Reminding Oneself of Winch's Context

Our strategy in this chapter has been to argue that Winch cannot, if he takes Wittgenstein seriously, be any kind of idealist, and for much the same reasons that he cannot, either, be a realist—to give loyalty to either of these positions, or to transfer it from one to the other would not put an end to the philosophical problems involved but would to a significant extent perpetuate the very same confusions (not least the idea that philosophers, whether dressed up as 'social scientists' or overtly speaking as philosophers, are tasked to adjudicate what is factually the case by non factual means). Besides, what Winch has to say cannot be a substantive doctrine about 'the nature of reality' since he is not trying to say *on his own independent behalf* what would in any case, or in general, stand as constituent of reality, for from that point of view both realism and idealism, not to mention any proposed alternative to them, are superfluous to the need to get a clear sight of what role *the expression* 'reality' (and related expressions) play in the language to which it belongs, that is to say, the place those words have in the lives of those who employ them. Winch's own contribution is entirely second storey, a matter of reflection on *the sense* that attaches to talk about 'reality', appreciating that the expression commonly invokes that which obtains independently of us, but derives its intelligible content from the discourse that draws upon it. 'Real' can join 'fact' and 'representations' as expressions which have no general application, finding their life and referents in discontinuous contexts of application.[10] That is, Winch *qua philosopher* does not try to tell us that God exists or that witchcraft does, as though he himself had established these things, nor is he busy denying that 'an external world' exists and that only thought is real. In the first case, he is attempting to pin down the sense that attaches to intelligibly evidencing the consequences of God's love or the consequences of witchcraft, seeking more scrupulous treatment of the forms of language intelligibly employed in practices to which he does not himself necessarily subscribe. He uses this order of reflection to indicate, with respect to the second case, that *in the mouths of philosophers* the

---

10 It is in this respect that we recommend highly the work of Charles Travis (2008); see particularly chapter 2, 'Annals of Analysis'. Also see Putnam (2002), 'Travis on Meaning, Thought and the Ways the World Is'. Review of Charles Travis, *Unshadowed Thought*.

expression 'an external reality' can carry the same definite sense of what is being affirmed—or of what would be denied—as it does when the reality of God's love or the reality of the defendant's guilt is insisted upon (or contested).

Chapter 3

Seeing Things for Themselves:
Winch, Ethnography, Ethnomethodology
and Social Studies

The Enchantment of Theory

In previous chapters we have frequently referred in passing to points of convergence between aspects of what Winch has to say about social studies and what has been written by ethnomethodologists. In this chapter we seek to conduct a more extended examination of these points of convergence, without underplaying divergences. In pursuing this task we shall also give some attention to other classic and prominent ethnographers, such as Erving Goffman. Our central claim will be that the social studies are, even in the work of the great ethnographers and some ethnomethodologists, too entranced by theory. For sure, ethnomethodology is often closest to being the sort of enquiry into social life which is least exposed to Winch's criticisms. For, while much social studies is resolutely theoretical, operating seemingly according to the principle that every perceived problem of social explanation requires a theory in order to explain away the perceived problem, ethnomethodology proceeds in such a way as to question whether the perceived (perceived by professional sociologists not their fellow members of the society) problems are indeed problems at all.

Resisting Theory's Spell

In the contemporary intellectual culture of the social studies, one of the most difficult challenges is to see things for themselves, to accept the validity and priority that attach to Wittgenstein's injunction 'Don't think – look!' and/or to phenomenology's 'Back to the things themselves!' In a theory-infatuated age that supports many academic factories it is near impossible to have it recognised that this is practically possible, let alone that it *needs to* be done.

The idea that perception is theory laden[1] is now very deeply entrenched and underpins an enormous range of otherwise very diverse points of view—it is thus

---

1   But doesn't Wittgenstein himself believe in the theory-ladenness of perception? Isn't that what his famous writings on aspect-perception, e.g. in section xi of Part II of the *Investigations*, are about? No. For a proper understanding of Wittgenstein on aspect-perception, see Guetti (1993) 'Idling Rules', and (especially) Avner Baz's (2000) marvellous work critiquing Stephen Mulhall and others on Wittgenstein on seeing aspects. See also Baker (2004), chapters 1 and 13. Kuhn at his best is compatible with Wittgenstein's non-theoreticistic

supposed that it is impossible to even recognise anything save through some theory, therefore even those who unregenerately insist that they have no theory nonetheless *must* have one—they cannot avoid presupposing a theory, regardless of what they say. The idea that there could be resistance to theory thus becomes a nonsense, and if one denies having a theory that can only mean that one is deluding oneself, and one's actual theory is implicit or tacit.[2]

Care is required in what one takes 'resistance to theory' to be. It does not arise from any generalised distaste for theory or science either—in natural science theories are both prominent and successful, even invaluable and unavoidable; however, the fact that they are does not validate the idea that they must be so in 'social science' too, for that is to presuppose that the problems in understanding our human neighbours are akin to those of understanding the remotest parts of the universe, the domain of microparticles or the chemical workings of genetic mechanisms. Winch's (and ours) is not resistance to all attempts to put together theories, even in the social studies. It reflects rather a resistance to a prejudice, a prejudice toward theory or what Wittgenstein called 'a craving for generality'. Whether a theory is needed, whether it can play a useful part, and what it explains are not matters to be decided programmatically, certainly not to be answered in the affirmative as a basis for *setting up* a new discipline or approach on the assumption that the absence of theory is *prima facie* evidence of the need for one. All serious questions meaningfully arise only in specific contexts, and in relation to particular puzzlements; recognising this fact, there is absolutely no point in being against theory in a general way, but neither is there any in being 'for' theory in an equally general and *a priori* way.

It is the rather ubiquitous inclination to be 'for' theory in a general way that provokes Winch's 'resistance to theory', where the latter does not seek to exterminate all theorising but, rather, to break the spell that the idea that to have a theory is to have understanding, to mitigate the craving for generality. What is being advocated here is not a scepticism about theory but cautiousness, not merely about claims that theory is needed, but also about accepting that what is on offer as theory does play the role that it is advertised as doing. Breaking the spell of theory requires showing that there are other forms of understanding than the theoretical—unless one begins to redefine 'theory' in a bloated[3] fashion: i.e. so freely as to encompass all forms of understanding, whatever these are (but then there would no longer be disagreement, except about terminology, and thus about what important differences such redefinition might obscure). A cautious resistance to theory bids only to show that there are other forms of understanding than through a theory, and that where these other forms are in operation there is no need for theory, since the kind of understanding they give is different from the kind that theory can provide.

It is not then generality that is the issue, but a certain attitude toward it—such that the understanding's satisfaction comes only from construction of a theory about

---

'account' of aspect-perception—that is how Sharrock and Read recommend interpreting Kuhn in their (2002).

2   Such alleged implicit theories are often referred to as 'tacit'. See Nigel Pleasants (1999, chapter 4) for an excellent deflation of the appeal to tacit knowledge.

3   For further explication of this notion of 'bloat', see Read (2000), and also his (2002).

that which one seeks to understand. One thing about the craving for generality is that in cases where theory is appropriate its returns do not come from merely accumulating thoughts that can be cast in the form of theories, but rather from the resolution of opaque puzzles. The craving for generality as such rarely issues in genuine explanatory theories at all—the main satisfaction seems to come from the righteousness of the conviction that, whatever the matter, there must be a theory that subsumes it—it is enough, that is, to make an *a priori* case that any phenomenon-in-question is amenable to theory. Indeed, Jurgen Habermas (1984 and 1987) for instance often proceeds seemingly on the assumption that any phenomenon-in-question *needs* a theory.[4] This is plain enough in the social studies, and in the debate that Winch initially continued, and which goes on still: is 'general theory' what is needed in the social studies?

The hold of the idea of theory encourages the high level of concern in the social studies (and, no doubt, across the social-studies-infected-humanities also) with *the form* of explanation. If there is only one proper form of understanding, then what form is that? What decides that something is an explanation is that it *has the form*. Deciding on the form, then, decides how things are *in general* to be explained, and it is this kind of generality that attaches to sociological schemes such as those of Giddens, Habermas, Bourdieu and other luminaries of Grand Social Theory; their sketches of social life are cast in the form that they have elected as *the* form of explanation. Naturally, in direct consequence, the disputes amongst them are over whether their own scheme gives the best form in which any phenomenon is to be explained. What, therefore, look like disputes over how *this* phenomenon is best explained will be revealed, on inspection, to be spats over how *any* phenomenon is rightly to be explained.

Despite the seeming self-evidence of these academic imperatives, Wittgensteinians and ethnomethodologists make the effort to break their hold over the life of thought, and, indeed, aim even to put them into full scale retreat, so pervasive and influential have they become—even though they seem so widely, deeply and unquestionably entrenched. The difficulty of the task cannot be under-estimated, since it involves breaking the spell that a self-reinforcing circle of reasoning can powerfully hold— it is *obvious* that theory is the thing, that thought and theorising are everywhere synonymous, and that there *just can't* be a plausible alternative to this (this is what we mean by 'prejudice'). Claims to be 'without theory' then can just be discounted in advance, without need to explore claims to an alternative, certainly without need to examine them with care and in depth, for, as is plain, they cannot turn out to be true.

Scaling these battlements is perhaps near impossible—though one may hope that the modern academy may before too long be recognised as by now having become in this respect the equivalent of the Catholic Church in the sixteenth century—but there is nonetheless a need to put the alternative point of view on the record and keep

---

4   Indeed, Habermas is not alone. Contemporary philosophy of social science is dominated by those who take Habermas's attitude to such matters. Anthony Giddens would be one prominent example, Bourdieu another.

it there.[5] It *is* possible to think differently than the orthodoxy imagines, but to do this calls for changes that, like turtles, go all the way down.

Wittgensteinians and ethnomethodologists have taken on this seemingly-futile task, in parallel much more than in common cause, though there have been attempts to bring them into closer alignment. This chapter will look at some of the features that make them seem rewardingly similar, but will also highlight the ways in which they are significantly—and at moments perhaps irreconcilably—different. The understanding of ethnomethodology that brings it closest to Winch's sociology is not one that would necessarily recommend itself to many ethnomethodologists, but that is precisely because of the above mentioned difference in understanding that keep them at arm's length.

If perception is theory laden, then so too must be description, which defuses the possibility of any alternative to the all consuming pre-eminence of theory being persuasively established by our advising of a relocation of the issues involved by placing description at the centre. If description is of necessity theory derived, then it cannot be meaningfully proposed that a concern *for* description could possibly displace the obsession with and obsessive production of theory. This, though, only reflects the circular character of the reasoning here—if we have *decided* that all description is of necessity theory-laden, then there is no further argument. It makes no sense to suggest that the issue of describing is a separate one from that of theorising, that discussing description could differ from, let alone replace, considerations of theory (save to the extent to which the salience of theory would be explicitly recognised). Such a disadvantage is ours. It has also always been such for ethnomethodologists and those who follow Winch.

Ethnomethodology's Program

Developed principally by Harold Garfinkel,[6] ethnomethodology was much influenced by the phenomenological tradition, an influence exercised on Garfinkel especially through the work of Aaron Gurwitsch, Alfred Schutz and Maurice Merleau-Ponty. Following Schutz's reconstruction of the philosophical premises of Max Weber's conception of social action, ethnomethodology continues in the 'social action' tradition. A revaluation of the idea of sociology as the study of social action, when applied in the theoretical and methodological doctrines of modern sociology, leads to the conclusion that the character of actual, real world, practical action will invariably escape the theoretical construals and methodological applications of those doctrines, that the organisation of everyday social life is *presupposed* in the practice of professional sociological inquiry, rather than portrayed by it. Such presupposition results in a systematic underrating of the extent to which the supposed problems of professional sociology are already solved in society and are resolved in

---

5   As C. Wright Mills held, in the darkness of certain times the best one can realistically hope to do is to keep hope alive for the future.

6   Garfinkel's *Studies in Ethnomethodology* is rightly, in our view, considered a classic; though it is still too little-read, suffering a similar fate to that we are essaying herein to have been suffered by Winch's writings.

and through social practice.[7] For example, because of its generalising ambitions, professional sociology aspires toward the production of a systematic vocabulary for the description of social action, failing to incorporate the fact that standards of 'adequate description' for practical affairs are provided and deployed in the everyday practices of society. Ethnomethodology therefore emphasises the extent to which social action—*competent* practical action—involves 'mastery of natural language'. Professional sociology too relies on such mastery, which is why social order is presupposed in its professional practices, rather than reflectively considered by them. Competent participation in social life irreducibly requires the capacity to express, to describe and report, what others are actually doing as well as what oneself is up to. Such competence must not be thought of as a generalised one, for what are the appropriate, recognisable things to be doing on any occasion depends upon the social setting of one's activities, of the practices that one is involved in, meaning that the requirements for the correct description of actions are connected to the socially organised occasions on which those doings take place. Ethnomethodology's studies are very prominently exercises in giving perspicuous display to the way in which 'language use' and 'social organisation' are interwoven on occasions of 'social action', thus demonstrating that attempts to develop generalised portrayals of social organisation and practices will unavoidably run up against the fact that, in order to say, appositely, what people are doing, a professional sociologist will require not only a knowledge of the official vocabulary and procedures constitutive of sociological theories and methods, but, invariably, a 'vernacular' familiarity with the practice and occasions about which their official sociology purportedly speaks.

As can be seen from this brief sketch, there are strong parallels with Winch's insistence that professional sociological researchers do not stand in the relation of external scientific witness to those that they purportedly 'observe', but are, rather more like apprentices and collaborators, appropriating their understandings from the members of the society at least as much, if not much more so, than from their formal sociological doctrines and procedures. The unreflective treatment of language-in-context, of language in its practical domains, is diagnosed, by both Winch and ethnomethodology, as causing considerable obscurity and confusion about the relationship between professional sociological discourse and 'vernacular' ways of speaking. In both cases, some of the cure is to be sought through perspicuous examples of the way in which the actual practices of language use in context are incongruous with the preconceptions that theorists would impose upon them.

Identity of Action

Colin Campbell (1996) is probably right to argue that identifying the subject matter of sociology as 'social action' is the recent and current orthodoxy, though in doing so he risks overstating the unity and coherence amongst 'social action' approaches. For many of those who adopt 'this' approach, the central issue remains that of explanation:

---

7   See Linblom and Cohen (1979) for an account of the way such problems feature in the policy sciences.

either (a) how are we to explain social action (for example, is it determined by structures or by subjectivity?) and/or (b) how are we to explain the part social action plays in generating social structures (e.g. do actions generate structures or do they stand in a relation of duality with structures)? So while the disciplinary orthodoxy is, at least nominally, as Campbell describes it, among those that claim to work within this orthodoxy there are still many who have yet to learn the true significance of the shift to social action. For it is not enough to merely talk of *social action*, as Giddens and Habermas do in their social theories. One has to have genuinely learned what the shift amounts to. Winch and Garfinkel's attempt to take the lesson that talk about 'social action' puts the issue of *the identification of social actions* (description) in prime position remains very much a minority and marginalised view.[8]

The simple point about 'social actions' is that the relevant criteria of identity belong to the social settings in which those actions occur, and are not contrived by or taken from the theories of social science (except in a secondary and derivative case). An action is such, as we have already stated in this book, *only* under a description. And this should not be confused with the thought that there are two things, action on the one hand and description on the other. Clearly, an action and a description of an action are two analytically distinct things such that the action identified is the action described, but this is, in the present context, an irrelevance—the point is that a description of an action identifies that action as what it is. It only does so—only successfully, correctly, identifies that action—if the action is as described. The action *is* the action described, otherwise it is misdescribed, and it is in *this* sense that action and description are internally related: in this sense to see the action, to identify it, is to see it under a description: action and description are as one (though this is of course not to hold that the "*act of* describing the action" and the "action described" are the same). The correct ways of speaking of action derive from the practices in which the actor is engaged, the criteria for correct description being those that are applied by *competent* participants in the practice—which is one reason why ethnomethodology regards membership as a matter of competences, and its own exercise as a depiction of competences. If one is blind to the description of the action as would be understood by the competent actor—what the action is, given the social setting, given the actor's purpose—then one has simply failed to establish what they are doing. And unless one has done that, established what they are doing, then one is in no position to explain why they are doing what they are doing—where the other

---

8   Authors such as Habermas and Bhaskar domesticate and thus marginalise Winch by depicting him as a hermeneutic stage—a mid twentieth century knee-jerk response to positivism—in the philosophy of social science, to be transcended by their own unifying critical social theories (again see Pleasants op cit.). Similarly, text books on sociology might have a chapter devoted to ethnomethodology (sometimes lumped together with the Chicago school, Symbolic Interactionism, Goffman et al.) which depicts it as just one of the many methodologies on offer to the student in the social studies: 'try this one' might be the implicit message. Here 'methodologies' are lined-up like different brands of shampoo on the supermarket shelves. While this one is good for combating alopecia it doesn't give your hair the all-day shine and body-lift of the other brand. Ethnomethodology then is, if given credit at all, seen as responding to one or two concerns while being weak its ability to acknowledge and respond to others.

horn of the dilemma for social theory is that, understanding *what* people are doing obviates the need for a *why* question, or put another way, means that the description of their action answers any *bona fide* why question; those *bona fide* 'why' questions are not the theorist's questions but those of e.g. beginners, learners, and strangers.

People—actors/members—don't merely make bodily movements in some extensionally-described type way which it is then down to sociologists (or psychologists) to render evaluative or intensional through some theoretical representation. People do things; very specific, variegated things. To ignore what it is they are doing, to simply set that aside in the name of one's theory, is to refrain from observing what they are doing. It is, in Harold Garfinkel's illustrative phrase, to tear down the walls to gain a better view of what is keeping the roof up.

Now, it is true that an action gives rise to a number of possible descriptive renderings and it is frustration at this point which sometimes leads to confusion. For example, compare Hillel Steiner's (1994) discussion of his going to see the auditorium performance of *Richard III*, which can be given various renderings. Steiner claims that there are numerous competing intensional descriptions of an act-token; he writes:

> "An act-token is fully identified, then, by an *extensional* description of the action in question: a description indicating the physical components of that action". There cannot be more than one act-token (of a particular act-type) answering to the same extensional description, i.e. having the same set of physical components. Purely *intensional* descriptions of actions, by contrast, do cover more than one act-token. Such descriptions are couched in terms of the purpose or meaning attached by the actor (or others) to what he does: my attending *Richard III*, my running for a bus, my throwing a ball and so on. It's true of each of these descriptions that there are many events that would answer to it (Steiner 1994, 36).

This passage is an exemplar of a particular, rather common, confusion; it is a confusion that we dubbed, in our *Introduction*, the fallacy of extensional primacy. For Steiner, the only description which correctly picks-out the act-token in question—picks out the event—is the extensional description: a description which brackets-out—sets aside—(on Steiner's own admission) the purpose and meaning of the action, one that merely describes the actor's behaviour in terms of the physical components of the action. All other descriptions are intensional renderings and thus glosses on the action. But think about the opening sentence: "An act-token is fully identified, then, by an *extensional* description of the action in question: a description indicating the physical components of that action". First, how is an action "fully identified" if that 'identification' involves leaving out that which makes it an *action* as opposed to mere movement or behaviour? Extensional renderings of actions are not, we submit, descriptions of *actions*. Or, put another way, so we are not taken to be simply policing the meaning of the word "action", if we accede to Steiner's claim that an "act-token is fully identified, then, by an *extensional* description of the action in question" the words "action" and "movement" become synonymous, thus leaving us with a diminution in the resources our language at present affords us, so that we can distinguish between actions people undertake and the movement of bodies. An act-token (to use Steiner's language) extensionally described does not actually identify the action that is supposedly being described but merely reports a physical state of affairs or process (we consider it misleading to even call it an 'event', as does Steiner).

The motivation for Steiner's position seems to be that a plurality of *possible* descriptions leads to each description being imprecise and thus open to contestation; that is, he sees 'numerous possible intensional descriptions' as equal to 'numerous competing candidate descriptions'. But it does not follow that different descriptions of an action are of necessity *competing* descriptions, as the whole idea of 'action under a description' that we have appealed to before is intended to explain. Equally, Steiner's account infringes the distinction between grasping a rule/seeing the action on the one hand and interpreting a rule/interpreting the action on the other that we discussed in chapter one. We suggest that Steiner is led to his position by assuming that all (intensional) descriptions are *interpretations* of pre-interpreted (extensionally-characterised) behaviour, as if the meaning of a piece of behaviour is projected onto that behaviour by observers: social scientists and psychologists (etc.); but such an understanding must presumably relegate the actors themselves to the status of observers of their own behaviour! What we have therefore, is the manifestation of a latent dualism in Steiner's thinking.

So, we wrote above, "Now, it is true that an action gives rise to a number of possible descriptive renderings and it is frustration at this point which sometimes leads to confusion". What we take the word "action" (and thus why some descriptions would be *renderings*) to denote in that sentence is evidently different to what philosophers (and social scientists) such as Steiner take it to denote. Steiner takes 'action' at bedrock to be extensionally-described movement: described in terms of physical components, the actor and spatial and temporal location, only. While we, following Winch (and Frank Ebersole,[9] too), take action to be bedrock, and thus, at bedrock to be meaningful action: on that (our) view, moving one's arm is an action, one's arm moving is a piece of behaviour. On Steiner's account then, any non-extensional description is a rendering. On our account only theoretical or interpretivist descriptions are best-termed as 'renderings', and we include Steiner's extensional descriptions in this category of rendering-descriptions. On our argument, there is a description which *identifies* the act, which is not a rendering, which is not an interpretation, and this is an intensional description. Steiner makes an oft-made mistake; it is a mistake which has its roots in scientism. The mistake is to assume the priority of extensional description, to assume that only this form of description is not an interpretation, to assume this is what actions are at bedrock. This is prejudice. This is to commit the fallacy of extensional primacy. Extensional descriptions are interpretations (just as much as Freudian explanation of an action in terms of the unconscious desires of the actor is an interpretation), to the extent that they are not identifications of the action but renderings of the action; a rendering of it exclusively into physical movement extended in space and time—and, of course, the prioritising of the extensional in this way is entirely notional, and no 'social scientist' is in any position to provide rigorously extensional descriptions of actions.

---

9   See Ebersole's (2001) (excellent) 'Where the Action is', chapter 15 in his *Things We Know: Fifteen Essays in the Problem of Knowledge*; also chapter 6, 'The Analysis of Human Actions', in his (2002), *Language and Perception: Essays in the Philosophy of Language.*

To repeat, 'at bedrock' the action is a meaningful action and its description-which-is-not-a-rendering is the description which correctly identifies the action in terms of the social situation and the purposes of the actor.

Steiner might object that we are being unfair to him; he is not in the business of social explanation; he is not a sociologist but a political philosopher. However, the mythological mistake he has made is crucial. Steiner's reason for translating actions into extensional language is to resolve normative disputes over matters of distributive justice. In rendering the action as he does through describing nothing but the movement of the physical components he *fails* to describe *the action*. Thus, in employing such a tactic in the attempt to arrive at conclusions as to whether a given actor is free or un-free to undertake a particular action Steiner unwittingly cuts himself adrift from the very thing he is seeking to adjudicate on: the freedom or un-freedom of an actor to carry out a particular action; for he has not uniquely identified the action but only rendered it.[10]

Winch and Garfinkel: Seeing an Action

The sociologist, qua sociologist of 'social action' is in no position to make an identification of any putative *explanandum* since the proper criteria for identifying the 'doing to be explained' do not belong to nor derive from theoretical schemes, sociological or other, but from the social settings within which the activities occur. This is not to say that sociologists *can't* make correct identifications of (some) social actions, but that their capacity to do this does not originate in their sociological training or distinctively professional expertise, but in their mastery of one or more of society's practices. It may come either from the diffuse and general familiarity that sociologists (as themselves members in the society they typically talk about) have with a range of everyday practices or it may derive from the 'anthropological' opportunities their professional role has provided to familiarise themselves with domains of expert technical practice they would not otherwise have come across in their own everyday experience (though these domains are those of *someone else's* everyday practice, and the sociologist researching them proceeds rather more like tourists than like any kind of natural science investigator). The identification of social actions is not an operation conducted by an observer using criteria independent of the occurrences being identified, but is a form of participation in the social setting to which the activity-in-question and the identification of it belong—at the very least, the sociologist is borrowing the criteria of the setting *if the identification of the action is indeed to successfully identify the occurrence-in-question as the action-it-performs.*

Again, there is no duality of action and description, for an action is the action it is correctly identified as being. To understand what an individual is doing is, by the same token, to understand a great deal about how the social setting featuring the doing actually works. It is to understand what is going on in and through the

---

10 How this plays out in Steiner's theory is that he is led to deny that threats are (in any way) restrictions on freedom. This will be seen to be pertinent to the arguments of the following chapter on conservatism.

application of mastery, of being personally competent to apply what we are calling, for convenience, 'the criteria of identity'. One can say on one's own behalf what someone is doing because one can satisfy certain socially required conditions for making such decisions. These may include occupying certain entitling social positions, which explains why many of professional sociology's identifications are, of necessity, second-hand. For a simple, but resonant, example, the determination of cause of death as officially suicidal is within the power of an appointed officer, and sociologists, not being coroners, cannot themselves make competent counts of suicide rates but must, rather, *if they are to be able to talk about suicides at all*, be dependent upon the determinations that coroners make for the location of instances of this activity. Further, as Harvey Sacks pointed out, the 'correctness' of an identification here is not a matter of evidentially satisfied criteria alone—perhaps even at all— ... identification is a normative matter, and 'correct' identifications are ones which are 'proper' or 'appropriate'. Bare correctness of an identification does not ensure its relevance: any person can be correctly identified in an open ended variety of ways in this 'bare' sense, but whether they are *correctly* (in a real world, practice sense) identified is sensitive to many features of the practice within which the activity is situated and the role that the identification plays there.

The criteria of adequate identification are not those of sufficiency to get a sociological discussion going, but those which apply within a social setting, and, as the preceding brief deliberation has indicated, if one gets to the point of being able to make genuinely adequate designations of actions then one already knows a great deal about how the social setting, within which the action is a point of reference, works.[11] Such knowledge is practical, built into the mastery of whatever range of practices is required to make competent designations, and it is, as such, amenable to being taken for granted to the extent that it disappears from view.

This is why Winch and Garfinkel direct our attention to, respectively, reflection and explication rather than to 'empirical research' in the canonical forms of sociology. Garfinkel, it is true, is intensely interested in studies in a way that Winch was not, but it should be noted that Garfinkel does not attempt to (artificially) dignify these efforts by making them out as methodology, but emphasises their commonplace status as matters of taking a look at activities, hanging around with practitioners, training up

---

11 There is an analogy here with the claim that Sharrock and Read (2002) made regarding the role of the philosopher or historian of science, in their *Kuhn*: throughout that book, and especially at its close, they argued that science is *difficult*, and that scientists' work cannot be gainsaid by the would-be normative intervention of philosophers etc. In order to actually make a difference to the science, *one has to be in-principle-competent in the given scientific speciality in question*. Likewise: in order to actually make a difference to the area of society (e.g. the level of suicide therein) that one is investigating, *one has to be competent in the art of (e.g.) being a coroner*. It is not enough to be a good philosopher, sociologist or historian. One cannot intervene in the object of one's study (be that, the work of some community of scientists, or the work of some community of social practitioners, and *ethnomethodologists*), except by virtue of one's mastery of *their* practice. A given scientific discipline or speciality is advanced by competent and intelligently innovative science; likewise, knowledge of the level of suicide in one's society is advanced by competent and intelligently innovative work by coroners etc. Not by sociological study that fails seriously to involve and refer to that work.

in the activity, and treats them as a means of accessing what, for any experienced participant, will be apparent and transparent matters.

Both are concerned with what is 'built into' the capacity to make identifications ('identifications' *means* 'successful identifications') of activities in which people are engaged, pointing towards what is involved in operating as a full-fledged participant in a practice. The concern leads in different directions—Winch's reflections focus upon what is 'built into' the diverse forms of language that we use in our affairs, the need carefully to differentiate one from the other, and to avoid being led into philosophical confusions by mistaking one form for another on the basis of superficial similarities—taking a linguistic stipulation for an empirical proposition, for example. For Garfinkel 'explication' is more a matter of giving attention to the extensive array of organisational and situational considerations that enable participants competently to 'speak definitely' of the passing scene of social affairs to which they are witness, to observe and report 'what is going on' before their eyes, to identify actions in the ways that they do. The repertoire of practical understandings (often, but sometimes confusingly, called 'common sense understandings') that is ubiquitously relied upon is illustrated by the activities that are reviewed, a tangible reminder that for *both* those being studied and those conducting the study, what Winch calls 'the intelligibility' of social life derives from the understandings indigenous to the social setting in question.

In other words, neither Winch's nor Garfinkel's investigations face the question that troubles so much of sociology: what empirical measures are adequate to establish the generality of connections between one aspect of social life and another? The connections that they are concerned with are already present in the very materials themselves, they are ones that are formed in and through social activities, and the effort is in tracing how intelligible connections between one activity and another are mediated by the ways of—what are, for those engaged in them—familiar practices. In many respects, the generality of practice is antecedent to the identification of occurrent instances, for the performance of actions is as an application of a social form (what is said is said-with-words-from-the-language, an advancing of a pawn one space is a-move-in-the-game-of-chess not barely 'a game of chess'), and its intelligibility involves seeing that the performer is e.g. acting as anyone might in this context, acting-according-to-a-rule, is applying what is for all players a mandatory policy, is performing the usual courtesies etc., *ad. inf.*

There is a comparable understanding between both Winch and Garfinkel that sociological thought is very much a second stor(e)y job, and that the exercise in which it is engaged—*as professional sociology*—is not description, but *redescription* (or representation rather than presentation).[12] Winch and Garfinkel concur that competence in social affairs involves the capacity to describe them, to say in ways intelligible/acceptable to fellow competents, what is being done and is going on as an *otherwise* unremarkable part of participation in those affairs. Professional

---

12 There is a sense in which this is overt and explicit in authors such as Habermas. Sociology's job is to *re*-present in such a way as to be liberationist or critical of current social practices, which prevent the realisation of the Enlightenment project. But as we've noted, unless one identifies the action (in its own terms) first one fails in any attempt at criticism.

sociologists are utterly dependent upon the availability of those forms of descriptions if they are to have anything whatsoever to talk about. Garfinkel is at pains to highlight the numerous practical circumstances which may need to be attended to on any occasion in which someone is to say definitely what they or someone else is doing, and the whole of conversation analysis may equally be seen to detailing the circumstances which require a very specific form of words as a proper contribution to the use of language in ordinary conversation. What parties in a practice are doing is intimately, intricately and inextricably interwoven with what they can be said to be doing, can be described, formulated or reported, as doing amongst themselves (account-able in Garfinkel's terms). Thus, what participants in a practice according to the ways of the practice can be correctly described as doing is the (intended) object of the professional sociologist's empirical reference (though due to inattention to the nature of identifying criteria they may, in actual cases, miss those references, but this is perhaps due to the fact that sociologists are very rarely interested in more than— perhaps even as much as—the roughest and readiest identification of anyone's actual actions).

On Sociological Redescription...

Despite doctrines premised upon the assumption that the professional sociologist's understandings are at odds with those of the 'ordinary members of the society' there is not really much disagreement *in sociology's actual practice* with the ways in which activities are indigenously identified. Professional sociology does not provide an extensive re-classification of things that people are doing. That is, they have no substitutes for commonplace descriptions such as 'standing six places from the front of the bus queue' or 'scoring an equaliser in injury time'. It is really the theme of the foregoing remarks that the availability of such actions, so described, is the taken-for-granted starting point for the professional sociologist's redescriptions, and those taken-for-granted identifications are *absorbed* into the redescriptions that are given as (professional) sociological descriptions. Professional sociologists do not *in actual practice* want to change or contest these everyday descriptions, but want to argue, instead, about the understandings that attach to these actions when they are considered from the point of view of their illocutionary or perlocutionary effects, or from the point of view of their placement in some postulated social system or some protracted span of historical time, or, again, from the point of view of an analogy with some other activity. Space allows little elaboration or illustration, so brief mention of that one man industry of redescription, Erving Goffman, will serve.

...the Case of Erving Goffman

Goffman's work was exceptional in the *number* of schemes for redescription that he sought to create, and may thus remind us that much of the sociology profession's motivation is to provide a general framework for redescription—many important sociologists labour lifelong on a single such scheme, but not Goffman. Goffman's work often begins with the most ordinary of occurrences—his best known work

(*Presentation of Self in Everyday Life*) literally begins with someone showing off on a beach (an illustration taken from a novel). Goffman does not wish to question that the person is indeed playing the show-off but wants to develop a general scheme based on describing this activity in terms of one of its effects (that of 'projecting a self') i.e. showing off on a beach might impress some people that you are a pretty striking individual or others that you are an exhibitionist pratt. All kinds of things, wearing white coats and stethoscopes in hospitals, sealing the restaurant kitchen off from customer view etc., will subsequently be redescribed in terms of this *scheme,* which is itself built on an analogy with the theatre, the idea of the stage and backstage.

The status and character of these things as occurrences on a beach or in the preparation and service of food is taken for granted and remains intact throughout as Goffman highlights formal similarities between *aspects* of activities with very different purposes, constituent concerns and participants. In another book, Goffman (1963) contrives a scheme to redescribe social relations in terms of the conventions found in etiquette books. These conventions are to be used to illustrate how the observance ensures the integration of the face-to-face encounter, the effects they have in allowing people to share a common focus of attention, to contain their embarrassment or inclination to embarrass others by laughing inappropriately. Again, and finally, though not exhausting Goffman's variety and invention, in yet another study (Goffman 1969) he adopted espionage as an analogy for social relations, treating these as a matter of 'the control of information', the concealment and discernment of which is—supposedly at least—a speciality of espionage agencies. In each case, the commonplace identity of all sorts of actions identified in quite ordinary terms provide Goffman's illustrative materials, though that level of identity is only superficially considered, and features noted only relative to their match with Goffman's reclassification of them in one or other of his schemes (which are, in fact as much dictionaries as anything else, with a very high definitional content). The things that, according to Goffman, people are doing are not rivals to the things they think they are doing. That is, it is not as though, when they think they are sharing a tasteful joke, they are, instead, achieving the integration of the face-to-face encounter. It is, rather, that *when* they are sharing a tasteful joke, they are, *by doing this* (unwittingly) effecting the integration of the face-to-face encounter.

Goffman's proprietory vocabulary does not describe anyone's actions *as such*— indeed, one cannot 'integrate the face-to-face encounter' as a direct action of one's own, but can only do such a thing by doing something else (telling a joke, concealing amusement, holding back embarrassing information etc.) The often considerable effect that Goffman achieves is not produced by his finding any new facts on his own behalf, for that whole effect depends upon making his readers feel that they are seeing things that they are entirely familiar with in a fresh light, inspecting them from an unusual angle, though people who feel that way often suppose that what Goffman has shown is that we are all very manipulative in all our dealings with each other, perhaps literalising Goffman's analogical use of confidence tricks as a way of generating formal resemblances.

Despite his peculiar and highly distinctive status, Goffman is not being singled out as singular, nor is his work being simply dismissed. It is not by producing schemes for the redescription of action that he achieves distinctiveness, but in the ingenuity of his schemes and his fertility with them. All this is invoked to make the point that Goffman's schemes, like theirs, are not rival to commonplace descriptions, but rework them in the context of a purportedly uniform scheme which pick out things about those actions, where their identity as the (everyday practical) actions that they are can be taken for granted, and to allow passing suggestion of the theme that there are always opportunities for considering the relation, and usually the difference, between what professional sociologists seem to be doing and what, in practice, their achievements amount to.

An exercise such as Goffman's does not enable us to understand an activity which really puzzles us, but seeks to relate those actions which do not (from the point of view of their intelligibility) puzzle us to the themes and preoccupations of his professional colleagues. Goffman is often associated with those who are suspicious of positivism, such as many symbolic interactionists, but Goffman's own broader views are often in deep sympathy with atomistic and mechanistic conceptions of understanding (hence the appeal of game theory and ecological biology to him.) Goffman saw himself as predominantly engaged in setting out a specialised area of analysis—the analysis of the face-to-face situation—which could occupy a place within a broader scientifically explanatory sociology.

Winch and Ethnomethodology: Some Differences

Whilst there might be broad agreement of the sort outlined between Winch and ethnomethodology, there are reasons for wondering whether the agreement can go much further, and whether, even, the extent of it can be fully recognised on either side. Ethnomethodologists are apt, like sociologists more generally, to think of philosophy as a non-empirical pursuit, and one which is to be disparaged as such (see Melinda Baccus's (1986) discussion of Winch; here it is clearly recognised that Winch has some relevance to ethnomethodology's concerns but where this is minimised as essentially programmatic and non-empirical). Clearly, Winch's whole campaign is to liquidate the idea that philosophy is an attempt at *a priori* knowledge of the world: that philosophy's problems are 'conceptual' in nature, and that they have no empirical content. Thus, it would be profoundly misguided to suppose that philosophy's problems can be taken over and answered by empirical investigations.

On What Ethnomethodology Should Not Be: Pollner's Scepticism

Melvin Pollner's (1987) *Mundane Reason* is often seen as affiliated with ethnomethodology, in a way which makes the latter seem able to issue a frontal challenge to our most fundamental assumptions, such as, for example, that we live in one and the same world. To summarise Pollner's argument rather baldly, it is addressed to the idea of the 'natural attitude', taken from the phenomenological tradition, that provides us with basic expectations such as that, for example, other people—from a different physical and temporal history, a different social background experience, perhaps—experience phenomena that basically correspond to the ones that one experiences. Pollner takes the idea that the natural attitude features certain 'theses', such as the 'thesis' that we inhabit a world known in common rather literally, i.e. as a proposition expressing an hypothesis (that the world is the same for you as it is for me).

As Pollner understands 'the natural attitude' it is the conviction that this hypothesis is true, that the *world* is the same for you as it is for me. An hypothesis is bivalent, capable of being both true and false, and empirical in nature, meaning that its truth is a matter of evidence. The natural attitude conviction that the world is the same for you as it is for me seems to Pollner to be one that is not empirically justified, for it is held in face of the fact that there is counter-evidence. Evidence, that is, that not everyone's experience is congruent with everyone else's, as is the case with mentally ill people who seem certain of things that the rest of us may suppose 'defy common sense'. In more mundane cases, there are discrepancies between the experience of individuals in their everyday affairs, as traffic court hearings reveal divergences between the testimony of witnesses as to the speed at which a motor cycle was travelling. Pollner sees these cases as potential counter-evidence to the natural attitude, its failure to refute the natural attitude despite the manifest nature of such purportedly 'perceptual' disjunctions being due to the way in which 'the natural attitude' *explains away* such counter evidence (bringing us very much into 'Understanding a primitive society' territory here). Rather than accepting that the experience of the insane, or the respective experiences of disputing witnesses, show that there is no 'world known in common', the natural attitude explains this 'counter-evidence' in its own terms i.e. it keeps the assumption of a 'world known in common' intact, and decides that the experience of the 'dissidents' is invalid, that there is something wrong with their perceptual capacities. These dissident experiences are not treated as standing on an equal footing with those experiences which conform with the world (conventionally) known in common.

Thus, the courtroom disagreement between a police officer and a motorcyclist over the speed at which the latter's motorcycle was travelling *could* be treated as a product of equally *bona fide* experience, causing us to review our supposition that a motorcycle can only travel at one speed at any given moment in favour of the alternative, that it might be capable of producing two different experiences. Thus, for Pollner, the hypothesis of the natural attitude is justified in only a circular fashion, for it uses itself to deny potential counter-evidence any admission. Pollner's 'radical' proposal is to put everyone's experience on the same footing, to accept that both our own and 'the deluded' person's perceptions are genuine experiences. In other words, in *our* reality there may not be any superhuman powers, but in *someone else's* reality there are. One is on the way to 'multiple realities' and a good deal of *metaphysical—* not sociological—confusion, indiscriminately mixing together empirical materials and conceptual confusions.[13]

Pollner's difficulties reflect the fact that it is a mistake to treat the 'thesis' of a world known in common as an empirical hypothesis (as though our expectation that our fellow pedestrians will not walk directly into us were some sort of theoretical

---

13 Compare here, once again, the wording of the last paragraph of the *Investigations*, Part II.

desiderate), when the 'assumption of a world known in common' does not function in anyone's life in such a way. Pollner's evidential demonstrations do not show that the 'thesis' is an empirically unjustified and evidentially asymmetric proposition, but only that it is not an empirical proposition, supported or undermined by evidence—in reality Pollner unwittingly highlights its *normative* status, as a standard of correctness, not an empirical generality. Pollner's confusions perhaps originate in a mis-taking of the phenomenological idea of a 'description of my experience' which slips from the idea of this as a 'bracketed' exercise, one abstaining from judgements of veracity, to the idea of it as a description of my experience *tout court*, exempt from the qualifying restraints of **phenomenology's specialist purposes.** The description ('reporting' would probably be a much better word) of my experience does not, as we normally understand it, outside the province of phenomenology's restricted exercise, depend for its correctness upon the sincerity or veracity with which I report how it was with me, but upon the states of affairs one claims to have experienced. 'Reporting my experience' is not a matter of engaging in a Cartesian style scrutiny of my personal 'subjectivity', as opposed to reporting on 'objective' states of affairs, but is a matter of reporting on those states of affairs that I have encountered, undergone etc., and the effects that they have had on me or the significance that they have for me. The claim to have seen a motorbike going forty miles an hour in a thirty mile an hour zone is not a cautiously hedged claim about my 'subjective experience', it is a claim about what *the bike* was doing. This latter claim is not to be established by my testimony alone, for it is part of the work of the court hearing to establish whether my testimony is to be accepted as a report of what happened, rather than a report of how things seemed to me, what I thought I saw and so on. That experiences and perceptions must satisfy certain conditions to count as authentic is not a supernumerary addition but an integral part of our practical understanding of what an experience or perception is (e.g. we look for a more appropriate light under which to view a fabric so as to decide whether its colour is the one we want).

Pollner's arguments seem to entail a radical ontological claim, abandoning the 'natural attitude' assumption of a world known in common, in favour of multiple realities, but this does not really invite us to now accept something we might have thought physically impossible—that a bike should go at two speeds simultaneously. Rather, Pollner's proposals are unintelligible. The courtroom claims—the bike was doing 30mph, the bike was doing 60mph—are rival claims not because of the assumption of 'a world known in common' but because of the nature of the numbering and measurement systems on which he and the parties to the courtroom are all relying. The number system and our conventional methods of speed assign unique numerical values. That is how they work, their logic. In effect, then, the number system and the speed values it is used to compute operate contrastively—to say that a bike is doing 40mph is to exclude or deny that it is doing 60mph. To say that the bike is going both 40 and 60mph makes no sense, since it is saying that the bike is both going and not going 40mph. What is someone who says this saying? How is it other than a contradiction? One could perhaps try to rescue this by saying that Pollner's proposals would entail that there are two bikes, each going a determinate speed in their own realities, but if one is prepared to say things like that, why suppose—as Pollner presupposes throughout—that there is only one courtroom, only two witnesses etc.?

There is no need to suppose that Pollner provides any serious challenge to the fundamental assumptions (about reality) of our 'natural attitude' in a way which threatens to destabilise them, his challenges are, rather to the numerical and calculational systems in current use—to realise his proposal we could possibly change the idea that objects have a unique speed (indeed relativity theory is sometimes understood as doing just that), but this would also require that in respect of everyday affairs we make changes to the organisation of the number systems that we use in calculating speed, and this would involve all kinds of very complicated consequences, leaving us perhaps inclined to see what the further benefit of going to all the trouble that would be involved (altering the odometers in cars etc.) would yield any real benefit, even with respect to traffic courts. Given we accept that systems of calculation are contingent, we certainly can't claim—and wouldn't want to be seen dead doing so—that there is any metaphysical or physical necessity which rules out all possibility of developing number systems that would allow a bike to be rated as going at 40mph and 60mph simultaneously, but,

a. we cannot see that such a system would necessarily conflict with our present understandings, since in all likelihood the sense of the expression 'mph' would be changed (as happens when we accept, as loyal British subjects, that our beloved Queen has two birthdays! We do not suppose that she was born twice, unlike everyone else who has only one birthday); and

b. the proposal involves inviting us to set aside our ways of telling whether a report on e.g. a speeding vehicle is correct, and then tries to persuade us that we have no *real* way of telling whether one person's claim or another is the correct one. The argument is simply a circular one, and derives not from finding any specific failings in our usual ways of making and assessing claims (because the discussion itself relies to a considerable extent on those) but from the usual sceptic's tactic of asking us to put our practices into doubt even though there are no genuine grounds for doubt. As hinted above, Pollner is much closer to Evans-Pritchard than he is to Winch, another victim of confusedly engaging in 'misbegotten epistemology' and traditional scepticism on the assumption that he is framing an empirical inquiry.

Pollner's position is closer to Evans-Pritchard in that it treats notions of 'error', 'delusion' and the like as if they were secondary terms, ones which are applied *after* an experience's authentic nature has been formulated. If one witness in traffic court says that a motor-cycle was travelling at 30mph and another witness says it was travelling at 50mph why not accept that both reporters are honest recorders of their experience, and accept, then, that the bike was travelling at two speeds? The idea that each witness did see what they testified to overlooks the nature of 'see' as, in Ryle's terminology, an achievement verb, one which intends in such contexts, saw *correctly*. This highlights how Pollner's argument short circuits the function of the traffic court, for the issue is not the sincerity with which a witness delivers testimony, but the capacity of the testimony to contribute to a determination of the speed that the motor bike was travelling. In other words, the quality of the experience is a function of what determinately took place, and the latter is determined by other evidential input in addition to the testimony of the two witnesses into the courtroom's adversary procedure—the nature of the facts and the relevant experiences are determined together. The witness's testimony only establishes the speed of the bike if the witness is accepted as e.g. having indeed been able reliably to determine and honestly to report the speed of the bike—otherwise, the witness's experience is/was guesswork, misjudgement, delusion etc. There is no logical connection between the sincerity of the speaker and the correctness of their claim.

Rather than an empirically inspired new radicalism, Pollner's efforts are merely another application of traditional scepticism, an attempt to raise a doubt where there is no (ultimately) intelligible basis for doubt. There are, of course, plenty of doubts in the courtroom: e.g. whether a witness is honest, whether a witness could possibly be correct in what they claim, whether a witness is well enough equipped to understand what they are attempting to testify to etc. Deciding these matters is what the courtroom practices are for. Pollner, however, wants to ask whether courtroom proceedings (conducted on the basis of 'the natural attitude') are capable of getting *anything* correct. Pollner's views originate in an attempt to raise the standard of proof for courtroom proceedings, raise the standard to a level which such proceedings cannot attain. Of course they cannot, for this is the sceptic's art, to insinuate standards which are unattainable and use these to indicate the presence of (possible) doubt. Pollner treats 'the natural attitude' as an ensemble of hypotheses which, considered as such, cannot be empirically grounded, for they are presupposed in the determination of what is and what is not empirical evidence. Therefore the proceedings in courtrooms cannot be *truly* justified by evidence, for they too must be circular. As we say, the ostensible space for 'doubt' comes not from any issues in the courtroom but from the treatment of the courtroom as an example of a procedure based on the natural attitude which is, on Pollner's understanding, a circular operation. Pollner overlooks, of course, the extent to which courtroom proceedings are a (so to speak) grammar of action rather than an ensemble of empirical hypotheses (whereas they provide the standards for deciding what can—for legally admissible purposes—count as an empirical hypothesis and what could comprise evidence for or against it, providing in various and complicated ways, the scaffolding which *gives sense* to factual claims, the validity of testimony and the like. The witnesses' rival claims can only be rival claims because both presuppose the same system for the determination of speed, one in which only a single velocity can be assigned—its not an empirical (im)possibility that is in prospect here but rather an adjudication between two applications of the same measurement system.

In consequence, there are, perhaps, misapprehensions as to what is going on when ethnomethodologists 'look at the data' and what the purpose of such exercises might be, especially in those sectors where there is almost a militant empiricism about resort to data.

Of Later Garfinkel

On Winch's understanding, philosophy is only *a priori* to the extent that (the grammar of) our language plays a shaping role in what it is possible (intelligibly, informatively) to say, and it is *the language,* not philosophical doctrines—or sociological approaches, for that matter—which *facilitates*—in advance, so to speak—what it makes sense to say about empirical instances of social action. Inattention to this means that what is going on in the consultation of empirical instances is lost sight of (such that, for example, there seems a strong strand in Garfinkel's later thought (Garfinkel 2002) that often features the idea that our 'ordinary language' cannot capture the nature and nuances of the activities he is trying to describe i.e. we don't have a word for it (in English)—though this involves only the adoption of Greek and Latin terms, and these, too, surely qualify as part of natural language; as expressions with perfectly 'ordinary' uses amongst Greek speakers and indeed, as possible extensions of English. Talking about the examples as 'data' can help obscure the fact that the materials sampled are not the sole or even necessarily main materials for the exercise, where the prime 'materials' are rather one's own, commonplace, understandings (ones which are commonplace in one's own life, or that one has learned are commonplace in the lives of some others) whose application is invoked and focussed through the example. What is going on is the spelling out—explicating—of what is being brought to bear (through the medium of an enculturated understanding of the language, of how to conduct oneself intelligibly) through consideration of the instance.

There are at least two conflicting ways in which ethnomethodologists can think of their inquiries: as either a beginning or an ending. One can—and Garfinkel sometimes seems to—think of ethnomethodology as a first step in the direction of a genuine sociological science, one which differentiates itself from sociology-at-large (or Formal Analysis (FA), as Garfinkel nowadays terms it) in being the only branch of sociology that addresses itself directly to actual and observable occurrences in and of the social order. By contrast, FA is perceived as typically addressing observable social activities (a) in forms that have been processed and reconstructed by sociological methods and/or (b) are construed as a function of the preconceived interests that sociological theorising has in turning to the social world, i.e. sociologists *project* their procedural forms onto their data, rather than exploring the data for itself.

Thus, one might think of ethnomethodology as attempting the beginning of a reconstruction of sociology, where the current investigations open up new directions of inquiry which, if cultivated, will produce much more striking and powerful results.

One might. Garfinkel himself does not consistently indicate that this is the direction he forsees, being inclined to destabilise any seemingly settled understanding of his work, to repudiate some of his own prior stances, and the attachment other ethnomethodologists might show to them. Looked at that way, ethnomethodology has a subversive, rather than a constructive role, is ultimately subversive even of its own apparently constructive contributions.

Garfinkel talks of ethnomethodology as an 'alternate' sociology, but this too might be understood in different ways. The possibility being explored here is that the 'alternate' registers ethnomethodology's interconnection to the enterprise of Formal Analysis. Rather than having an independent platform from which to launch itself as an autonomous form of sociology, it may be better understood as existing in response to and reaction against Formal Analysis. As, that is, countering the theoretically and methodologically top heavy renderings of social affairs with displays of the way in which the observable doings making up the society's practical life elude representation by those renderings, with recovering what is otherwise readily recognisable and eminently well known to practitioners from beneath the overload of professional interpretation.

Another of Garfinkel's turns of phrase acquiring latter day popularity is that of 're-specification'. This term can also fit the idea of an umbilical affiliation of ethnomethodology to Formal Analysis. Re-specification is a matter of taking the topics and problems of sociology done in Formal Analysis, and turning them into topics of ethnomethodological inquiry. This was reflected in Garfinkel's 'studies of work' programme—take sociological topics and themes and ask, 'Who in society has the work of dealing with this problem as their daily work?', then go and study how those people, as part of that work, encounter and deal with these problems. Rather than, for example, worrying about sociology's problems of measurement, investigate, instead, people whose job it is (within the state, in organisations, in educational organisations, *wherever*) to measure social phenomena and understand what measurement is for them, and how they achieve it.

The idea of re-specification is that this can be done ubiquitously with Formal Analysis's themes and pre-occupations, and as such can be understood as an ending for the idea of 'a sociology' as the proprietary possession of a profession of investigators. The work available for such a sociology has been, so to speak, handed over to the members of the society, the themes and pre-occupations making up the putative work of such a profession, having their problematic character resolved in *socially organised indigenous practice* not by theoretical and methodological contrivance and fiat. The ethnomethodologist's own work is not itself that of proposing solutions to 'sociological problems' on his or her own behalf, of offering 'an ethnomethodological account' of 'locating lost property', 'accepting patients for treatment', 'joining a queue for service' or whatever else it might be. It is, instead, a matter of producing exhibitions of what it could be—in social life's practical affairs—that sociological theoretical and methodological discourses are talking about, to recover (from the supervision of theorised discourses) the everyday social world as a place recognisable to those who inhabit it.

Providing displays of this kind could function very much as reminders' and 'perspicuous presentations' in Wittgenstein's—and thus Winch's—sense, though clearly, in many cases, these do not serve as reminders of one's own personal practices specifically, but as a means of relaying the understandings that those involved in unfamiliar activities—mathematics, observatory astronomy, martial arts training, truck wheel repair, industrial print production, loan suitability assessment—employ to organise their activities. The function, in either case, can be an emancipatory one, enabling the breaking of an intellectual spell. The spell is that cast by the idea of theory-and-method as essential precursors to understanding, where the only alternative to any given theory has to be some other, and different, theory.

Ethnomethodology's studies illustrate the way that social affairs are *already* understood, prior to the appearance of professional sociologists on the scene, by those who possess a purely practical understanding of those affairs, and who resolve 'problems of social order' for and by themselves through the practical organisation of their affairs, i.e. by arranging their affairs in ways that are satisfactory according to the standards that come with the practice. Exhibitions of the ways of less familiar activities (less familiar, that is, to sociologists), with a strong emphasis upon their irreducible detail and specificity, is a forceful counter to the 'craving for generality' that comes with the aspiration to theory-and-method or which continues to infect disappointment with, alienation from, and reaction against such 'universalising' aspirations.

The exhibitions make vivid the numerous specific and localised demands which the circumstances of action make in every case, and the distinctive competences that are involved in adequately (in a practical sense) responding to them. The dense and diversified array of conditions involved in putting together intelligible social actions can be left out of, overlooked by, attempts to give theoretical portrayal of action-in-general, but they cannot be disregarded by those who must, in real time, under real circumstances, carry out 'the affairs of society' in the form of their everyday practical affairs.

Empirical investigations in Formal Analysis are designed to capture empirical cases in a way which will yield generalities that absorb the case into a whole genre of activities (e.g. Goffman's example of making confidence tricks, waiter service, hotel reception, medical encounters, moments of socialisation all examples of 'presentation of self'). In such a context, studies of cases are ends to means, rather than as, for ethnomethodology understood as here, ends in themselves. Understanding is thus effected through clarifying how specific activities are embedded in the social settings to which they belong, and the setting-specific practices which they enact. The connections which are made between one action and another, between actions and their social settings, between one setting and another are not to be understood as instantiating theoretical axioms, but as forged in and by those activities themselves.

Critical Social Theory and the Charge of the Reification of the Contingent

With an eye to the topic of our next and final chapter on Winch and the charge of conservatism, we wish here to briefly address charges, such as those levelled by Jurgen Habermas (1988), that views like those of Winch and the ethnomethodologists are dangerously conservative, in that they serve to reify the *status quo*, thereby intimating that the social order cannot be changed. Such a criticism is really an expression of Habermas' preoccupations and the way they shape his reading of other people's work and, apparently, blind him to all kinds of important aspects of their thought which don't fit within his own—somewhat restrictive—framework for social science—that social science should pursue the goal of completion of the Enlightenment project (as Habermas understands that project, in (post-)Kantian terms).

In their parallel efforts to bring gross and misguided philosophical and theoretical abstractions back down to earth, Winch and Garfinkel both put the contingency of existing practices front and centre—there are no (metaphysical) necessities involved in them—though one (more than) suspects that desire for metaphysical necessities lingers on in Habermas.[14] Such necessities as there are should be understood as functions of how our practices are contingently organised (even the necessities of logic and mathematics!) i.e. as stringent requirements of the practice, not the other way around. The 'status quo' is the ensemble of our current practices, but that ensemble has changed in order to arrive at its current state, is likely changing even now in respect of many aspects of any of our many practices, and will no doubt see further subsequent changes, involving the mutation of some of those practices and even the abandonment of others. But these are banalities, not dogmatics, banalities whose recognition fully obstruct the effort to read-off any implication of the immutability of 'the *status quo*'. Whether *Habermas'* political programme offers ways of transforming existing society in the way he aims for is simply immaterial to the issues that Winch and Wittgenstein address. Habermas wants to derive a political programme from a sociological theory, and, in that respect Winch and Garfinkel are a deadly threat to his project. Even there, it is only because they are—very much unlike Habermas—utterly unimpressed with the idea of 'a sociological theory', and regard acquisition of one as supernumerary to the creation of a political programme.

---

14 Exchanging Kantian talk of the 'transcendental' for post-Kantian (C.S. Peirce-inspired) talk of the allegedly post-metaphysical '*transcendent*' leaves these authors unconvinced that either metaphysics or their lure have been overcome.

Chapter 4

Winch and Conservatism: The Question of Philosophical Quietism

Can we Criticise, from 'Inside'; from 'Outside'?

The charge of conservatism, so often levelled at Wittgenstein and Winch is mistaken. It is a mythic and oft-repeated mistake. How can so many people be so wrong (so often)? Their thought seems to be that as Wittgenstein allegedly advanced the claim that truth is internal to language-games,[1] Winch advanced the claim that rationality, if one could talk of such a thing, was internal to a culture.[2] This we might call, for shorthand, the **charge of relativism**. If accepted, both (related) positions, it is thought, render otiose any attempt at logical or rational critique, respectively, or scientific critique, generally, and have paralysing political consequences.[3]

As if the charge of relativism wasn't damning enough for Wittgenstein and Winch, their accusers also point to Wittgenstein's claim that (his) philosophy "should leave everything as it is" (*PI*, section 124), and Winch's implicit endorsement of this in his explicit rejection of the underlabourer view of the philosopher's task, in *ISS*. This we will call the **charge of quietism**.

Wittgenstein, Winch and those who follow them, are therefore taken to hold and endorse a position which entails relativism about truth and reason: a rejection of

---

1   See the essays in Crary and Read (2000), especially Crary's own essay, for efficacious disputation of this claim and allegation. See also the 1990 Preface that Winch added to *The Idea of a Social Science*, where he makes very clear that he himself does not accept the claim.

2   Johann Hari, columnist for the *Independent* newspaper in the UK, when writing a rather ill-tempered article marking the occasion of Jacques Derrida's death, invoked language-games as the problem. He wrote: 'If reason is just another language game, if our words cannot match anything out there in the world without doing "violence" to others—what can we do except sink into nihilism, or turn to the supernatural?' (http://www.johannhari.com/archive/article. php?id=461). As we shall see (below), Hari's claim has more than a passing resemblance to claims made by Norman Geras. Hari's target is Jacques Derrida, Geras's, as we shall see, is Richard Rorty. We do not seek, in what follows, to defend Derrida, post structuralism or Rorty. We seek only to clarify what talk of language-games (following Wittgenstein and Winch) amounts to and why talking of 'truth internal to a language-game' does not *entail* an inability to talk meaningfully about injustices. For now it is enough to note that contrary to what is strongly implied by what Hari writes, language-game is not a term employed by Derrida. For a critique of Derrida on deconstruction (which Hari might find is consonant with his views) see Hutchinson 2008, *Shame and Philosophy*, chapter 2.

3   Compare here the similar charge made against Kuhn, disputed by Sharrock and Read in their (2002).

the critical force of scientific reason: the charge of relativism. And to advocate that philosophers stay quiet about the world (everything): that philosophy is not a servant of the natural sciences, sweeping aside irrationality (narrowly construed) so as to pave the way for the march of science: the charge of quietism. It is this pair of charges that underpin the charge of conservatism often levelled at Wittgenstein, Winch and Wittgensteinians, as though they advanced the plainly implausible idea—the quite *absurd* idea—that cultures, being closed to external realities, cannot change. Those holding such a view of Winch are legion, and we cannot possibly deal with each and every one of them in what follows. However, this is, in any case, unnecessary. For the argument, where there is one, is generally the same. Here's a sample from Gerard Delanty:[4]

> The implication of Winch's contribution to the philosophy of social science was relativism. Winch followed Wittgenstein with the notion that reality is structured by language, a position that entailed relativism since linguistic rule systems were seen as specific to concrete forms of life. As with Gadamer, his conception of social science, was rooted in a conservative view of the interpretive capacity of social science, which was for ever context bound (Delanty 1997, 55).

Previous chapters have dealt with many of the canards one finds in the above quote, from Delanty—see specifically chapter two, though also chapter one and, regarding the specific accusation of conservatism in the last sentence, the final section of the previous chapter, above, where we briefly address Habermasian concerns. In this chapter we seek to show that one cannot generate a charge of conservatism from the charges of relativism and quietism; for both those charges, when levelled at Winch, are misplaced in that they do not follow from anything Winch writes, when read aright. We endeavour to show such by first clarifying the philosophical remarks made by Wittgenstein and Winch regarding language-games and truth-claims, and the remarks about criticising other cultures. We then progress to discuss in more detail the very notion of critiquing another culture with reference to Wittgenstein's discussion of Frazer and Winch's discussion of Evans-Pritchard.

---

4   We could easily fill a whole book with quotes similar to this. This one from Gerard Delanty will serve as an example. What is common to all such accusations is a seemingly complete and utter failure to have grasped what Winch is saying; indeed, there seems to be very little effort made to even attempt to have grasped what he is saying. It can often seem that what is being commented on is not Winch's writing on these issues but other people's summaries of that writing. Note, in the case of Delanty, that this quote comes from a book published some seven years after the second edition of *ISS* appeared, with the new Preface, which directly addressed these issues, in response to misreadings of the 1st edition; Delanty's bibliography contains only the first edition of *ISS*: thus no Preface to the 2nd edition and no other writings by Winch on these issues are consulted (including, 'Understanding a Primitive Society'). Why?

The Charge of Relativism

If one holds that truth is internal to particular language-games, then, the fear seems to be, one rules out any possibility of showing the language-game-bound truth-claim to be false through resources employed from without the language-game. This has seemed to give rise to two concerns:

a. that truth is not answerable to the world 'outside' language. In this case we are said to be denying the world-answerability of truth-claims; and

b. that one cannot employ the resources of one language-game (say) that of empirical science, to draw in to question the truth-claims made in another language-game (say) that of religion; Christianity, for example. In this case we are said to be cutting ourselves off from the ability to engage in *rational critique*.

(a) World-answerability

The first concern (a) is neatly stated by Norman Geras (1995), in a paper criticising Richard Rorty; Geras writes:

> I shall be travelling in what follows a somewhat winding road, and so here is my central thesis. If there is no truth, there is no injustice. Stated less simplistically, if truth is wholly relativized or internalized to particular discourses or language games or social practices, there is no injustice. The victims and protesters of any *putative* injustice are deprived of their last and often best weapon, that of telling what really happened. They can only tell their story, which is something else. Morally and politically, therefore, anything goes (Geras 1995, 110).

Geras's objection relies on two intimately related confusions. First, Geras misunderstands, along with Rorty,[5] the nature of the Wittgensteinian claim about truth and language-games as a relativist thesis. It is nothing of the sort. And Second, Geras assumes "language" and "world" to be externally related, and thus he is led to the thought that something being internal to a language-game implies it not having contact with or being answerable to the world: linguistic non-cognitivism.[6] In response to the second of Geras's confusions therefore, we need only note that one of the pictures from which Wittgenstein helps us free ourselves, is the picture of language as externally related to the world; indeed, language and world are better understood as internally related; grasping concepts is to further come to see, to grasp, our world. Put another way, 'world' (in this context of use) is not taken by Wittgensteinians to denote some un- or pre-conceptualised brute given world on to

---

5   Unless, perhaps, one engages in a charitable reading of Rorty, along the lines essayed by Alan Malachowski in his (2002).

6   Of course there is no reason to suppose such follows from Wittgenstein's remarks on language and rule-following. See John McDowell's papers on rule-following, particularly 'Non-Cognitivism and Rule-following' (reprinted in his (1998)).

which we project meaning through our linguistic capacities, but "world" is rather taken to be the conceptualised world in which social actors, people, reside.

Now Geras takes this thought to imply that the world is, for such philosophers, merely socially constructed. Again, this doesn't follow. Rorty might say such things, or imply such things, but such thoughts are not entailed by the claim that truth is internal to language-games. Therefore, there is no implication in saying that understanding the truth of a claim is to understand it in terms of the 'language-game' in which it is made as entailing that the truth-claim is not answerable to the world. In some 'language-games' it clearly is, in others maybe not. But the 'language-game' being played, or, put another way, the idiom in which the truth claim is made, tells you to what the truth claim is answerable.[7]

The worry seems to be that this leads to a form of linguistic idealism; that in talking of the conceptualised world and eschewing talk of, or appeals to, the pre- or un-conceptualised world, we in some sense lose the (Real) world. But, again, that does not follow. Nor does it follow that creatures without linguistic abilities have no world. Both would be particularly odd claims—though this is not to say that some have come very close to saying as much.[8] We, of course, are arguing nothing of the sort.

"Truth" is a word like any other and its criteria for assessment or verification might vary with use.[9] We come to understand the use through coming to understand the language-game in which the particular truth-claim has its home.[10] Therefore, Geras's claim (above), that if truth is internalised to language-games then there is no injustice, arises from confusion. For Geras assumes that "truth being internal to the language-game" entails truth being "not answerable to the world". When it is the identification of the language-game in which the truth-claim is made which tells you to what the claim is answerable.

Now, Geras is taking issue specifically with Richard Rorty here, and we would not want to defend a 'Rortian position' on the matter. However, while Geras's essay focuses particularly on Rorty it does capture a widespread misunderstanding—albeit a misunderstanding which might well unfortunately find support in Rorty's writing, i.e. a misunderstanding which Rorty is at times equally guilty of holding—of what is entailed by Wittgenstein's discussion of truth. To say that truth is internal to a language-game is not to advance a relativist thesis about truth but merely to say that

---

7   For detailed argument regarding issues of world-answerability and a nuanced defence of the possibility of singular thought, see Charles Travis (2005 and 2006).

8   Rorty, at times seems to say as much (though he generally denies that he does); Stanley Fish has built a career on making such claims. Neither can claim Wittgenstein or Winch's writings as support for their positions.

9   It is in this sense that we here depart from the attempt in the contemporary philosophy of language to advance a general theory of truth. And this is not to say that truth is relative, only that there are many different applications of the word 'truth' and related expressions such as e.g, accurate.

10 Of course one is not obliged to use Wittgenstein's terminology here. We could just talk of examining the context or occasions of use. Wittgenstein was always very concerned that terms he employed for analogical and therapeutic purposes, such as language-game, would be read in a quasi-methodological manner.

to identify the nature of a truth claim, to understand what the claim is claiming, to understand what would be the case if the claim were true, and to understand how one might tell whether the claim is true or not—is to comprehend the claim against the background of the language-game in which the claim is made. To understand *a truth-claim* is to understand *a language-game*. No understanding of the latter, no *identification* even of the former.

Now, employing the expression 'language-games' in connection with 'truth being internal to language-games' is somewhat problematic if it is intended as a forceful allusion to Wittgenstein, whose own notion of 'language-game' was more sparingly used than 'the literature' would lead one to think. Wittgenstein introduced the term as a sort of contrivance for imaging alternative possibilities to some standard patterns of linguistic usage specifically for clarificatory purposes. *It was never intended as a technical term to be developed as part of the apparatus of a theory*—on the contrary.

Furthermore, 'language-games' have, frequently and somewhat troublingly, come to be treated as equivalent to cultures or institutions, and the idea that 'truth is internal to a language-game' (see Chapter 2, on Linguistic Idealism) has come to be understood as saying that the prevalent or dominant doctrines found within a national or tribal culture or within an institution such as law are true because they are defined as such within 'the language-game' of community life or institutional practice. Thus, the logic underlying Geras' anxiety that the possibility of damning injustice is being excluded is that the idea of 'truth being internal to a language-game' cashes out as 'if people believe they are just, then they *are* just, and so it is impossible to say that people who believe that what they do is just are nonetheless engaging in injustices. (Thus Geras and the Relativism that he opposes are *merely two sides of the same unhappy coin*.) Indeed, taken seriously, such a line of thought would require that 'establishes what justice is' be given further specification, to accommodate the fact that the same argument could be applied to each and every community or institution. Thus, there could be no notion of 'justice' as such but only of justice in this community, justice in that community etc., where 'justice' may be in each case something very different. If it is additionally assumed that what is meant by each community determining justice is that each community counts its own ways as just, and then the very notion of 'injustice' is eradicated, for the ways of a community are, *now by definition*, just. It is this kind of logic which reinforces, for those who share Geras' general concerns, the idea that they are defenders of a necessary and universal conception of justice which can be used to measure each and any culture to determine whether it is or is not just. However, at least as far as Wittgenstein is concerned—Rorty being a very different matter—the threat against which they defend is an imagined one, and their perceived need for a 'universal' conception much attenuated. After all, and somewhat ironically, if the above *were* Wittgenstein's argument or implication then the charges of quietism would be instantly rebutted, for such arguments are surely massively revisionist of a language which features such extensively employed expressions as 'unfair', 'unjust', 'exploitative' etc.

Some alleviation of the anxiety about the import of the (badly expressed) proposal that 'truth is internal to a language-game' might be dispelled if it is noticed that we are quite comfortable with talk of e.g. and *inter alia* 'the truths of science', 'the truths of religion', 'the truths of poetry', 'valid in law', 'mathematically speaking' and so on, where it is quite intelligible to talk of truths belonging to, in the casual use of that expression, specific 'language-games'. That is, those expressions are perfectly intelligible, and objection to assertions involving them would not be to the suggestion that certain truths are associated with, even the property of, science, but to any suggestion that the findings of science or the truths of religion were thereby necessarily being endorsed.

To understand the claim that 'truth is internal to language-games' in the way that Geras conceives it, does not relate to anything that can be found in Wittgenstein or in Winch. The latter's disagreement with Oakeshott (*ISS*, pp. 62-66) is partly about the importance of conceiving of rules in relation to the possibility of 'reflection'. For Winch, to talk of something as a rule is to at least imply the possibility of understanding that one could have done otherwise. Thus, the example he gives: to be able to behave honestly one must at least understand what it would be to behave dishonestly—after all, the idea of what makes something a matter of honesty is the contrast with its other.[11] The notion of 'justice' seems much akin to that of 'honesty' in that seeing

---

11 Again there is much confusion over Winch's discussion of rules in *ISS*. His critics seem unable to see that discussion as anything other than an attempt to provide a rule-following conception/theory of society, so as to replace a positivist conception. Where, in brief, Winch is only concerned to bring to light what it is to identify an action as what it is. Winch is not talking about what it is to do things correctly. Thus, Bohman's (1992) criticism, which draws on MacIntyre (1970 [1967]), 'that it is not true that all social actions can be done correctly and incorrectly, and hence they do not all refer even implicitly to rules as constituting part of their description: for example, how do we go for a walk "incorrectly"?' (Bohman 1992, p. 62). Of course, this criticism is 'loaded' in its employment of the word 'correctness'. If we rather say with Winch that a rule is what tells you when something being done is something other than going for a walk (e.g. when the person is going for a run, when the person is going for a ride on their bike or going for a drive in a car, and so on) we can, on occasions and in contexts, specify what we mean by 'going for a walk' when we say of Reuben that he went for a walk. Specifying what we mean by 'going for a walk', such that we can say with clarity that that is, indeed, what Ruben did, is done by our invoking a rule for what counts as going for a walk. This rule can be said to be established by something like the following: should I have said that Reuben had gone for a swim I would have said something incorrect, for Reuben, in fact, went for a walk through the woods that day and at no time swam. Had Reuben donned his swimming attire and swam, and not 'gone for a walk', that day, then he would not have 'gone for a walk' incorrectly, as Bohman and MacIntyre seem to think Winch must hold, Reuben would have gone for a swim, and *not* gone for a walk. We are simply talking about the meaning of to walk, hereabouts. Questions as to correctness, *if* they are appropriate, if they do indeed arise, come later.

Now, Winch does say—and qualifies in the Preface to the 2nd edition—that following a rule and making a mistake are interwoven (overgeneralising some kinds of rules). However, he does not say that all actions are rule-following. And he certainly has no need to say it. All he needs is the—obvious point—that many connections in social life are made by rules. This is all that is required to combat the (related ideas) that all explanations invoke causal connections (since rules are used in explaining), and that all relations between actions are causal (since the relation between one action and its successor or between my action and yours are rule related). Whilst it is correct that not all actions are amenable to correct/incorrect assessment, this does

what makes something just involves understanding how it would differ from what is unjust—as incarceration at Guantanamo is conceived as unjust, not because people are imprisoned, but because they are imprisoned without opportunity to have their imprisonment adjudicated by a court and in violation of existing international laws governing prisoners of war. This point would have to hold for anything that we would want to translate as 'justice' from another community, and would require that, in that community, there be an intelligible difference between what is just and what is not. What might count as justice and injustice in another community might differ significantly from what we count as justice in ours, just as what is legal and illegal do, but this does not mean that the possibility of asking whether *by our standards* their practices are just is not intelligible—as critics of Guantanamo illustrate by their doubts that military justice is not good enough in the current cases and that the standards of the civil courts should be applied.

Some truth-claims are answerable to the way the (conceptualised) world is—to empirically established facts—while some might not be. The truth (or otherwise) of a claim that God exists might be an example of a truth-claim which is not made on the assumption that it can be shown to be true or false in light of empirically established facts about the world. The truth of a claim as to the meaning of life might similarly not be verifiable by reference to facts. It might well be that one takes these latter two types of truth-claims not to be truth-evaluable at all, but, whether they are or not is an open question, as such claims are certainly not, *prima facie*, nonsensical.

The point, therefore, is once again—as it was in the case of actions—a point about identification, not about what can or cannot be done. The point of talking about language-games at all when talking about truth is merely to emphasise this point about identification of the particular truth-claim. If one fails to identify the nature of the truth-claim as what it is then one will simply fail to understand what is being claimed and miss one's target in attempting to assess or criticise the claim.

As with the identification of an action, the point is to look and see, to observe what the relevant criteria of identity are, and not, to abstractly theorise (about) what truth must be. The production of one's theory as to what is the appropriate general form of truth is almost always treated as prior to any attempt at identifying the criteria for assessment of the truth-claim. Indeed, philosophers often seem so absorbed in debates over which form of truth—which theory—should be employed in the philosophy of language that assessment of how people ordinarily employ the word truth is seemingly thought irrelevant.

(b) Rational critique

What of (b)? As we noted above, here the concern seems to be that the indexing of the truth-claim to the language-game entails an inability to criticise the truth-claim by drawing on the resources of another language-game. To illustrate: if one takes the language of religion to be a 'language-game' and thus providing its own criteria for truth and falsity, the conclusion is thought to follow that the discoveries

---

not preclude the fact that many of them are, and it is the consequences of this fact, not the propsing of a universal hypothesis, that Winch was trying to develop.

of the experimental natural sciences, or the insights provided by certain fundamental and basic principals of logic cannot be garnered as support for a claim, say, that the Roman Catholic Church's doctrine of the Unity of the Trinity is, as a matter of logical or scientific fact, false. What counts as true in formal logic and what counts as true in the experimental natural sciences is internal to the logic of those two—maybe closely related—language-games: that of formal logic and that of the experimental natural sciences. The criteria that need to be fulfilled for a claim to be accorded the status of a true proposition in each language-game is different and is different again to that required in the language-game of religion (specifically Catholicism).

Similarly, if one holds that rationality is internal to a culture, then providing a criticism of the reasoning within that culture by drawing on the resources of reason found in another culture is either illegitimate or merely forlorn. To illustrate: if one takes a hypothetical isolated hunter-gather people in a remote part of the Amazonian forests to have their own culture, thus having their own criteria for what is counted as rational and irrational, the conclusion seems to follow that the principles of Western scientific rationality cannot be employed as support for the claim, say, that taking precious time to chant over one's arrow before shooting the arrow at one's prey (food), is irrational. What counts as rational in twenty-first century Western culture is internal to that culture: that of a scientifically rational (disenchanted, to coin Weber's term) culture. The criteria to be fulfilled for a practice to be accorded the status of a rational practice are different in the culture of the twenty-first century West (advanced, late-capitalist, yada yadda yaddda…) and the culture of our (hypothetical) Amazonian hunter-gatherers.

Fortunately, *neither Wittgenstein nor Winch make such claims*.[12] Wittgenstein and Winch are best understood not as telling you what you cannot do, but rather offering advice, reminders, as to what criteria you must fulfil or observe if you are to do what you, as would-be critic, claim/aim to do.[13] If you wish to subject the proclamations of the church or serious people of faith to critical scrutiny then you had best understand those proclamations: you must understand the 'voice' in which they speak, the 'game' they are playing. Similarly for Winch: if you wish to criticise the practices of another culture you had better understand those practices in their terms, first and foremost: you had better understand their reasons for engaging in those actions, their purpose, the social setting, and so on. Only then might one's criticism be of what they are saying or what they are doing.[14] But this is only part of the story. For to understand another's claims, to understand the practices of another culture, one will need, for those claims and/or practices to be intelligible to one, to understand them in terms of things you might say or you might do. And this is

---

12 This is clearest of all in Winch in the 1990 Preface to *ISS*, where, following Rush Rhees, he makes absolutely explicit that it is an illusion, and profoundly un-Wittgensteinian, to treat 'language-games' and 'communities' as isolatable *entities*, independent of one another. This is most strikingly a criticism of Norman Malcolm, whose interpretation of Wittgenstein *vis-à-vis* the matters presently under discussion has much to answer for.

13 The kicker is that having fulfilled the criteria you realise that you might well find that you no longer wish to pursue your goal of criticism. Not, at any rate, in the manner you had assumed hitherto that you did. (More on this below.)

14 For a more detailed account of this part of the story, see Chapter 1.

what makes both Wittgenstein's and Winch's remarks, hereabouts, not, as generally understood, methodological—showing the philosopher or social scientist a new method or methodology—but *a work on oneself*,[15] work in self-understanding as much as in the understanding and criticism of others.

For in attempting to reach understanding of the 'voice', or idiom, in which the serious person of faith speaks, one might be best served in examining one's own articles of faith and weighing them against the claims of the religious. In attempting to reach understanding of the practices of another culture, such as the practice of chanting over an arrow before loading the bow and releasing the arrow at the prey, one might be best served in examining one's own culture's employment of ritual or ceremony in analogous situations. One might reflect, for example, on the soldier's practice of polishing boots and ironing 'kit' in the armed forces. One might well find that the language-game of experimental science does indeed allow for articles of faith; that, as Kuhn and Feyerabend showed, progress (as Kuhn understood such) can often rely on *commitment*, which does not follow from any experimental results (i.e. commitment *as* faith) just as much as it can and does follow from experimental results. Similarly, one might find that many of the practices central to twenty-first century scientifically rational cultures do not conform to the strictures of scientific reason, narrowly construed. One might well find that ritual and ceremony provide both motive for and sense to many of our practices. Understanding this aids us in our understanding of other cultures; it enables our criticism, if such is still relevant, once we have understood. Just ask yourself the question: have you ever kissed a photograph, or an envelope that you were about to post, or for that matter (since you were small) a teddy bear? If you have, then you ought to be hesitant to condemn 'primitive' cultures as unreasonable; not because you ought not to have kissed the photo or the envelope—far from it. Rather, because you ought to be readier to try to make sense of *what* it is they are doing, before you criticise or condemn.

The recruit who simply fails to get to grips with polishing his boots to a 'mirror-like' shine and fails to master the task of ironing a 'razor-like' crease in his uniform trousers will either fail to achieve the status of soldier (he will not pass-out (graduate basic training)) or he will be labelled a poor soldier and constantly subject to disciplinary procedures and failure to progress through the ranks. Poor creases and dull boots do not mean he has failed to incorporate the heroic virtues into his character, much less that he is more likely to be subject to accurate and thus fatal, enemy fire. A dull boot and dull crease will not slow him down, make him less fit, make his shot less straight, nor does he believe they will do so. The practices of polishing one's boots to a 'mirror-like' shine and ironing a 'razor-like' crease in one's trousers are not instrumental in that sense. To take them to be such is to fail to understand what the soldier is doing (or failing to do, in the case of our example). In acknowledging that such practices are not instrumental we might therefore grant that our hypothetical Amazonian archer's chanting over his arrow is, similarly, not (at least, not necessarily) undertaken for instrumental reasons—at least not directly instrumental ones, for they are part of 'military discipline' and strict compliance in

---

15 For discussion, see once more Winch's intriguing and too-little-read late (1992) paper, 'Persuasion'.

military discipline is conceived as contributing to the kind of performance essential to effective combat organisation. It is crucial to entertain the possibility as a live one that the archer does not believe that, in some mystical way, the words of the chant make the arrow direct itself to the heart of the prey or even fly true. And that this is neither the motive for nor the sense of his actions, that it fails to identify the action within its social setting.

As we have noted in previous chapters, the thought that the action under scrutiny needs rendering through description-in-terms-of-instrumental-reason (or in Freudian terms, or in extensional terms, and so on) is born of a (scientistic) preoccupation with the form of explanation. The production of one's theory as to what is the appropriate general from of explanation is almost always treated as prior to any attempt at description/explanation of an action. Indeed, sociology and similar 'social science' enterprises often seems so absorbed in debates over which form of explanation—which methodology—should be employed in social studies that the actual studies seem tangential to the whole subject area. This is, then, how social studies go awry. For our attempt to understand should be read-off the action in question: "How do I/we make sense of/understand this action, in this social setting, given that my/our goal, first and foremost, has to be identification of the action?"

Perhaps like many soldiers in our own culture the archer simply does this, does what he does, because it is part of what archers/hunters do in his culture and he is an archer/hunter—it is how the practice was taught to him and its teaching was intimately related to his inculcation into the arts of the archer/hunter. And furthermore, were we to insist on finding ('the') rationale for the chant or the polishing and ironing we might feel our best explanation was that it is the 'ritualistic' nature of such acts that provides their sense. In each case, the ritualistic activities are conceived as indispensable preparations for the further activities that are to be undertaken, in the first case, getting the individual in the right spiritual state for hunting, in the second, developing the character of a fighter.

Where does this then take us? In trying to understand the practices of the archer/ hunter we look for analogous—*genuinely*, not merely[16] superficially, analogous— practices in our own culture; in doing so we disabuse ourselves of a propensity to see scientific (instrumental) reason everywhere before us in our own culture and a propensity to assume irrationality in the non-instrumental practices of those from other ('non-scientifically rational')[17] cultures; in doing so we do *not* rule-out the possibility of criticism of the practices of those from other cultures;[18] we merely note that criticism which depicts the motive for and sense of an act, such as chanting over an arrow, as instrumental seriously risks misunderstanding and thus misinterprets (we might say fails to see) the act before one.

In understanding the act of chanting over the arrow as analogous to that of polishing one's boots to a mirror-like shine and ironing a 'razor-like' crease in one's trousers, we understand that the motive for and sense of the act might be ritualistic

---

16 As in Evans-Pritchard.

17 The reason for the introduction of scare quotes at this point should be obvious.

18 Compare for instance the interesting (political) criticisms made of Zande culture by Nigel Pleasants (2000a and 2000b). See also his 2002 and 2004.

or ceremonial (we can allow for more possibilities here). In coming to see this, much of the *social scientist's* motivation for the criticism ebbs. It ebbs because the anthropologist's/social scientist's motive stemmed from the thought that our own culture was exclusively (or at the very least predominantly) one of (scientific/ instrumental) reason and theirs was one which saw instrumental value in non-instrumental acts. Neither assumption is worthy of the honorific label 'science'.

Winch was concerned to critique traditional social science's overwhelming propensity to see other cultures, more 'primitive' cultures, continually, even habitually, as committing the *post hoc ergo propter hoc* fallacy (after this therefore because of this), while simultaneously 'bracketing-out' all evidence counter to the (misattributed) causal connection. Other cultures, then, are said to be more primitive because they engage in such rampant bracketing of counter-evidence to their (mistaken) assumptions about causal relations. On this view, they engage in practices such as that of chanting over an arrow before shooting because they think after that the prey will always be struck to the heart by the arrow: i.e. the prey is struck by the arrow because of the chanting that went before. Their primitivity resides in their resolute attachment to this commitment in the face of evidence to the contrary—the prey frequently not being struck to the heart by the arrow following the chant; the archer/hunter bothering to spend time engaged in target practice; and so on. Winch and Wittgenstein seek to avail social scientists of reminders such that they will not themselves fall prey to such misunderstandings and thus misattributions.

Wittgenstein's and Winch's point is a basic one: *understand the practice under study before criticising the practice.* However, it is the upshot of this that troubles traditional social scientists. For as we have seen, if the path to understanding entails anything it is the realisation that one's own claim to reason is not as utterly secure as one had probably assumed[19] and that the practices of the objects of study, when truly understood, when seen as the practices that they in fact are, are little or no different to practices of ours which we had, hitherto, felt no desire to charge with irrationality on scientific grounds.

Is such a view likely to bring-forth or foster conservatism? We can see no grounds for such an assumption. Having come to see the analogy between certain practices in our culture and certain practices in the culture 'we' (as traditional social scientists) had already depicted as primitive we begin to understand our own lives more clearly. In doing so we are better placed to put those (our) lives and the practices that are partially constitutive of them under critical scrutiny, should we be inclined to do so. However, that—the inclination to criticise—is up to you. Wittgenstein and Winch provide you with reminders as to the necessary conditions for critique of another's words or practices: i.e. what amounts to a perspicuous presentation of those words or practices. They do not provide you with an explanation and, except occasionally and

---

19 If space allowed, it would be interesting to consider here why this assumption is so often taken to be self-evidently a good thing. As if a life lived according entirely to 'reason' would obviously be a good life. After all, there has been a long standing tradition in 'critical social science' of delineating what we might call the night side of reason. One ought therefore to ask whether the application of the idea of reason to all aspects of life itself involves genuinely rational understanding of the task or its consequences.

fragmentarily, *they do not provide you with the critique*. That (developing a critique) is up to you, and you must take responsibility for it. And it is in these senses then that *their* philosophy leaves everything as it is.

In sum, it is not 'criticism' that is the target, but a certain sort of criticism, which presents the terms of criticism as though these cast doubt on the target practice/culture for failing to be empirically well-founded, and as though the criticism were made from the standpoint of another practice which is, in contrast, empirically well-founded. It is the sort of criticism which, further, arises from the post-seventeenth century intellectual's fixation on method, and the treatment of understanding as though it must consist in only one singular form, and that a general and impersonal one. This view does not, perhaps cannot recognise, that there are diverse forms of understanding and (that) many of these have a personal character.

Far from finding our own critical capacities disabled by taking this line, we find that they lead us to take a certain line toward and against some of the main tendencies in contemporary intellectual culture, as above, where we are really accusing it of a kind of bad faith, of attempting to reify the sources of its judgements, to dissociate these from their roots in the commitments of people, as if only the deliverances of a mechanically applied moral/political/empirical calculus were respectable.

Philosophy Leaves Everything as it is: Wittgenstein and Quietism

This brings us directly to the charge of quietism.

Wittgenstein was reluctant to be a philosopher (at all), profoundly despising the idea of the professional, academic Philosopher, and being sufficiently critical of that role to hope that his philosophical policies would eventually more or less liquidate it. Wittgenstein rejected the whole idea that engagement with practical and political affairs need authorisation by way of philosophy, seeing engagement in philosophy as distancing one from real engagement with affairs (which is why he tried on more than one occasion to give up philosophy altogether). Perhaps, in this, Wittgenstein is not all that far removed from Karl Marx (1998 [1845]), who declared that philosophers had only interpreted the world, when the point is to change it. This can be understood to mean that previous philosophers had only sought to interpret the world, whereas future philosophers should attempt to change it. Equally well, though, it might be understood as saying that interpreting the world is the best that philosophers can do (rather more than Wittgenstein thinks they can) and that if changing the world is to be seriously undertaken, then it best be done by others than philosophers, or by philosophers when not doing philosophy.[20]

Understanding Wittgenstein's view of philosophy is essential to understanding what 'philosophy leaves everything as it is' could possibly mean. Throughout, Wittgenstein's basic supposition is that philosophy has nothing to say, which is why the only form that his philosophical thought could take was that of a 'method(s)' (though we must not conceive of even that method, 'our method', in too rigid or

---

20 For development at some length of this idea, see Read's 'Marx and Wittgenstein on Vampirism and Parasitism', in Pleasants and Kitching (2002).

formulaic a way).[21] For Wittgenstein, philosophy has nothing to say, has no content, can advance no doctrines, can perform only a negative, but nonetheless emancipatory (liberatory)[22] role, that of enabling people to release themselves from illusions—those that insinuate that philosophy does have something to say, that it must, and rightly, put forward doctrines, and that those doctrines will feature a privileged, even final, understanding.

Wittgenstein's own, life-long, view of what he was about is not one that can perhaps easily be taken *seriously* in the social studies, and consideration of his meaning for the social studies almost invariably discounts Wittgenstein's insistence that he has nothing to say. Wittgenstein's first alleged error is to suppose that he could be free of doctrines. Thinking necessarily involves theories, so Wittgenstein must have theories too. Wittgenstein-for-social-studies is therefore reconstructed as an ensemble of positive doctrines, and it is these which are appealed to in drawing the conclusion that Wittgenstein's thought threatens the imposition of awful and, in any case, invalid restrictions on thought.

If Wittgenstein is instead taken at his word, then it becomes apparent that no such restrictions can possibly be involved. Wittgenstein places no limitation whatsoever on what can be thought or said (indeed, his whole project, throughout his life, is to question the very *sense* of any such 'limitation'), arguing only that whatever can be thought or said gets said outside of philosophy. Wittgenstein's philosophy does not leave everything as it is, in respect of its (sometimes) successful effect to emancipate individuals from the impulse to philosophise. Philosophy leaves everything as it is in respect of the fact that someone so emancipated is otherwise no worse off than they were, for they can still say everything that they want to say, except for the things that, through philosophical therapy—which is extensively self-therapy—they have come to recognise do not make the kind of sense they had previously imagined them to.

This should make it clear that one can't treat Wittgenstein's disavowal of doctrines, of theories, as involving only an 'overlooking' of the 'fact' that he is busy putting up doctrines of his own. As mentioned, Wittgenstein was profoundly opposed to the idea of the philosopher as some kind of professional, whose work was the pursuit of a philosophy. People who need philosophical therapy are not, *per se*, professional philosophers, but those who, without necessarily being philosophers by profession, have become enmeshed in certain kinds of confusions. Much of Wittgenstein's philosophical therapy was directed towards those involved in mathematics—mathematicians—who find themselves drawn into puzzling reflections on the nature and status of mathematics.[23] The philosophical therapy, if effective, would enable

---

21 See Read's (forthcoming) review of McManus's *The Enchantment of Words* for development of this important point; compare also Hutchinson and Read's joint writings on Wittgenstein (op cit.).

22 See the Afterword to Read's *Applying Wittgenstein*, for development of this point.

23 Indeed: Soren Stenlund argues that confusions over mathematics were *the main focus* of Wittgenstein's philosophy in an unpublished paper 'Continuity and Change in Wittgenstein'. What is undoubtedly true is that the sheer numerical majority, measured in words/pages, of Wittgenstein's *nachlass*, consists of writings broadly in the philosophy of mathematics.

those involved in these reflections to recognise them for the distraction that they were from mathematics itself, and leave them free to return to mathematical work itself.

The roots of the 'prisoner of language' misconception are perhaps best exhibited in the 'rationalists' conception that change in cultures and societies are a product of falsification—rational people, at least, give up their convictions when these are falsified. The distinction between what is represented in language and the way things are 'in themselves' is essential to the conviction that practical refutation is both necessary and possible—reality can on occasion 'break through' the representations and reveal their falsity. Hence, the projection onto Wittgenstein and Winch of a picture of culture as a closed circle, closed against both incursions from reality and against validly grounded pre-emption by other cultures. This is because, it is supposed, for Wittgenstein and Winch, reality and representation are entirely coincident, (for discussion see Chapter 2, on Linguistic Idealism). For Wittgenstein and Winch, then, it must be that the limits of a culture are fixed by what it can represent and it is then a tautological consequence that nothing from outside the culture can intrude into it for there are no other accepted cultural resources to enable contrary representations. Not only is there no possibility of change through refutation, whether from 'another culture's point of view' or 'from reality'; there is really no possibility of change at all. Presumably a closed circle of this kind cannot be moderated at all.

We touched on the mythologically mistaken assumptions that led to such a view, above; but, to explore further: to start dismantling this point of view it is perhaps wise to begin with the fact that Wittgenstein's philosophy is concerned with 'concepts' rather than convictions. The rationalist conception betrays the shared attachment to the *intellectualist* fallacy that runs through sociology and related disciplines. We mean by this, the notion (naturally attractive to many *academics*) that all human activity originates in ratiocination, and that action is premised in belief (which is itself an inheritor of the deep fixation of philosophy on the form of the proposition, especially in its hypothetical role—thought is the formation of hypotheses, beliefs are those hypotheses we elect to affirm, etc.). The assumption is, then, that the starting point for understanding a culture is the identification of the beliefs that are expressed in and that underpin the actions of the culture's individual members. If a person's actions are premised in their beliefs, then changes in their actions will be consequent upon changes in their beliefs, and the way in which beliefs change is by being refuted—rationality, as noted above, is identified with the virtue of giving up a conviction when it is proved false.

As always, the mistake is to review Wittgenstein and Winch as though they too shared these intellectualist preconceptions. If one does this, then the conclusion that they postulate closed and incorrigible cultural systems is inevitable. The depth and ubiquity of the intellectualist presuppositions is perhaps such that these are not recognised as presuppositions at all, but are taken for self-evident truths. The possibility that someone—Winch and Wittgenstein for example—might not share these presuppositions is barely conceivable, and so the counter-case is not recognisable for what it is. Nonetheless, Wittgenstein and Winch do *not* share intellectualist presuppositions, but rather *consistently campaign against them.*

Winch saw much of the import of Wittgenstein's philosophy as condensed into the quotation from Goethe that Wittgenstein appropriated: In the beginning was the deed! In the context of the present discussion, the remark can be understood as going up against the intellectualist supposition that in the beginning there is the word (or: that in the beginning there is the belief). For Wittgenstein and Winch it is—in a sense—the other way around; though really the contrast between belief and action itself needs to be rotated into one between *practices and opinions.*

The consequence of doing that is, we will show, to liquidate the impression that a culture is, for Wittgenstein and Winch, a closed system of beliefs that are immune to refutation. We will thus expose the weakness of the rationalist equation of change in a culture with refutation of beliefs (not that no beliefs are ever refuted, just that rationalists make much too much of this possibility).[24] It is only if one accepts this equation that one could possibly construe Wittgenstein and Winch as precluding the very possibility of change. One can come to see that Wittgenstein and Winch are arguing that whilst cultures change they do not do so primarily as a consequence of the refutation of beliefs. But this does not entail that cultures do not change, only that the rationalists have, at best, a very partial handle *on the ways in which change can take place.* Conceptual change, Winch, Wittgenstein (and Kuhn) remind us, is rarely an effect of empirical information; or, at least, certainly not of empirical information *alone.*

Please note that the claim is *not* that refutation of beliefs never takes place, but that the possibility of such an occurrence requires quite specific conditions, and yet can be prompted by and can take form via quite varied matters. Think of it this way—the rationalists think of the relation between two cultures as equivalent to the relation between rival scientific theories (construed, crucially, in pre-Kuhnian fashion), as involving cultures which make different hypotheses about the same domain of facts, and which differ, then, primarily in respect of their truth value. They are rival hypotheses, and consequently cannot both be true. Unless, that is, one is, as many opponents of the rationalists are, at least tempted by the idea that they can both be true—that truth is, in some sense, relative. Rather than holding that the rival hypotheses subscribed to by different cultures might both, in their respective contexts, be true, Wittgenstein and Winch insist that many of the main differences between cultures do not consist in hypotheses, and that these differences do not involve cognitive or factual rivalry in the way that competition between scientific hypotheses (at least, within the enterprise of 'normal science') do.

Anyone familiar with the debates in and around sociology over the last six decades can recognise the lineaments of a recurrent opposition that appears there, and one which, for many, seems to involve Wittgenstein and Winch as central figures—they are the patron saints of relativist social science. However, this is not the game in which Wittgenstein and Winch are engaged *at all,* for to take the view that relativists are (usually in a very confused way) drawn toward *is to share far too much with*

---

24 A very vivid picture of this 'too much', and of the alternative—in which refutation is a feature of 'small' changes, rather than knock-out blows—can be obtained by a right understanding of Kuhn's philosophy.

their rationalist opponents. This whole picture of the difference between cultures is drawn in entirely the wrong way as far as Wittgenstein and Winch are concerned.

Here is the moment to notice that Winch's criticism of Evans-Pritchard, echoing Wittgenstein's objections to Frazer, is for supposing that all thought is an attempt to understand reality after the fashion of the formation of a scientific theory, and that Winch's counter is that there are different ways of attempting to 'understand reality', not all of them of the same form as or comparable with those of science. Specifically, Evans-Pritchard is guilty of identifying, for example, deliverances of the oracle as equivalent to hypotheses when they do not, in their home context, function as hypotheses at all.

More generally, Winch's objections to Evans-Pritchard are motivated by rejection of the idea of a scientific critique of religion. That idea is appealing to those who suppose that religion consists in doctrines compounded of empirical hypotheses, but mistaken ones, and that can be shown to be so through scientific evidence. But, for Wittgenstein, religion is not necessarily superstition. Religion is not primarily a set of doctrines *at all*, but much more importantly a set of maxims for a way of life. A set of practices. Both Wittgenstein and Winch try to show that religious expressions that might look like scientific hypotheses are not actually hypotheses and do not play a part in magical practice which is analogous to that which the hypothesis plays in scientific practice. This is one reason why Wittgenstein and Winch are not advancing relativism, for they are indicating the extent to which the scientific tradition is distinctive.[25] Winch tries to explain this by showing that the notion of 'understanding reality' does not signify a single kind of activity which is being pursued by different means (science, religion etc.) but that it encompasses many different kinds of affair, some of which are very unlike science. It makes no sense to say that religion and science are as good as one another, since the question 'good at what?' would indicate that what one is 'good for' the other is no use at. It is not as if science itself achieves the fulfilment of a pre-existing task—the understanding of nature, say—for any history of science will show that the development of science has itself involved a matter of developing and changing (the understanding of) what science is doing, of what 'understanding nature' might both encompass and consist in. 'Understanding' does not, even amongst the sciences, identify one single sort of operation, and science both changes and varies internally with respect to what can be understood, and what kind of thing comprises understanding of it.

The argument does not rule out the possibility of criticism[26] though does lead one to a deep scepticism regarding the idea that the only *real* criticism consists in logico-

---

25 In this respect, their enterprises resemble Kuhn at perhaps the most founding and critical moment at which he was understood: Kuhn intended the concept, 'paradigm' precisely to 'demarcate' the huge difference between the sciences on the one hand and disciplines without a paradigm (e.g. the 'behaviourial sciences') on the other.

26 See once again Crary's essay in Crary and Read (2000). Her argument is essentially that Wittgenstein must be read as preserving the possibility of criticism. See also Pleasants's work (op cit.) on Wittgenstein and Winch. Since much of the discussion of 'criticism' is premised upon arguments about whether the latter's thought rules out the possibility of criticism in face of that fact that criticism is both possible and necessary, it is worth erring on the side of caution and pointing out that 'preserving the possibility of criticism' does not mean that

empirical refutation. This way in which this latter kind of criticism is envisaged and practiced often seems effective only because its enthusiasts are actually talking mainly to themselves and talking past those whom they purportedly target. Criticism as a logico-empirical demonstration is possible, but only under restrictive conditions, where there is substantial agreement in place amongst the disputants such that their differences can be focused on a single—empirical—point and adjudicated according to a method that both parties will accept as appropriate for matching the disputed hypothesis against the facts.[27] If the (largely benighted) studies in the Sociology of Scientific Knowledge (which often anoint Wittgenstein, Kuhn and Winch as patron saints) have shown anything, it is that even in science, the exemplar of hypothetical reasoning, scientific disputes don't by any means always achieve the kind of consensual close focus that facilitates decisive resolution of the demonstrative kind. If such conditions are hardly satisfied within science, then how can anyone imagine that they could be meaningfully satisfied in any disagreement between religion and science (a disagreement which is often proposed without recognition of how many scientists do not find an inherent conflict between them)? Attempts to make comparisons on the basis of science's experimental methods simply beg the question, just as would the attempt to test science's validity in terms of magical or religious trials.

The notion of 'rationality' has been very narrowly identified with the kind of debate that takes place over (some—relatively 'contained'/'small-scale') rival scientific theories which can be resolved through the confrontation of hypotheses with evidence, which is why the argument that criticism is possible will nonetheless seem disappointing to many insofar as anything other than the kind of criticism which involves scientific-style refutations will be considered irrational. Wittgenstein's philosophy is intended to be descriptive, and, *as such cannot legislate on whether people are allowed to criticise either another culture, or their own.*

At the same time, it is part of Wittgenstein's task to suggest that and how philosophical thought suffers from one-sided diets of examples, and it is therefore consistent for we Wittgensteinians to observe not only that criticism does take place, but that criticism takes different forms, and there is no reason to identify 'criticism' with any one of these nor, without reviewing other kinds of criticism, to decide whether any one of these forms is the sole paradigm of rational criticism. The fact that there are deep incongruities between standpoints and practices does not preclude all possibility of rational disagreement between them, if one accepts that 'rational discussion' is not confined to stating contesting hypotheses and reporting evidence to adjudicate between them, but recognises that rational discussion can involve attempting to gain a better understanding of respective standpoints, even a realisation that no agreement can be had, and where the arguments are offered *persuasively.* Indeed, within the social studies themselves the likelihood of demonstrative resolution of even a single dispute between 'social science' approaches is unlikely,

---

Wittgenstein and Winch are trying to legislate on this possibility, as though *they* could decide whether people can criticise or not. It means rather that their arguments do not determine *a priori* whether criticism does or can occur in any specific case.

27 See Sharrock and Read on 'incommensuraibility', in their (2002).

for 'social scientists' disagree with each other in their whole conception of what their subject might be about,[28] what things are worth knowing, how to proceed, how to assure the acceptability of an account, what is acceptable as evidence *inter alia*, but this does not prevent them from criticising each other, nor sometimes—even though much of the argument amongst sociologists may be based on mutual misreadings (as we are arguing has been the case with much of Winch's readership)—need this lead to them talking past each other rather than to effective critique. One would not necessarily want to condemn all this discussion as irrational—though there is little realistic possibility of refutation of one social studies viewpoint by another.

We are making and re-making this point, but it is *well worth* turning and returning to, in differing formulations that can get it right for each one of us: The relevant issue is not whether criticism is possible or not, but where criticism is appropriate ... And whether something deserves to be criticised or not depends critically—*as a matter of logic*—upon *whether or not it has been understood to begin with*. Wittgenstein against Frazer, and Winch against Evans-Pritchard are both opposing particular forms of criticism of magical practices which are misplaced. The argument is not that such practices must not be criticised, but that if more attention is paid to understanding how the practices work, then one wouldn't want to criticise them as being, for example, based on an empirical mistake (which is the kind of criticism that Fraser and Evans-Pritchard want to make).

This point of view invites us to recognise rather more baldly that criticism of another society is a matter of conflict between cultures which stand on the same level as each other, *so far as the job of the sociologist or anthropologist is concerned.* The idea of rational criticism is often used as though it involved us in becoming dissociated from our own home culture, towards which we can take the same fundamentally questioning attitude as we might to any other, thus enabling us to deliver impartial assessments of the respective merits of each of those cultures, convincing ourselves that we are acting as the representatives of a universal rationality, overlooking the extent to which our conception of rationality is itself a product of cultural traditions, those of our own culture. Recognising that this is so only creates judgemental paralysis of a relativist kind if one accepts the philosophical fantasy of culture-free understanding as an appropriate conception of what 'rationality' is; if one does accept this, then withdrawing from the idea of a 'universal' standpoint entails giving up on the idea of rationality altogether. However, this is to give too much credit to what is, after all, an utterly-unrealistic fantasy, and there is no reason why anyone should suppose that this is the only, let alone the best, way of understanding what rationality is. One can then ask about rationality not as an inhuman demand, but as a humanly achievable matter, and thus be liberated to recognise that there are many and varied forms of e.g. rational disagreement that are not much like the fantasy version.

As recent controversies over science and religion (in the form of debates about intelligent design and creation science) indicate, the parties are very far apart, and there is no meeting of minds between them; the criticisms that are exchanged follow from rather than antedate the fact that each party rejects the other's way of

---

28 Once again, this insight is crucial to Kuhn's (1996 [1962]) genesis of the notion of paradigm: see the Preface to his *Structure of Scientific Revolutions*.

thinking. The opposition between them isn't over any specific hypothesis, but is wholesale dismissal of the parties' respective ways of thinking. Though the apparent focus of the controversy is Darwinian evolution, it is clear that those who defend Darwin do so 'on behalf of science' in opposition to 'religion', whilst those arguing for creationism are effectively objecting to what we would call the scientism that motivates the Darwinist's most vociferous defenders. The writings of someone like Richard Dawkins (2007) are clearly driven by generalised hostility toward religion, and, though his writings may advocate rationality in the narrow sense described above, they are not themselves notable examples of rational debate in either that or even a broader sense—at best they are polemics, and are perhaps fairly viewed as a manifestation of Dawkins' difficulties in getting any grasp on his opponents' point of view.[29]

There remains a sense in which those that comprise each of the parties to the 'intelligent design' versus Darwinism debate are not all that far apart (and in which there is a greater cultural distance between them and the Azande than between them among themselves)—they carry out their debate *in the form of* a scientific evidence-based dispute. And although, as we have just suggested, this form is deeply misleading, it does at least make perspicuous a respect in which, roughly speaking, would-be scientific advocates of 'intelligent design' are vulnerable to criticism in an important respect as pseudo-scientific/'superstitious' in which (e.g.) the Azande on Winch's construal are not, for they pledge allegiance to a standard of rationality that they then tend to lose their grip on. This is a flaw by *their own standards.*

This difference between the 'intelligent design' advocates and the Azande is itself a for instance of the way in which the determination of the conception of rationality of a given group or community requires context-sensitivity and philosophical subtlety—of exactly the kind that Winch recommended and demonstrated. It implies no commitment whatsoever to conservatism and does not place any kind of denying-ordinance upon criticism.

Limits to Cultural Understanding

Wittgenstein doesn't say that cultures can't be criticised, either our own or another, and neither he nor Winch suggest that a culture can only be criticised by those who belong to that culture. Winch and Wittgenstein in fact had much to criticise, themselves, in their own societies, and sometimes in others. What they jointly object to is that there is some simple and general way in which a culture can be understood. Many people will think they do have a grasp on what understanding another culture involves, for there is the example of the Azande (and one or two other anthropological instances that get endlessly re-circulated in this discursive context). However, to reiterate our key criticism of the elitism of social science in this context: before one imagines that one understands another culture better than its inhabitants do one ought to be confident that one understands it at least as well as its inhabitants do.

---

29 This line of thinking is followed through in detail in Terry Eagleton's (2006) review of Dawkins's most recent book, *The God Delusion.*

The claim that one does so is a logical prerequisite to securing the demonstration that the inhabitants are, after all, subject to misunderstandings of, or as a result of, their culture. However, those who are confident about their capacity to understand better than the natives are typically confident on *a priori* grounds that this must be so. They have little time for wondering whether they could be so assured in their implied claim to understand cultures even as well as its inhabitants themselves do.

The obstacles that Wittgenstein sees do not arise from the (logical) inaccessibility of a culture to those who are not full blown participants, but in the way that Winch tries to describe in his challenge to Evans-Pritchard, from the obstruction placed in the way by adopting *a priori* conceptions of what understanding has to be. The treatment of prominent cases of misunderstanding involve Wittgenstein and Winch with Frazer and Evans-Pritchard, where the Wittgenstein-Winch argument is that Frazer's and Evans-Pritchard's own data is incongruous with the *interpretation* they offer of another culture, and where their method blinds them to the extent to which they occlude their (own) understanding. Thus, Frazer registers the terrible situation of the priest king of Nemi in his own prose, but not in his arguments, and does not see that the potency of the practice derives from its configuration as a menacing and eerie affair, not from the influence of any extrinsic [explanatory] factor. If we are shown the configuration of the rite in a perspicuous way, we do not need an explanation of how this practice came to be adopted in the first place—about which, of course, in fact nothing is actually known—in order to understand how the practice works, for we can see from the practice itself its role as a significant ceremonial way of transferring power. Frazer himself cannot see that he has done enough to enable us to understand the rite for simply describing the ceremony does not satisfy his demand for what he conceives to be the proper sort of explanation—one that will be entirely general, and that will construe the event in utilitarian terms: there 'must be' some directly practical purpose underlying any practice, even if it is a misguided one—it is this assumption that *gives* Frazer what seem to be puzzles: what *practical* purposes could conceivably motivate doing things in this way? Given the utilitarian conception of practicality, the underlying purpose which Fraser will ascribe to the practice will prove to be a misguided one.

Note that neither Wittgenstein nor Winch treat 'understanding' here as coming to *believe in* these practices as their possessors do (which does not in any case contradict our early remark about practices not being founded in beliefs since 'believe' here is more 'believe in' than 'believe that'), and thus do not require one to become an 'insider' in the sense of subscribing to the practice. Indeed, for the cases that Wittgenstein and Winch concern themselves with, the simple fact is we can't bring ourselves to believe in them, very much in the way that the postmodernists tell us we just can't say 'I love you' seriously anymore.[30] If one of us tried going down to the bottom of the garden with a collection of hens and some erratically-acting poison, he would feel like an utter fool, and couldn't act out the rite with anything like the commitment that the diviner brings to his role—he could say the words, but just like 'I love you' in the mouth of a postmodernist, they would be empty of any conviction. Evans-Pritchard pretty much understood the mechanics of oracular

---

30 Not that *we* really believe this but the *analogy* helps clarify what we are saying.

consultation and magical rites, but *partially* misunderstood the … *spirit* in which those mechanics are employed.

Religion is a rather different matter, and the notion of 'understanding' often plays a rather different role in that context than it does in the 'primitive magic' case. In the latter, we can feel that we have an understanding of witchcraft and oracular consultation on the basis of an anthropologist's report, where the puzzlement is: how can they possibly believe that that works (and the resolution of the puzzlement can sometimes come in coming to see that it is not *intended* to work in just the way we fantasise)? With religion, however, there are important connections in which the religious belief sets limits to the extent to which we can claim understanding without accepting the practice in question—to 'understand' in that context is more like 'feeling the full force' of the religious experience. To understand a religious tradition can be to genuinely experience one's own life in its ways, and in that way, there can be no gap between understanding and accepting: to understand one's life as e.g. being wholly in God's hands is to possess faith, one cannot genuinely experience things that way on the basis of an intellectual simulation or pretence—understanding the mechanics of the outer forms is a long way away from being acquainted with the spirit that animates those. So: the challenge with religion is often: to find a way of imaginatively understanding without joining in believing—*and* without misrepresenting the faith or its practices.

As much as anything else, the argument here is about the contrast between (1) the social science urge for a general method and contempt for the particular case, and (2) the difficulties attending spiritual practices illustrating the fact that there is no general methodology that facilitates understanding, and that, for sure, there is no guarantee that any method will assure understanding. In the first instance, understanding is not a social science problem. The anxiety that Wittgenstein and Winch provoke in this connection is not toward the idea that understanding another culture is possible, but toward the *idea that it can always be achieved without a great deal of personal effort*, that one could seriously claim to understand another society without 'immersing' oneself in it, and without reflecting on it and upon oneself and 'ourselves' in ways that are not just intellectually but also imaginatively, philosophically, morally, spiritually, personally and psychologically demanding. The problem of understanding another culture is a problem that people practically overcome, or fail to do so, every day, but social scientists in the midst of their general explanatory project have no particular society or practice that they want or need to understand where they are utterly baffled by what people are doing such that they can't make head nor tail of it. Without a good deal of sensitive familiarity with a society or some aspect of its practices, one is not going to be able to get a good grasp on the sense that its practices have.

Perhaps a way to defuse the problem here is to point out that 'participation' in another culture may include a variety of forms, ranging from reading about a culture (which is how Wittgenstein and Winch, reading Frazer and Evans-Pritchard respectively, came to understand much about the culture of the 'classical civilisations' and the Azande) to joining in the daily life of that culture—signing up for a job on the production line to understand shop-floor culture, say. There is no denying that (some) understanding of another culture can be obtained in the first manner, though the capacity to achieve such understanding will presuppose that others have undertaken a much more intense immersion in the culture in question (to provide good written sources) but there are, nonetheless, points at which one cannot get any significant understanding without being a participant in the practice in question. Winch instances the case of the arts and of mathematics, thus clarifying what 'participation' might mean in this connection—one doesn't have to be a painter or working musician to understand the practice of the relevant arts, but one does have to be able to apply the aesthetic assumptions and criteria involved in painting, improvising or whatever, just as one does not have to be a working mathematician to follow some of the proofs that mathematicians produce but one cannot understand mathematics at all if one cannot follow any of the proofs. For Winch, these are perhaps limiting cases, where—to an extent—being able to understand what other people are doing involves being able to do, yourself, at least to some substantial degree what they are doing. Their significance is that they subvert—they completely turn over—the social science ideal that the correct way to understand human activity is from the outside (which, in the extreme, can demand that anthropomorphism not be employed in understanding human beings), where the better understanding allegedly results from the greatest remoteness from engagement with the affairs in question. They also subvert the other key social science assumption, that understanding people's activity is one single kind of thing which could be pursued (and taught) by one general method, which, if only it could be identified and mastered, would secure the prospect of universal understanding, such that, for the follower of the method, it would be possible to understand all of every people's activities merely by following the time-saving procedure. Winch is casting doubt on any such assumption—the best way to understand the practice of mathematicians is to learn some maths, but there is absolutely no guarantee that the average social scientist will be able, no matter how hard they try, to grasp much mathematics beyond the relatively elementary forms; the demands which mathematics makes on the understanding are peculiar and not easily, or at all, available to many very clever people.

In Conclusion

It is not that one can or cannot 'translate' between cultures, but that translation is not to be thought of as a formulaic matter. One should not be tempted into the thought that translation can be undertaken mechanically, through our having being availed of a methodology for such understanding, which one then applies. It can often be (rather) an imaginative exercise that is dependent upon 'embodied' information—prior understanding of the instance under translation on both sides of the translational equation. Further, the difference between better and worse translations is, in part at least, a function of the sensitivity, care, and contextual alertness and attentiveness that goes into producing the translation. Deciding what translation best fits their way of proceeding involves sensitivity to what, amongst our ways of doing things, is the best comparison to that. The fact that we can do many ready translations between cultures is the accumulated result of extensive experience by innumerable individuals, of contacts between cultures. From the point of view of sociology and broadly cognate 'social/human science' disciplines, which is (are) resource-poor and possessed of an urgent yearning toward generality, to make these observations probably is equivalent to saying that understanding another culture is impossible for them, since adoption of these policies would—as Wittgenstein and Winch were well aware—obstruct pursuit of standard 'social science' ambitions, and would postpone and redirect effort in a way which would make the sought for objectives of comprehensive schemes for understanding society seem utterly remote, if not wholly unattainable.

Notice, though, that the possibility of understanding another culture is nowhere being ruled out. *Not at all*. Rather, a contrast is being made between what counts, when language is at work, as understanding and what 'understanding' is dogmatically imagined to be under the influence of social science preformations.

Isn't the problem of understanding, though, that of bridging the gap between our concepts and theirs? Doesn't comparison of two cultures show that people in them have different concepts? And, if people have different concepts, and if understanding is achieved through the use of concepts how can we understand them? If our understanding is achieved through our concepts, and theirs through their concepts, then our understanding and theirs are different, and radically so, since our concepts are variant. Their concepts won't fit with/into ours, so we will only be able to understand them through our concepts, not through their indigenous ones: trying to absorb their concepts to ours will only distort them. We cannot really grasp their concepts, any more than they can grasp ours.

Our response is: isn't this, latter, conviction, and its powerful hold, more a product of a subliming of the idea of understanding than it is an expression of experienced insuperable difficulties? Isn't it an expression of an old and entirely-confused philosophical faithful, the idea that the only way to really understand what it is like is to be that person. This old staple, a legacy of all three of Rationalism, Idealism and Empiricism, has its current life in philosophy as the idea that we are stymied by the question: what is it like to be a bat? The way that question is put is meant to insinuate that we can't even really imagine what it is like to be a bat, that our being us gets in the way. Real understanding involves experiencing what a bat experiences, just as the bat experiences it, which we can't imagine because we can't dispense with the understandings etc., that we have as humans, and which, therefore, get in the way of our grasp on the bat's experience which is undergone in complete unawareness of any human concepts. The 'can't' here is surely a stipulative one, stipulative of what is to count as understanding (really), meaning that the many things we can say that we understand about what it is like to be a bat are not to be flatly denied, but to be denied the status of real understanding. Similarly, the idea of radical conceptual closure between cultures is a misbegotten child of a similarly sublimed notion of understanding—those in another culture have their own concepts and lack ours, therefore the only way we could (really) understand them would be if we could dispense with all our concepts, since understanding the world authentically in terms of their concepts involves complete unawareness of our concepts. (Really) understanding them involves getting outside of our culture and being wholly immersed in theirs, but this would of course mean—even if *per impossibile* we could do this—that we could never bring any (real) understanding of their culture back home. So it would be a profitless performance. As well as subliming "understand" so as to be able to voice a dissatisfaction with anything that we might call 'understanding their culture' there is perhaps too hasty invocation of ideas of being 'in' and 'outside' a culture. Wittgenstein and Winch regard the foregoing kinds of worries as symptoms of the problems they think are spurious, and never in any way faithful to their own. Their concern is absolutely not to show that understanding another culture is *a priori* impossible, but to show how some philosophical preconceptions *get in the way of* understanding some important aspects of some other cultures, a demonstration that requires a distinction between understanding and misunderstanding. Isn't understanding, as we practice it, often a matter of considering the similarities and differences between our ways of doing things and someone else's ways, of grasping where and how what they do diverges from what we do, being something which is a matter of greater or lesser difficulty, depending upon the cases involved?

That last sentence might sound like a rhetorical question, a banality, hardly worth saying. Quite right too. Winch is not a promulgator of any conservative doctrine; he is simply returning us to common sense in its true sense. He offers no revisionist doctrine, but only 'reminds' us of what we have all always-already known. He enables one to retrieve society as it actually is, by enabling one to overcome the delusions that 'social science' and its apologists have placed in the way thereof.

Conclusion

The Idea of a Social Science and its Relation to Philosophy was a young man's book. Peter Winch was 28 years of age when he wrote it. It is big in its claims and somewhat polemical in much of its delivery. However, the corrective to dominant misunderstandings of the social studies, both at the time that Winch drafted *ISS* and today, is of crucial importance. We have sought to convey to the reader this importance. We have not been concerned to rescue Winch from his critics (and those who would subject him to 'friendly fire') for scholastic reasons. We share Winch's concerns, and his sense of the importance of these concerns.

How the present book has unfolded might to some seem a little unconventional. One might have expected more textual commentary and explication of *ISS*. One might have expected chapters on such things as rule-following and on language-games. It is our view that Winch speaks for himself. His work is accessible and clear enough, read in the right spirit.

It is this, however—the right spirit—that has often been lacking in those that have read Winch over the fifty years since publication of *ISS*. There seems to be a number of things afoot that serve as barriers to much in way of accurate representations of Winch in the literature. We here take a stab at identifying some candidates.

One failure to read Winch's work in the right spirit, evident in some of the original responses to *ISS*, seems to be borne of those respondents having been affronted that someone (maybe particularly someone as young as Winch was then) would write such radical book, critical of the very idea of a social science. It's not a great feeling to be told that you are well and truly barking up the wrong tree—barking up the tree of the empirical sciences, when that cat one was chasing is sitting up the tree of philosophy, to maybe stretch the metaphor a little. But to be told that you are so along with everyone else who calls themselves a social scientist might well lead to anger. So much for our psychological diagnosis.

Other failures to read Winch in the right spirit seem to be based in a failure to have grasped the philosophical voice in which Winch, following Wittgenstein, is speaking. For, if so many have failed to grasp the therapeutic nature of Wittgenstein's philosophy, then why might we expect a better state of affairs in the secondary literature on Winch? Winch had no interest in and made no attempt to advance philosophical theses. That was not his method of philosophising. Many then, unfortunately, read Winch's broadly 'therapeutic' moves as if they were advancing doctrines.

Some seem not to have read more than the first edition of *ISS*. This leaves out most obviously the Preface to the 2nd edition, "Understanding a Primitive Society", "Can We Understand Ourselves" and "Persuasion". Now, of course one is not obliged to read everything we recommend. Nor is one obliged to read what Winch writes after *ISS* (even if it is clearly directly related to what he said in *ISS*) if one is concerned to generate a criticism of *ISS*. But, if one does marshal such a defence one might find it difficult to respond to the question as to what purpose one's criticism serves? For are we in the business of philosophy to score points off our interlocutors or to engage in dialogue aimed at furthering (our) understanding?

What we have therefore sought to show in the preceding pages is that read in the correct spirit—read by one who is free of the anger that someone who feels under attack often harbours; read by one who acknowledges the 'therapeutic' voice in which Winch writes philosophy; read by one who cares to engage in meaningful dialogue with Winch—Winch is not the philosopher one might hitherto have assumed him to be.

As we noted toward the close of our Introduction, we make no apology for any repetition. We are trying to make sense, and to find 'the liberating word': the right word(s) to help one (including: to help ourselves) to avoid delusions of sense, as well as of grandeur. We circle around and around these difficult waters, of the desire to reach for a scientific understanding of ourselves (our society/societies), sketching the seascape again and again, looking to help one to get to know this familiar place for the first time. It isn't easy reflectively to know one's way about that with which one is so familiar. To do a decent job of work in philosophy, one has to be prepared to continue to explore familiar routes and paths anew.

Furthermore, as we mentioned in our Introduction there are certain (repeated) features of thought in this area from which many misunderstandings of Winch can be seen to stem. These features will likely be clear to our readers now. They are, in addition to the 'therapeutic' voice in which Winch writes, *the identity of action and the character of understanding*. The starting point we should like to say is that people constantly grasp the meaning of actions in everyday transactions and interactions. This is where one ought to look for guidance. It is tempting to begin with cases where breakdown of understanding has occurred or where understanding what someone is doing is difficult (where we have failed to grasp what they're up to). It is tempting to begin with cases where we just find it difficult to discern what someone is up to (we find it difficult to identify their action). If we begin here, then it is tempting to think we need a general method for understanding, which will tell us in all contexts, on all occasions, what the identity of the action is.

We say: don't begin from here (with cases of breakdown or difficulty in understanding). That might superficially sound like the old joke about the man who is lost asking for directions, only to be told that he should not begin his journey here. Of course the joke is, in the case of that old joke, that one *is* here and one *needs* directions from here. However, our advice, following Winch, is that students in the social studies have a choice as to where they begin. We recommend that the starting point be with how people constantly grasp each others' meaning, without the need for a sociological method; without familiarity with the methods of Giddens, Bhaskar, Habermas, Bourdieu and so on.

To, in some sense come full circle and end as we began by quoting J.L. Austin, only this time we'll paraphrase. Everyday understanding might not be the last word, but it certainly ought to be the first.

Bibliography

Alcock, J. (2001), *The Triumph of Sociobiology*. Oxford: Oxford University Press.

Anscombe, G.E.M. (2000 [1957]), *Intention*. Cambridge, MA: Harvard University Press.

Ashmore, M. (1989), 'The Reflexive Thesis: Wrighting Sociology of Scientific Knowledge'. Chicago: University of Chicago Press.

Austin, J.L. (1962), *Sense and Sensibilia*. Oxford: Oxford University Press.

Baccus, M. (1986), 'Sociological Indication and the Visibility Criterion of Real World Social Theorising', in Garfinkel, H. (ed.), pp. 1-19.

Baker, G. (2002), 'Quotation-marks in *Philosophical Investigations* Part I', *Language and Communication* 22, pp. 37–68.

—— (2004), *Wittgenstein's Method: Neglected Aspects*. Edited and Introduced by Katherine Morris. Oxford: Blackwell.

Baz, A. (2000), 'What's the Point of Seeing Aspects', *Philosophical Investigations* 23:2, pp. 97-121.

—— (2003), 'On When Words are Called for: Cavell, McDowell, and the Wording of the World', *Inquiry* 46, pp. 473-500.

Bennett, M., Dennett, D., Hacker P.M.S. and Searle, J. (2007), *Neuroscience and Philosophy: Brain, Mind and Language*. New York: Columbia University Press.

Bennett, M. and Hacker, P.M.S. (2003), *The Philosophical Foundations of Neuroscience*. Oxford: Blackwell.

Bhaskar, R. (1998 [1979]), *The Possibility of Naturalism*, 3rd edition. London: Routledge.

Bloor, D. (1983), *Wittgenstein: A Social Theory of Knowledge*. New York: Columbia University Press.

Bohman, J. (1992), *New Philosophy of Social Science*. Cambridge: Polity.

Bourdieu, P. (1998), *Practical Reasons*. Cambridge: Polity.

Button, G. (ed.) (1991), *Ethnomethodology and the Human Sciences*. Cambridge: Cambridge University Press.

Button, G., Coulter, J., Lee, J.R.E. and Sharrock, W. (1995), *Computers, Minds and Conduct*. Cambridge: Polity Press.

Campbell, C. (1996), *The Myth of Social Action*. Cambridge: Cambridge University Press.

Cavell, S. (1976), *Must We Mean What We Say?* Cambridge: Cambridge University Press.

—— (1979), *The Claim of Reason*. Oxford: Oxford University Press.

Churchland, P. (1988), *Matter and Consciousness*. Cambridge, MA: MIT Press.

Churchland, P. (1989), *Neurophilosophy*. Cambridge, MA: MIT Press.

Clifford, J. (1986), 'On Ethnographic Allegory' in Clifford, J. and Marcus, G.E. (eds), pp. 98-122.

Clifford, J. and Marcus, G.E. (eds) (1986), *Writing Culture: The Poetics and Politics of Ethnography*. Berkeley: University of California Press.

Cole, S. (ed.) (2001), *What's Wrong With Sociology?* London: Transaction Publishers.

Coulter, J. (1994), 'Is Contextualising Necessarily Interpretive?', *Journal of Pragmatics* 21, pp. 689-698.

—— (1996), 'A Logic for "Context"', *Journal of Pragmatics* 25, pp. 441-445.

—— (2008), 'Twenty-Five Theses Against Cognitivism' in Coulter, J. and Watson, R. (eds).

Coulter, J. and Watson, R. (2008), 'On Cognitivism', A Special Issue of *Theory, Culture and Society* 25:2.

Crary, A. and Read, R. (2000), *The New Wittgenstein*. London: Routledge.

Davidson, D. (2001), *Inquiries into Truth and Interpretation*. Oxford: Oxford University Press.

Delanty, G. (1997), *Social Science: Beyond Constructivism and Realism*. Buckingham: Open University Press.

Dawkins, R. (2007), *The God Delusion*, new edition, with additions. London: Black Swan.

Dennett, D.C. (1995), *Darwin's Dangerous Idea: Evolution and the Meanings of Life*. London: Penguin.

Derrida, J. (1973), *Speech and Phenomena*, trans. Allison, D.B. Evanston: Northwestern University Press.

—— (1988), *Limited Inc.*, trans. Bass, A. and Weber, S. Evanston: Northwestern University Press.

Diamond, C. (1989), 'Rules: Looking in the Right Place' in Phillips and Winch (eds).

—— (1992), *The Realistic Spirit*. Cambridge, MA: MIT.

Dilman, İ. (2002), *Wittgenstein's Copernican Revolution: The Question of Linguistic Idealism*. Basingstoke: Palgrave.

Dupré, J. (2001), *Human Nature and the Limits of Science*. Oxford: Oxford University Press.

—— (2001a), *Humans and Other Animals*. Oxford: Oxford University Press.

Eagleton, T. (2006), 'Lunging, Flailing, Mispunching', review of Richard Dawkins's *The God Delusion*, first edition, in *The London Review of Books*, 19 October [http://www.lrb.co.uk/v28/n20/eagl01_.html].

Ebersole, F. (2001), *Things We Know: Fifteen Essays in the Problem of Knowledge*. Philadelphia: Xlibris.

—— (2002), *Language and Perception: Essays in the Philosophy of Language*. Philadelphia: Xlibris.

Evans-Pritchard, E.E. (1976), *Witchcraft, Oracles, and Magic among the Azande*, abridged edition. Oxford: Clarendon.

Feyerabend, P. (1975), *Against Method*. London: Verso.

Fielding, N.G. (ed.) (1988), *Actions and Structure: Research Methods and Social Theory*. London: Sage.

Gaita, R. (2007), Introduction to the Fiftieth Anniversary Edition of *Idea of a Social Science and its Relation to Philosophy*. London: Routledge, pp. xix-xxix.

Garfinkel, H. (1984 [1967]), *Studies in Ethnomethodology*. Cambridge: Polity.

—— (ed.) (1986), *Ethnomethodological Studies of Work*. London: Routledge.

—— (2002), *Ethnomethodology's Program* (Book One of *Working Out Durkheim's Aphorism*), edited and introduced by Anne Warfield Rawls. New York: Roman & Littlefield.

Gellner, E. (1970), 'Concepts and Society' in Wilson, B.R. (ed.).

Geras, N. (1995), 'Language, Truth and Justice', *The New Left Review* I/209, pp. 110-135.

Giddens, A. (1976), *New Rules of Sociological Method: A Positive Critique of Interpretative Sociologies*. London: Hutchinson.

Goffman, E. (1990 [1959]), *The Presentation of Self in Everyday Life*. London: Penguin.

—— (1963), *Behavior in Public Places: Notes on the Social Organization of Gatherings*. Glencoe: The Free Press.

—— (1969), *Strategic Interaction*. Philadelphia: University of Pennsylvania Press.

Goldfarb, W. (1985), 'Kripke on Wittgenstein on Rules', *Journal of Philosophy* 82:9, pp. 471-488.

Goldstein, L. (1999), *Clear and Queer Thinking*. London: Duckworth.

Guetti, J. (1993), *Wittgenstein and the Grammar of Literary Experience*. Athens, GA: University of Georgia Press.

—— (1993a), 'Idling Rules', *Philosophical Investigations* 16:3, pp. 179-197.

Guetti, J. and Read, R. (1996), 'Acting from Rules: "Internal Relations" versus "Logical Existentialism"', *International Studies in Philosophy*, XXVIII:2, pp. 43-62.

Habermas, J. (1984), *The Theory of Communicative Action: Volume One: Reason and the Rationalisation of Society*, trans. McCarthy, T. Cambridge: Polity.

—— (1987), *The Theory of Communicative Action: Volume Two: The Critique of Functionalist Reason*, trans. McCarthy, T. Cambridge: Polity.

—— (1988), *On the Logic of the Social Sciences*, trans. Weber Nicholsen, S. and Stark, J.A. Cambridge: Polity.

Harris, M. (1974), *Cows, Pigs, Wars and Witches: The Riddles of Culture*. New York: Random House.

Hoyningen-Huene, P. (1993), *Reconstructing Scientific Revolutions: Thomas S. Kuhn's Philosophy of Science*, trans. by Levine, A.T., with a Foreword by Thomas S. Kuhn. Chicago: University of Chicago Press.

Hunter, J.F.M. (1973), *Essays After Wittgenstein*. London: George Allen & Unwin.

Hutchinson, P. (2004), 'Steiner's Possession: As it Were', *European Journal of Political Theory* 3:3, pp. 245-265.

—— (2005c), 'An Elucidatory Interpretation of Wittgenstein's Tractatus: A Critique of Daniel D. Hutto's and Marie McGinn's Reading of Tractatus 6.54', *International Journal of Philosophical Studies* 14:1, pp. 1-29.

—— (2006) 'Unsinnig', *International Journal of Philosophical Studies* 14:4, pp. 569-577.

—— (2007), 'What's the Point of Elucidation', *Metaphilosophy* 38:5, pp. 691-713.

—— (2008), *Shame and Philosophy: An Investigation in the Philosophy of Emotions and Ethics*. Basingstoke: Palgrave.

Hutchinson, P. and Read, R. (2005), 'Whose Wittgenstein?' *Philosophy* 80:3, pp. 432–55.

—— (2008), 'Towards a Perspicuous Presentation of "Perspicuous Presentation"', *Philosophical Investigations* 31:2, pp. 140-160.

Keita, L.D. (1997), 'Winch and Instrumental Pluralism: A Reply to B.D. Lerner' *Philosophy of the Social Sciences* 27, pp. 80-82.

Kitching, G. (2004), *Wittgenstein and Society: Essays in Conceptual Puzzlement.* London: Ashgate.

Kitching, G. and Pleasants, N. (eds) (2002), *Marx and Wittgenstein: Knowledge, Morality and Politics.* London: Routledge.

Kuhn, T. (1996 [1962]), *The Structure of Scientific Revolutions*, 3rd edition. Chicago: University of Chicago Press.

Lassman, P. (ed.) (2000), *History of the Human Sciences: Peter Winch and the Idea of a Social Science*, Special Issue, 13:1.

Lerner, B.D. (1995), 'Winch and Instrumental Pluralism', *Philosophy of Social Science* 25:2, pp. 180-191.

—— (2002), *Rules, Magic and Instrumental Reason: A Critical Interpretation of Peter Winch's Philosophy of the Social Sciences.* London: Routledge.

Linblom, C. and Cohen, D. (1979), *Useable Knowledge.* New Haven: Yale University Press.

Louch, A.R. (1963), 'The Very Idea of a Social Science', *Inquiry* 6, pp. 273-85.

Lyas, C. (1999), *Peter Winch.* Teddington: Acumen.

Lynch, M. (1993), *Scientific Practice and Ordinary Action.* Cambridge: Cambridge University Press.

—— (2000), 'Against Reflexivity as an Academic Virtue and Source of Privileged Knowledge', *Theory, Culture and Society* 17:3, pp. 26-54.

MacIntyre, A. (1962), 'A Mistake about Causality' in Laslett, P. and Runciman, W.G. (eds), *Philosophy, Politics and Society*, pp. 48-70.

—— (1970 [1967]), 'The Idea of a Social Science' in Wilson, B.R. (ed.), pp. 112-130.

Malachowski, A. (2002), *Richard Rorty.* Teddington: Acumen.

Manicas, P.T. (2006), *A Realist Philosophy of Social Science: Explanation and Understanding.* Cambridge: Cambridge University Press.

Marx, K. (1998), *The German Ideology (Including the 1845 Theses on Feuerbach).* New York: Prometheus Books.

McDowell, J. (1994), *Mind and World.* Cambridge: Cambridge University Press.

—— (1998a), *Mind, Value and Reality.* Cambridge, MA: Harvard University Press.

—— (1998b), *Meaning, Knowledge, and Reality.* Cambridge, MA: Harvard University Press.

McGowan, J. (1991), *Postmodernism and its Critics.* Ithaca: Cornell University Press.

McIntyre, L.C. (1996), *Laws and Explanation in the Social Sciences: Defending a Science of Human Behaviour.* Oxford: Westview Press.

—— (2006), *Dark Ages: The Case for a Science of Human Behaviour.* Cambridge, MA: MIT Press.

McManus, D. (ed.) (2004), *Wittgenstein and Scepticism.* London: Routledge.

—— (2007), *The Enchantment of Words.* Oxford: Oxford University Press.

Merton, R.K. (1968 [1949]), *Social Theory and Social Structure, Enlarged Edition.* New York: Free Press.

Monk, R. (1990), *Ludwig Wittgenstein: The Duty of Genius.* London: Vintage.

Mounce, H.O. (1973), 'Understanding a Primitive Society', *Philosophy* 48, pp. 347-362.

Mouzelis, N.P. (1995), *Sociological Theory: What Went Wrong?—Diagnosis and Remedies.* London: Routledge.

Phillips, D.Z. (2000), 'Beyond Rules', *History of the Human Sciences* 13:2, pp. 17-36.

Phillips, P. (1997), 'Winch's Pluralist Tree and the Roots of Relativism', *Philosophy of Social Science* 27:1, pp. 83-95.

Pinker, S. (2002), *The Blank Slate: The Modern Denial of Human Nature.* London: Penguin.

Pleasants, N. (1999), *Wittgenstein and the Idea of a Critical Social Theory.* London: Routledge.

—— (2000a), 'Winch and Wittgenstein on Understanding Ourselves Critically: Descriptive not Metaphysical', *Inquiry* 43:3, pp. 289-318.

—— (2000b), 'Winch, Wittgenstein, and the Idea of a Critical Social Theory', *History of the Human Sciences* 13:1, pp. 78-91.

—— (2002), 'Toward a Critical Use of Marx and Wittgenstein' in Kitching and Pleasants, pp. 160-181.

Pollner, M. (1987), *Mundane Reason.* Cambridge: Cambridge University Press.

Putnam, H. (2002), 'Travis on Meaning, Thought and the Ways the World Is', review of Charles Travis, *Unshadowed Thought. Philosophical Quarterly* 52:2, pp. 96-106.

Read, R. (1997), 'The Career of "Internal Relations" in Wittgenstein's Thought', *Wittgenstein Studies 8* [http://www.phil.uni-passau.de/dlwg/ws08/22-2-97.TXT].

—— (2000), 'Wittgenstein and Marx on "Philosophical Language"', *Essays in Philosophy* 1:2 [http://www.humboldt.edu/~essays/read.html].

—— (2000/1), 'How I Learned to Love (and Hate) Noam Chomsky', *Philosophical Writings* 15/16, pp. 23-48.

—— (2002), 'Marx and Wittgenstein on Vampires and Parasites: A Critique of Capital and Metaphysics' in Kitching and Pleasants, pp. 254-281.

—— (2003), 'On Delusions of Sense: A Response to Coetzee and Sass', *Philosophy, Psychiatry, and Psychology* 10:2, pp. 135-141.

—— (2004), 'Wittgenstein and Faulkner's Benjy: Reflections on and of Derangement' in Gibson, J. and Huemer, W. (eds), *The Literary Wittgenstein.* London: Routledge, pp. 267-288.

—— (2004a), 'Throwing Away "The Bedrock"', *Proceedings of the Aristotelian Society* 105:1, pp. 81-98.

—— (2007), *Applying Wittgenstein.* London: Continuum.

—— (2007a), 'Economics is Philosophy: Economics is not Science', *International Journal of Green Economics* 1:3/4, pp. 307-325.

—— (2008), 'The "Hard" Problem of Consciousness is Continually Reproduced and Made Harder by all Attempts to Solve it', *Theory, Culture and Society* 25:2.

—— (2008a forthcoming), 'Review of Denis McManus's The Enchantment of Words' in *Philosophy*.

Read, R. and Goodenough, J. (eds) (2005), *Film as Philosophy: Essays on Cinema After Wittgenstein and Cavell.* Basingstoke: Palgrave.

Read, R. and Guetti, J. (1999), 'Meaningful Consequences' in *Philosophical Forum* XXX:4, pp. 289-315.

Ryle, G. (1949), *The Concept of Mind.* London: Hutchinson & Co.

Schatzki, T. (1991), 'Elements of a Wittgensteinian Philosophy of the Human Sciences', *Synthese* 87, pp. 311-329.

Sharrock, W.W. and Anderson, R.J. (1985), 'Understanding Peter Winch', *Inquiry* 28, pp. 119-122.

Sharrock, W. and Coulter, J. (2007), *Brain, Mind and Human Behavior in Contemporary Cognitive Science: Critical Assessments of the Philosophy of Psychology.* New York: Edwin Mellen Press.

Sharrock, W. and Read, R. (2002), *Kuhn: Philosopher of Scientific Revolution.* Cambridge: Polity Press.

Sharrock, W. and Watson, R. (1988), 'Autonomy Among Social Theories: The Incarnation of Social Structures' in Fielding, N.G. (ed.), pp. 56-77.

Skinner, Q. (ed.) (1985), *The Return of Grand Theory.* Cambridge: Canto.

Sluga, H. and Stern, D. (eds) (1996), *The Cambridge Companion to Wittgenstein.* Cambridge: Cambridge University Press.

Sorokin, P.A. (1957), *Fads and Foibles in Modern Sociology and Related Sciences.* Chicago, Ill: Henry Regnery & Co.

Steiner, H. (1994), *An Essay on Rights.* Oxford: Backwell.

Stroll, A. (1998), *Sketches of Landscapes.* Cambridge, MA: MIT Press.

Travis, C. (2000), *Unshadowed Thought.* Cambridge, MA: Harvard University Press.

—— (2001), 'Annals of Analysis', *Mind* 100:2, pp. 237-264. Reprinted in Travis (2008).

—— (2005), 'The Twilight of Empiricism', *Proceedings of the Aristotelian Society* 104:2, pp. 245-270.

—— (2006), *Thought's Footing: A Theme in Wittgenstein's Philosophical Investigations.* Oxford: Oxford University Press.

—— (2008), *Occasion-Sensitivity: Selected Essays.* Oxford: Oxford University Press.

Wilson, B.R. (1970), *Rationality.* Oxford: Blackwell.

Winch, P. (1964), 'Understanding a Primitive Society', *American Philosophical Quarterly* 1:4, pp. 307-24. Reprinted in Wilson, B.R. (ed.) (1970), and in Winch (1972).

—— (1972), *Ethics and Action.* London: Routledge.

—— (1987), *Trying to Make Sense.* Oxford: Blackwell.

—— (1990 [1958]), *The Idea of a Social Science and its Relation to Philosophy.* 2nd edition. London: Routledge. Reprinted in 2007 (with altered pagination) as the 50th Anniversary edition, with an introduction by Raimond Gaita.

—— (1992), 'Persuasion' in *Midwest Studies in Philosophy* XVII, pp. 123-137.

—— (1995), 'Review of James Bohman's *New Philosophy of Social Science*', *Philosophy and Phenomenological Research* 55:2, pp. 472-475.

—— (1997), 'Can We Understand Ourselves' in *Philosophical Investigations* 20:3, pp. 193-204.

Wittgenstein, L. (1922), *Tractatus Logico-Philosophicus.* London: Routledge.

—— (1958), *Philosophical Investigations*, 2nd edition. Oxford: Blackwell.

—— (1967), *Remarks on the Foundations of Mathematics*, 2nd edition. Oxford: Blackwell.

—— (1969), *The Blue and Brown Books: Preliminary Studies for the 'Philosophical Investigations'*. Oxford: Blackwell.

—— (1975), *On Certainty*. Oxford: Blackwell.

—— (1978), *Philosophical Grammar*. Oxford: Blackwell.

—— (1978), *Remarks on Frazer's Golden Bough*. Doncaster: Brynmill Press.

Index